Contents

Teaching notes for Clic! 1

**Symbols used in this Teacher's
Resource Book:**

🎧	listening materials
▶	video clip on OxBox *Interactif* CD-ROM
🅖	support on OxBox *Interactif* CD-ROM
W1	consolidation and extension activities available in the *En solo* Workbook
C1	consolidation and extension activities available on Copymaster
AT 1.1	reference to National Curriculum attainment level

CLIC! 1 SUMMARY OF UNIT CONTENTS

	Contexts	Grammar	Language strategies	Pronunciation	Cultural focus	Framework
Départ	**Introduction to French** • Greetings • Names and nationalities • Classroom language	• *je suis...* • *tu es...* • Masculine and feminine agreement of nationality adjectives		**Workbook:** • Key pronunciation points		L – 7W3. 7W4, 7W8, 7S3, 7S8, 7T1, 7L1, 7L4, 7L5, 7L6, 7C5
Unit 1	**The French language; France and other countries** • Things that make you think of France • Numbers 1–10 • The alphabet • What there is/is not in a town • Country, nationality, languages • Colours • Jobs and languages	**Nouns and gender** – Determiners: *le, la, les; un, une, des* – Agreement of nationality adjectives – Masculine/Feminine forms of job titles • *Il y a un/une/des...* • *Il n'y a pas de/d'...*	• Recording and remembering new language **Workbook:** • Using reference materials • Differences between French and English (accents)	• Nasal sounds	• Symbols of France	L – 7W1, 7W2, 7W6, 7W7, 7S1, 7S4, 7S5, 7S9, 7T4, 7T7, 7C1, 7C2, 7C3, 7C4 R – 7W3, 7W4, 7S3, 7S8, 7L1
Unit 2	**Favourite things** • Things that you like and don't like • Pets • Special occasions • Numbers 11–31 • Dates, age, birthday • Weekend activities you like or dislike • You and your friends	**French verbs (1)** – The infinitive – Subject pronouns *je, tu, il, elle* – 1st/2nd/3rd person singular present tense of regular *-er* verbs – *ne... pas* – *j'aime/je déteste* + infinitive – *j'ai, tu as, il/elle a* – *je fais, tu fais, il/elle fait* • *mon/ma/mes, ton/ta/tes, son/sa/ses* • *je n'ai pas de/d'...*	• Using a bilingual dictionary **Workbook:** • Listening strategies • High-frequency words **Copymasters:** • Cognates, false friends	• Silent letters	• French festivals	L – 7W5, 7S2, 7T2, 7T3, 7T6, 7L2 R – 7W1, 7W2, 7W6, 7W7, 7W8, 7S1, 7S3, 7S4, 7S5, 7S9, 7T1, 7T4, 7L1, 7C2, 7C3, 7C4
Unit 3	**School** • School subjects you like and don't like • Numbers up to 60 and how to tell the time • School timetable • School objects • *En plus*: Problems and excuses	**French verbs (2)** – *-er, -ir* and *-re* infinitives – Introduction to irregular verbs – *nous, vous, ils, elles* – *on* + 3rd person singular – 1st/2nd/3rd person plural of *-er* verbs – Full present tense of *avoir* and *être* – *En plus*: Introduction to the perfect tense of regular *-er* verbs with *avoir*	• Learning vocabulary **Workbook:** • Cognates, false friends	• The *é* sound **Workbook:** • How to sound more French	• School life in France	L – 7S6, 7S7, 7T5, 7L3 R – 7W1, 7W3, 7W5, 7W6, 7W7, 7W8, 7S4, 7T2, 7T3, 7L1, 7L4, 7L5, 7L6, 7C2, 7C3, 7C4, 7C5

CLIC! 1 SUMMARY OF UNIT CONTENTS

	Contexts	Grammar	Language strategies	Pronunciation	Cultural focus	Framework

Unit 4	**Homes and regions**
	• Your area and the weather
	• Where you live
	• Flats and houses
	• Things in your bedroom
		• **Adjectives**
		  – Adjective agreement
		  – Position of adjectives
			• How to listen well
			Workbook:
			• Why literal translations don't always work
			• Out-of-school learning
				• Pronunciation of adjective endings	• Geography of France	**R** – 7W1, 7W2, 7W4, 7S1, 7S2, 7S6, 7S9, 7T3, 7T5, 7T6, 7L2, 7C1, 7C2, 7C3, 7C4

Unit 5	**Family and other people**
	• Family
	• Morning routines
	• Descriptions of appearance and personality
	• *En plus*: Relationships
		• **French verbs (3)**
		  – Present tense of common irregular verbs
		  – Reflexive verbs
		  – Negatives with reflexive verbs
		• Adjective agreement
			• Using connectives
			Workbook:
			• Speaking strategies
			• Using visual and context clues to help with reading
				• The *è/ais* sound	• French surnames	**R** – 7W4, 7W5, 7W7, 7S1, 7S2, 7S3, 7S5, 7S6, 7S8, 7S9, 7T1, 7T3, 7T4, 7T5, 7T7, 7L1, 7L3, 7L5, 7C2, 7C3, 7C4

Unit 6	**Food and meals** • Eating out • Numbers 70–100 and above • Ordering food • Recipes: ingredients and quantities • Healthy eating • *En plus*: Quantities and packaging	• *au, à l', à la, aux* • *du, de l', de la, des* • *… pas de/d'* (revision) • Present tense of *aller* • *aller* + infinitive	• Asking questions **Workbook:** • How to prepare for listening tasks • Checking written work	• Intonation	• "Food facts" relating to France	**R** – 7W2, 7W5, 7S4, 7S5, 7S7, 7T1, 7T2, 7T4, 7T5, 7T6, 7T7, 7L2, 7L3, 7L6, 7C2, 7C3, 7C4, 7C5

Year 7 Long Term Plan							
	Départ	Unit 1	Unit 2	Unit 3	Unit 4	Unit 5	Unit 6
W1: Everyday words		L	R	R	R		
W2: High-frequency words		L	R		R		R
W3: Classroom words	L	R		R			
W4: Gender and plural	L	R			R	R	
W5: Verbs present (+ past)			L	R		R	R
W6: Letters and sounds		L	R	R			
W7: Learning about words		L	R	R		R	
W8: Finding meanings	L		R	R			
S1: Typical word order		L	R		R	R	
S2: Sentence gist			L		R	R	
S3: Adapting sentences	L	R	R			R	
S4: Basic questions		L	R	R			R
S5: Basic negatives		L	R			R	R
S6: Compound sentences				L	R	R	
S7: Time and tenses				L			R
S8: Punctuation	L	R				R	
S9: Using simple sentences		L	R		R	R	
T1: Reading using cues	L		R			R	R
T2: Reading aloud			L	R			R
T3: Checking before reading			L	R	R	R	
T4: Using resources		L	R			R	R
T5: Assembling text				L	R	R	R
T6: Texts as prompts for writing			L		R		R
T7: Improving written work		L				R	R
L1: Sound patterns	L	R	R	R		R	
L2: Following speech			L		R		R
L3: Gist and detail				L		R	R
L4: Classroom talk	L			R			
L5: Spontaneous talk	L			R		R	
L6: Improving speech	L			R			R
C1: Geographical facts		L			R		
C2: Everyday culture		L	R	R	R	R	R
C3: Contact with native speakers		L	R	R	R	R	R
C4: Stories and songs		L	R	R	R	R	R
C5: Social conventions	L			R			R

L = opportunity to **launch** a Framework objective
R = opportunity to **reinforce** a Framework objective

Introduction

The course

Welcome to **Clic! 1**!

Clic! is a broad-ability course for 11–14 year olds with two levels of coursebook (*Star* and *Plus*) for each part of the three-stage course. The course has been written in response to an ever-growing need for greater flexibility and relevance in the early stages of teaching and learning French.

How does *Clic!* differ from other courses on the market?

Clic! has been designed to take account of:

- greater diversity in Year 7 due to language learning in many primary schools
- raised expectations in learners, regarding the range and differing formats of content
- the revised (2008) Modern Languages Framework
- alternative styles of learning and assessment
- increased demands on teacher time in terms of planning, presentation and assessment
- greater variations in timetabling for Modern Foreign Languages.

To achieve this, **Clic!** offers:

- full differentiation using alternative pathways to teach the whole ability range
- motivating themes and topics, including more "real world" and vocational links
- a more personalised approach, including on-screen assessment *of* and *for* learning, and alternative ways of summative assessment supported through OxBox Assessment CD-ROM
- video, interactive activities, games and songs in an integrated multimedia package (OxBox *Interactif* CD-ROM)
- fully editable lesson plans to allow teachers to customise and deliver exciting structured lessons with minimal hassle (OxBox *Interactif* CD-ROM).

How does *Clic!* make it easier for you to meet the needs of your students?

Firstly, **Clic!** provides *clarity*:

- **a clear structure**
  - There are six units per part, which makes it easy to teach one unit per half-term.
  - Each unit has four core spreads, plus a grammar and skills spread, which makes it easy to teach one core spread per week.

  - Additional (optional) spreads provide extension, further practice and cultural focus, a vocabulary résumé – and a song!
  - There are regular formative assessments in each unit and summative end-of-unit tests, end-of-term and end-of-year tests.

- **clear presentation**
  - In the Students' Books, scene-setting unit opener spreads provide clear contexts and a grammar focus.
  - Activities are colour-coded by skill so that students can find their way easily around a spread.
  - Key language is highlighted and core grammar and skills are presented in special *Labo-langue* spreads.

- **clear progression**
  - Clear teaching and learning objectives show students exactly what they will learn.
  - Key grammar, skills and pronunciation points are presented and practised carefully and systematically.
  - A *Blog-notes* page linked to a video diary recycles key language of the unit.

- **clear differentiation**
  - There are two levels (*Star* and *Plus*) of coursebook for each year, with common core for term 1 to allow for mixed-ability teaching.
  - Two levels of *En solo* Workbook and Copymasters allow for fast- and slow-tracking learners.
  - Two levels of presentation and practice material are provided on OxBox *Interactif* CD-ROM, including gap-bridging texts.

In addition, **Clic!** provides *comprehensive* and *flexible support* to ensure that *lesson planning and teaching are as easy as possible*:

- In this Teacher's Resource Book, in addition to a clear, at-a-glance lesson planner page for each core spread, notes and suggestions have been reduced to a punchy minimum to save preparation time.
- On OxBox *Interactif* CD-ROM, you'll find an editable scheme of work, as well as ready-made lesson plans that allow you to build and modify your lessons to suit your students' needs.
- Other useful features on OxBox *Interactif* CD-ROM include customisable teacher's notes, recording transcripts in Microsoft Word, audio recordings in MP3 format – and the facility to incorporate all your own lesson resources, including worksheets and photos.

To find out more about individual components, please read on!

The components of Clic! 1

Students' Book

The 160-page Students' Book consists of six main units, plus two introductory spreads (*Départ*). This allows one unit per half-term's work. Each unit is divided into an opening spread, presenting the themes of the unit, four core spreads, and a grammar and skills spread. This allows time to cover the additional practice material provided in the course, including cultural and reading pages, revision and assessment. Part 1 ensures that students have appropriate activities for their first year of learning French, providing the necessary programme of teaching, practice, revision and reference materials. Full attention has been given throughout the course to the revised (2008) Modern Languages curriculum (see page 10).

The Students' Book contains the following sections:

Départ

This initial four-page unit raises students' awareness of different languages and introduces them to the sounds and written appearance of French, as well as to aspects of the French-speaking world. It is intended to whet students' appetite and draw on their previous experience and knowledge. Page 4 of the *Départ* section introduces some key classroom language.

Unités 1–6

There are six 18-page units set in different contexts. Each unit has been planned to be interesting and motivating, as well as to provide a coherent and systematic approach to language development in terms of grammar, pronunciation and study skills. An outline of the content of each unit is given on pages 4–5 of this book. For a detailed description of the features of a **Clic! 1** unit, see pages 10–11.

Lecture

Clic! 1 has a substantial 12-page reading section towards the end of the Students' Book, designed to encourage independent reading and help students develop reading strategies. There are two pages of reading per unit: the texts and activities on *Lecture A* should be suitable for all, whereas *Lecture B* is more challenging and may be suitable for more able students only. Students may attempt the *Lecture* pages once they are confident with the core language of the unit. The activities can be used by students who finish other activities quickly or as alternative class and homework activities.

Grammaire

A grasp of grammar and structure lies at the heart of language learning. Each unit in **Clic! 1** focuses on a key aspect of grammar on the *Labo-langue* spread, and this is supported by lively presentations on OxBox *Interactif* CD-ROM. Grammatical items are also incorporated into

the regular sequence of activities running through the units, so that they are seen as an integral part of language practice.

The grammar explanations within the main teaching units are complemented by the detailed grammar reference section at the back of the Students' Book. Here, additional grammar practice activities are integrated into the corresponding grammatical explanations, enabling students to consolidate or revise further their knowledge of grammar. The answers for these activities are at the end of the grammar section in the Students' Book for self-checking.

Expressions utiles

Following the grammar reference section, there is a small section containing useful general vocabulary for easy reference, including numbers, times, days, months, quantities and connectives.

Glossaire

A French–English and English–French glossary contains the words in the Students' Book for students' reference.

Teacher's Resource Book

Each unit contains the following detailed teaching notes:

- a Unit Overview Grid, providing a summary of the unit
- a Medium Term Plan, showing coverage of Framework objectives
- notes to accompany the unit opening page, including unit objectives and assessment opportunities
- a Planner section for each core teaching spread for ease of lesson planning, including suggestions for starter and plenary activities
- ideas for presenting and practising new language
- detailed notes on all the Students' Book material, including answers to all activities
- suggestions for further activities to reinforce and extend the content of the Students' Book
- cross-references to other course components, e.g. margin icons indicate where corresponding resources are available on OxBox *Interactif* CD-ROM, on Copymaster or in the *En solo* Workbook
- information about the Copymasters and *En solo* Workbook activities, including answers
- transcripts for all listening material and video clips.

Audio CDs and MP3 files

The CDs provide the listening material to accompany the Students' Book, Copymasters, *En solo* Workbook and assessment material. The listening material was recorded by native French speakers. The material is scripted and contains a range of text types, including monologues, short dialogues, longer conversations, and songs. Sound files are also available in MP3 format on OxBox *Interactif* CD-ROM. All recorded material may be copied within the purchasing institution for use by teachers and students.

CD contents:
CD 1   *Départ*, Units 1–2 (including Copymasters)
CD 2   Units 3–4 (including Copymasters)
CD 3   Units 5–6 (including Copymasters)
En solo Workbook CD

Copymasters

The Copymasters, located on the CD that accompanies this Teacher's Resource Book, are an integral part of **Clic!** and there are cross-references to them throughout. Notes and transcripts for each unit's Copymasters are provided together at the end of the teaching notes for each unit in this book. The Copymasters provide opportunities for further practice and extension of the language of the unit.

Each unit has the following Copymasters:

- *Vocabulaire*: a list of key vocabulary from the unit, which students can use as a reference or as an aid to learning
- *Je sais…*: a checklist of the core language of the unit, providing an opportunity for students to review their progress and reflect on areas for improvement
- *À tes marques!*: starter activities
- *Bilan de leçon*: plenary activities
- *Écouter*: listening activities
- *Parler*: speaking activities
- *Lire et écrire 1* and *2*: two pages of reading and writing activities
- *Labo-langue*: consolidation and practice of key grammar points
- *Bien apprendre!*: language learning strategies
- *Bien parler!*: pronunciation practice
- *Culture*: activities based on the cultural focus of the unit.

En solo Workbook

Reinforcement and extension activities are provided in the *En solo* Workbook. There is a double-page spread for each of the core spreads in the Students' Book, followed by:

- *Labo-langue*: two pages focusing on key grammar of the unit
- Checklist: a checklist of the core language of the unit, providing an opportunity for students to review their progress and reflect on areas for improvement
- Top tips and strategies: language learning strategies
- *Vocabulaire*: a list of key vocabulary from the unit, with accompanying activities including a listening task.

The Workbook is designed for students to write in, so is ideal for setting homework. Rubrics are provided in English throughout so that students can work independently. Most activities are reading/writing tasks that can be completed without a lot of teacher input, but there are also some listening activities and opportunities for speaking.

OxBox CD-ROMs

See **An integrated approach: How OxBox works** on page 11 of this book.

Course progression

Completing Clic! in a year

Clic! has been designed so that it is possible to complete each part in a single year. Each part has six units and each unit is divided into four core spreads plus a grammar and skills spread. It is estimated that each core spread will take a week to complete and each unit will cover approximately half a term's work.

If you have limited contact time with your students, you can cover the essential language points within a year by concentrating on teaching the core spreads in class and using the additional material (e.g. *En plus*, *Clic.fr*, *Lecture*, *En solo* Workbook and Copymaster activities) selectively for students to work on independently.

Detailed plans are included on OxBox *Interactif* CD-ROM so that lesson planning and delivery can be done flexibly.

Managing the transition between primary and secondary French

Widespread take-up of modern languages in primary schools means that many students are arriving in their first year of secondary school with prior knowledge of French, and may also have acquired transferable language learning skills learned from another language.

It is important to know what level of French or language learning skills your students are bringing with them to secondary school. You may already have links with your feeder primary schools and may have helped to draw up a scheme of work with them. Try to plan your schemes of work together and share information on methodology and resources.

When students transfer to the secondary school, they may bring a record of their achievement in listening, speaking, reading and writing and the National Curriculum levels obtained, a Junior version of the European Languages Portfolio (a Council of Europe initiative), or another similar document detailing exactly what they have learned in their French lessons. The Portfolio and Teacher's Guide are freely downloadable from the NACELL website (www.nacell.org.uk/elp.htm).

You may wish to put students with a prior knowledge of French in a separate group until the spring term, or make use of their extra knowledge to help out the rest of the students in the class. Guidance on transition can be found on the NACELL website.

Clic! and revisions to the Modern Languages curriculum (2008)

Review of the Key Stage 3 Programme of Study

The Modern Languages Key Stage 3 Programme of Study has been revised following consultations to increase curriculum flexibility and improve coherence and progression across Key Stages 2 to 4. The review builds directly on the existing Framework, but reorganises the

Programme of Study to match a common format. It also aims to align level descriptions with Languages Ladder statements.

The new Programme of Study identifies a number of *key concepts* – linguistic competence, knowledge about language, creativity, and intercultural understanding – that students need to deepen and broaden their skills and knowledge. It also identifies *key processes*, in the form of language learning strategies – identifying patterns, memorising techniques, applying knowledge of English, etc. – and specific language skills, for example listening for gist, initiating and sustaining conversations, re-using language in new contexts, etc. Many of these will be familiar to language teachers, but in the writing of **Clic!** we have taken care to ensure that the development of strategies and skills is specifically addressed and practised throughout the course.

The Dearing Review

The Lord Dearing Languages Review (2007) made a number of recommendations aimed at increasing take-up of languages at Key Stage 4. These include providing greater variety and relevance in subject matter and the use of ICT, and looking at alternative forms of certification and recognition of language achievements.

In terms of content, **Clic!** seeks to bring in new themes and topics as well as to explore new angles on more established contexts. The ICT element (see OxBox *Interactif* CD-ROM and OxBox Assessment CD-ROM on page 11) is an integral part of the course, intended to enhance all phases of teaching and assessment and to ensure that learning French is an enjoyable and interactive experience. As regards alternative forms of assessment, in addition to an extensive range of formative assessments on OxBox Assessment CD-ROM, we are working closely with Asset Languages to provide examples and ideas to support Asset tests at suitable points in the course. These relate directly to National Curriculum levels and the Languages Ladder.

Teaching with Clic!

Features of a Clic! unit

Unit opening spread

Each unit begins with a double-page spread designed to set the scene for the unit. These opening spreads provide a clear overview of the contexts and grammar to be covered, with starter activities to introduce students to the core themes of the unit.

Core spreads

There are four core spreads per unit, via which the key language is presented and practised. Each double-page spread includes:

- a clear statement of what students are going to learn on the spread, given in English in student-friendly language
- activities in all four skills to practise the key language of the spread: rubrics on the core spreads are bilingual throughout the Lower book (*Star*); in the Higher book

(*Plus*), they are bilingual in Units 1 and 2, and from Unit 3 onwards in French only

- colour-coding to identify each skill (listening, speaking, reading, writing)
- clearly identified key language panels, providing support and reference for students
- clearly presented grammar boxes to introduce grammar points. Key grammar is then further developed on the *Labo-langue* spread (see below).

Labo-langue

Each unit features a *Labo-langue* spread, which is divided into three sections:

- *Bien comprendre!*
  This page focuses on key grammar points that have been introduced on the four core spreads. Further grammar practice activities are provided in the grammar reference section at the back of the Students' Book, on OxBox *Interactif* CD-ROM, on Copymaster and in the *En solo* Workbook.

- *Bien apprendre!*
  This section promotes language learning strategies. The development of language learning skills is considered to be an integral part of the language learning process and should be given sufficient time during whole-class work. Students who are given opportunities to practise these skills from the start will develop into effective independent language learners. See also the *Bien apprendre!* pages in the *En solo* Workbook and on Copymaster for further development of language learning strategies.

- *Bien parler!*
  This section focuses on key pronunciation points. See also the *Bien parler!* Copymasters for further pronunciation practice.

An overview of the grammar, language learning strategies and pronunciation points covered in each unit of **Clic! 1** is provided on pages 4–5 of this book.

Blog-notes

This page summarises the main points of the unit in context in the form of an Internet video blog – a format that students should find fun, familiar and motivating. It provides a model for students, enabling them to personalise the language of the unit, and is designed to work in tandem with the *Je sais…*/Checklist page on Copymaster and in the *En solo* Workbook. The *Blog-notes* page also provides extended listening practice together with opportunities for students to ask as well as answer questions.

Tu sais tout?

This revision page recaps on the language and structures of the unit, and can also be used as a quick formative test of all four skills. The page is divided into four sections: listening, speaking, reading and writing.

En plus

This page provides extension material for able students who are confident with the core language of the unit. It can be used by students who finish other activities quickly or as alternative class and homework material. Sometimes new language points are introduced via this page.

Clic.fr

The *Clic.fr* page promotes intercultural understanding by focusing on different aspects of French culture and providing opportunities for comparison with students' own culture.

Vocabulaire / On chante!

This double-page spread is divided into three sections:

- *Vocabulaire*
  This theme-based summary of the key language of the unit can be used by students as a reference or as an aid to learning. The *Vocabulaire* list is also provided on Copymaster and in the *En solo* Workbook.

- Extra tips and activities to promote language learning strategies and help students develop as independent learners.

- *On chante!*
  This regular feature recycles the language of the unit in the form of a song.

Lecture

Each unit has a corresponding *Lecture* spread at the back of the Students' Book, designed to encourage independent reading and help students develop reading strategies. There are two pages of reading material per unit: the texts and activities on *Lecture A* should be suitable for all, whereas *Lecture B* is more challenging and may be suitable for more able students only.

An integrated approach: How OxBox works

What is OxBox?

OxBox is a "toolkit" of electronic resources that is designed to facilitate lesson planning and delivery, and provide an effective way of assessing students' progress through the **Clic!** course. Think of OxBox as a virtual filing cabinet with three main folders: one for lesson plans, one for teaching materials and one for tests.

Each folder comes filled with pre-prepared resources to supplement and support the **Clic!** course, ranging from well-structured schemes of work that take the stress out of lesson planning to stimulating interactive activities that

will motivate your students as they learn. OxBox also contains a "User Management" folder, into which you can import class registers and create user accounts for your students.

Fully customisable

OxBox is compatible with all standard Microsoft Office programs so, as well as being able to create new plans and interactive exercises using the OxBox interface, you can also import your own Word or Excel-based lesson plans and materials into OxBox and file them in one centralised location. Many of the resources included in OxBox are themselves fully editable Word and PowerPoint files, permitting you to adapt them to the needs of a particular class or combine them with your own materials as you see fit. Because OxBox comes with a site licence, it can be installed on your school's local network, thereby additionally enabling you to share materials with other teachers if you wish to do so.

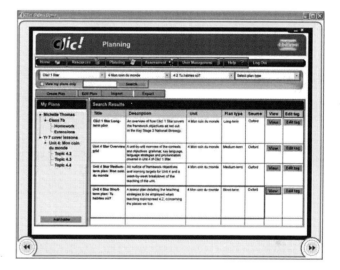

Different access levels for teachers and students

OxBox provides two separate environments, one for teachers and one for students, giving access to different resources. If you log in as a teacher, you have complete access to all of OxBox's resources: you can import class registers, devise new exercises and assessments, and assign assessments to particular groups of students. You can also see individual or aggregated test results for any assessments you have set. Students, on the other hand, have only limited access to two areas within OxBox: **Clic!** *Interactif*, where they can complete interactive exercises, and **Clic!** Assessment, where they can take the tests that you have assigned to them. This means that students can work on OxBox activities and assessments at individual workstations in the classroom using individual log-in IDs.

Lesson planning

The planning section of OxBox contains a variety of resources designed to help you teach the **Clic!** course effectively from the very outset, and reduce the burden of time-consuming lesson conception and planning:

- Course overviews and unit plans familiarise you with the objectives and contents of each unit, allowing you to map out the term's work quickly and easily.

- Schemes of work provide a clear picture of the context for learning and give an outline of how the Framework objectives may be taught.
- Lesson plans offer ideas and strategies for delivering the **Clic!** course, and suggestions on how you can combine the different resources available in the **Clic!** Students' Book and on OxBox. They also point to extension activities from the *En Solo* Workbooks.
- The lesson planner provides a simple template in which you can write additional lesson plans which link to resources in OxBox. Using the lesson planner, you can also customise existing plans, tailoring them to different classes by changing the materials used in the lesson.

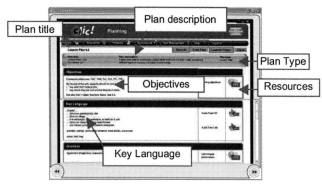

Interactive activities

Interactive exercises in **Clic!** for OxBox take six different forms, which are straightforward enough to be navigated intuitively by students and teachers, yet also provide sufficient scope to develop students' skills in the four key areas of listening, speaking, reading and writing:

- **Flashcards**: an interactive version of the classic vocabulary tool, Flashcards in OxBox use audio-visual stimuli to present vocabulary and encourage speaking practice. Textual clues can be displayed on-screen to help less able students.

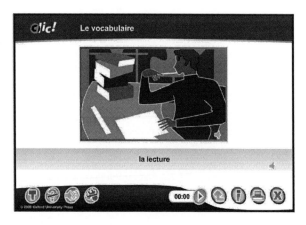

- **Linking lines**: students match audio clues with pictures and/or text to reinforce vocabulary learning and grammar points.
- **Sequencing**: students rearrange elements from a sentence, or reorder information heard in a listening comprehension to underscore syntax rules and practise cloze listening.

- **Drag and drop**: students categorise different words and concepts in accordance with written or spoken instructions, thereby developing their understanding of underlying grammar rules and word categories.

- **Multiple-choice quiz**: students answer questions relating to a text or recording to hone their comprehension skills.
- **Fill the gap**: a chance for students to practise what they have learned in a more active way, testing their ability to recall precise spellings and verb conjugations.

Using the OxBox exercise builder, you can create your own interactive exercises based on these models by filling in simple templates.

Assessments

A subset of these exercise types, including sequencing, drag and drop, multiple choice and fill the gap, is also available for assessment purposes. As part of an assessment, the number of times that each screen can be seen and each question attempted is restricted, and time limits can be set for how fast the assessment should be finished. Assessments in OxBox fall into two categories: formative and summative:

- **Formative**
  Formative assessments are designed to be completed by students as they progress through the course, helping them to master what they have learned and improve any areas of weakness. Students are asked to predict how well they will answer each question before attempting it, and are given two chances to get it right. If they answer incorrectly, they are given feedback on why their answer was wrong and, ultimately, told the right answer. At the end of the test, they are not given an overall score.

- **Summative**
  Summative assessments provide you with a simple and effective way to chart your students' progress at regular intervals throughout the **Clic!** course. Summative assessments are provided as end-of-unit, end-of-term and end-of-year tests. In a summative assessment, students may only attempt each question once and are given an overall result at the end of the test. Once all the members of a class have sat a summative test, the results are aggregated

automatically so that teachers can identify any areas that caused particular difficulty. The feedback from the first end-of-term test can be used as a way to decide which students should follow the *Star* (Lower) and which students should follow the *Plus* (Higher) **Clic! 1** course after term 1.

Presentation and practice of new language

Clic! 1 provides extensive visual and audio-visual support for presentation and practice of new vocabulary via the digi-flashcards and other interactive activities on OxBox *Interactif* CD-ROM: see **Interactive activities** on page 12.

In the Students' Book, new language is presented via the core spreads in a variety of ways, through photos, illustrations and different types of text. Recorded material is provided on CD or as MP3 files on OxBox *Interactif* CD-ROM, and may be used for repetition by students in order to ensure the best possible pronunciation and intonation.

Once presented, the key language of each unit is developed through a wide variety of mixed-skill practice, with activities to ensure language development from supported/guided to more open-ended. **Clic!** intends each activity to have a purpose for students, and to be interesting and motivating as well as promoting linguistic development. Students should be encouraged to learn by heart on a regular basis, not only items of vocabulary but also short conversations. This promotes good language learning habits and ensures that students are able to transfer language learned to new contexts.

Additional reinforcement and extension activities are provided on the *Blog-notes*, *En plus*, *Clic.fr* and *Lecture* pages, with further consolidation and practice on Copymaster, in the *En solo* Workbook and on OxBox *Interactif* CD-ROM. Extra grammar practice is available at the end of the Students' Book in the grammar reference section.

Please refer to OxBox *Interactif* CD-ROM for guidance on:

- ways to use the digi-flashcards
- general strategies and games to present and practise new language using interactive flashcards and other visuals
- activities to present, consolidate and revise the alphabet
- activities to practise numbers.

Target language in the classroom

Clic! aims to maximise the use of French as the means of communication in the classroom by providing rubrics in French wherever appropriate. In the Lower Students' Book (*Star*), rubrics on all the core spreads are in both French and English; in the Higher (*Plus*), rubrics on the core spreads are bilingual in Units 1 and 2, and in French from Unit 3 onwards.

Planned progression ensures that students have opportunities to develop their ability to use target language spontaneously. The *Départ* unit introduces some target language phrases, with a particular focus on communication between student and teacher, and Unit 3 includes a section on using perfect tense phrases to

explain problems and excuses in class (e.g. *J'ai oublié mon cahier, J'ai laissé mon cartable dans le bus*). It is worth spending time on a regular basis revising classroom language, so that students are reminded of the key phrases and encouraged to use them as much as possible.

Differentiation

Particular features of **Clic!** that make it easier to differentiate work include:

- There are two levels (*Star* and *Plus*) of coursebook for each year, with common core for term 1 to allow for mixed-ability teaching.
- Two levels of *En solo* Workbook and Copymasters allow for fast- and slow-tracking learners.
- Two levels of presentation and practice material are provided on OxBox *Interactif* CD-ROM, including gap-bridging texts.
- The *Défi!* activities on some of the Students' Book spreads provide more challenging opportunities for able students.
- *En plus* (towards the end of each unit) provides extension material for students who are confident with the core language of the unit.
- The *Lecture* reading section at the back of the Students' Book features two pages of graded reading material per unit.
- The teaching notes for individual activities often provide suggestions for differentiation, e.g. varying the amount of support offered and adapting the tasks slightly to suit different students.

The following additional classroom management suggestions may help teachers wishing to further differentiate activities:

- Listening activities: provide individual copies of listening material for less able students to work on at their own pace, allowing them to play the recording several times, possibly with the transcript. Encourage more able students who complete a listening task on the first hearing to note any other information they hear and check this against the transcript.
- Paired/Group listening, reading and writing: students can usefully work together on many activities. Two weaker students working together will usually tackle a task with more success than one. An able student working with a less able student will have the dual effect of helping one student while consolidating language for the other.
- Writing activities: encourage students to prepare a first draft of longer writing activities. They could then improve this in consultation with you or other students. This helps less able students to avoid making basic errors and encourages more able students to use a wider variety of vocabulary and structure.
- Regular groupwork lessons: organise groupwork lessons on a regular basis to provide students with appropriate consolidation and extension work. For example, a groupwork lesson towards the end of a unit might involve some students in revising basic vocabulary by playing language games, another group working on Copymasters or on the *En solo* Workbook,

and others working on the *Blog-notes* page or on *Clic.fr*. If a computer is available in the classroom, some students could work on drafting and redrafting written work or on OxBox activities.

Independent learning

In the early stages of learning a language, students are reasonably dependent on their teacher for presentation of new language. However, the following features of **Clic!** are designed to encourage learner independence:

- The *En plus*, *Clic.fr* and *Lecture* pages in each unit are ideal for independent work.
- The *Blog-notes* page provides opportunities for students to work independently and personalise their responses to the themes of each unit.
- Each unit's *Je sais…*/Checklist page on Copymaster and in the *En solo* Workbook encourages students to take responsibility for their own learning by providing opportunities for them to review what they have learned and reflect on areas for improvement
- The *Vocabulaire* pages at the end of each unit, on Copymaster and in the *En solo* Workbook can be used independently by students as a reference source or as an aid to learning.
- The *Grammaire* section at the back of the Students' Book provides full explanations of all the grammar points in English together with additional practice activities, so that students to use it independently as a reference source.
- A strong emphasis on language learning strategies throughout (via the *Bien apprendre!* sections in the Students' Book, on Copymaster and in the *En solo* Workbook) encourages students to progress as independent learners.
- The *En solo* Workbook is designed for independent work, with rubrics in English throughout.

Thinking skills and creativity

One of the key aims of **Clic!**, and of the MFL Framework as a whole, is that students should be able to learn in a meaningful way. This means, for example, thinking flexibly, analysing language and problem-solving, justifying answers, and making predictions based on previous knowledge. It encourages students to move towards becoming independent learners. Once students take a more active role in their language learning, they make quicker progress and the thinking skills learned can be applied to other curriculum areas.

Creativity in language learning is not simply imaginative use of language, such as poetry, creative writing, etc. It also refers to resourcefulness, e.g. finding ways to express oneself using only a limited range of language, taking risks and experimenting with language.

See **Independent learning** above for examples of features of **Clic!** that encourage students to take a more active role in their learning. In addition, the following types of activity used in **Clic!** help to promote thinking skills and creativity:

- Encourage students to deduce new language for themselves (e.g. verb endings, adjective endings) by working from what they already know.
- Ask students to spot the odd-one-out in a group of words/phrases, giving a reason. All appropriate answers should be accepted, provided that students can justify them, e.g. answers may be based on meaning, grammar, pronunciation, etc.
- Encourage students to apply previously learned language in different contexts.
- Provide opportunities for students to use language spontaneously. This promotes the development of coping strategies, since students need to find ways of communicating when they don't know the word for something, dealing with unpredictable situations, etc.
- Ask students to write something within an exact word count, e.g. 100 words exactly. This type of task encourages students to experiment with language and take risks, because in order to arrive at the precise word count they will need to paraphrase.
- Provide opportunities for students to share their knowledge in pairs/groups or during whole-class feedback.

Assessment

Assessment of learning

Regular assessment of student progress is an integral part of the learning process. **Clic!** offers an approach to assessment in line with the National Curriculum and the 5–14 National Guidelines.

A range of formative and summative assessment opportunities are provided on OxBox Assessment CD-ROM: for details of this, see **An integrated approach: How OxBox works** on pages 11–12 of this book. In addition, **Clic!** provides the following **assessment opportunities**:

- The *Tu sais tout?* page at the end of each unit in the Students' Book can be used either as a revision page or as a quick formative test of all four skills.
- At the start of the teaching notes for each unit in this book, the **Assessment opportunities** section suggests activities from the forthcoming unit that may be suitable for formative assessment. Two skills are suggested for assessment in each unit, with each skill being covered three times during the year.

Assessment for Learning

Assessment for Learning (AfL) helps students to know and understand the standard they are aiming for, and also to understand what they need to do in order to achieve their objectives. It involves not only sharing learning goals with students, but also involving them in both peer- and self-assessment. AfL stresses the importance of ensuring that the information gained about students' progress is used, by both teachers and learners, to identify the next steps for learning. This might involve giving students opportunities to talk about what they have learned and what they have found difficult.

In **Clic! 1**, each unit's *Je sais…*/Checklist page on Copymaster and in the *En solo* Workbook is specifically

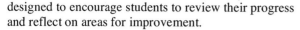

designed to encourage students to review their progress and reflect on areas for improvement.

Further guidance on AfL can be found in *Training Materials for the Foundation Subjects* (Module 1 "Assessment for learning in everyday lessons"), which is available to download from The Standards Site (managed by the Department for Children, Schools and Families) (www.standards.dfes.gov.uk). For further guidance on AfL, see also the website of the Qualifications and Curriculum Authority (QCA) (www.qca.org.uk).

Clic! and Asset Languages

Asset Languages is the assessment scheme for the DCSF Languages Ladder and is offered by OCR as part of the National Languages Strategy.

Each of the four skills, listening, speaking, reading and writing, forms a separate qualification. There are two forms of assessment:

Teacher assessment

Learners may take teacher assessment for one or more skills at each grade and are then eligible for a Grade Award issued in the centre by their Accredited Teacher. Teachers may adapt or replace some tasks in the Asset Languages Teacher Assessment Pack with other equivalent tasks. Some activities in this course have been identified by Asset Languages as suitable for this purpose.

External assessment

Learners receive an accredited OCR qualification for a particular stage and skill once they have taken the appropriate external assessment. This consists of one test that covers all three grades in the stage for one skill, for example, French Breakthrough Reading. Some activities in this course have been identified by Asset Languages as suitable for helping to prepare learners for external assessment at Breakthrough Stage.

For more information on Asset Languages visit the website **www.assetlanguages.org.uk**

How to teach the MFL Framework with Clic!

Long Term Plans, Medium Term Plans and Lesson Plans

Clic! has been carefully planned to ensure that all Framework objectives are covered in familiar contexts.

- **Long Term Plans (LTPs)**

  These provide an overview of objectives to be covered in each year of Key Stage 3. Each objective is to be specifically launched (L) and reinforced (R) at least once within that year.

  – Year 7 objectives are covered in **Clic! 1** Units 1–6.
  – Year 8 objectives are covered in **Clic! 2** Units 1–6.
  – Year 9 objectives are covered in **Clic! 3** Units 1–6.
  See page 6 of this book for the **Clic! 1** Long Term Plan.

- **Medium Term Plans (MTPs)**

  These relate to individual units within the course and aim to cover six weeks' work. The MTPs provide a

clear picture of the context for learning and give an outline of how the Framework objectives, identified in the LTP, might be taught. See the beginning of each unit's teaching notes in this book for a copy of the Medium Term Plan for each unit.

- **Lesson Plans**

  These focus on teaching strategies, specific resources and activities to meet objectives within each unit. All the lesson plans are provided on OxBox *Interactif* CD-ROM in an editable format, together with an editable lesson plan template.

Key areas of teaching and learning

Clic! reflects the focus of the MFL Framework on key areas of teaching and learning. These include:

- **Starters**

  – Suggestions for starter activities for each core spread are given in the lesson plans (on OxBox *Interactif* CD-ROM) as well as in the Planner sections in this Teacher's Resource Book.
  – Additional starter activities are provided on the *À tes marques!* Copymasters.

- **Setting lesson objectives**

  – The Planner sections provide a clear list of objectives for each spread in terms of contexts and grammar. These can easily be adapted into individual lesson objectives, as shown in the lesson plans.

- **Modelling**

  – **Clic!** provides clear examples for all activities, where appropriate, so that students have a visual demonstration of how to complete the activity.
  – Selected written texts are provided on OxBox *Interactif* CD-ROM so that you can work on them with the whole class.
  – Specific guidance is also given in the teacher's notes.

- **Questioning**
- **Practice**
- **Plenaries**

  – Suggestions for plenary activities for each core spread are given in the lesson plans (on OxBox *Interactif* CD-ROM) as well as in the Planner sections in this Teacher's Resource Book.
  – Additional plenary activities are provided on the *Bilan de leçon* Copymasters.

Launching and reinforcing Framework objectives

All Year 7 Framework objectives are launched and reinforced via activities in the Students' Book, or via the language strategy pages in the Workbook and on Copymaster. In this Teacher's Resource Book, there are cross-references to the objectives in the Long Term Plan, Summary of Unit Contents grid, Medium Term Plans, Unit Overview Grids, and Planner sections.

The grids on page 16 show how Framework objective 7W7 is taught using **Clic! 1**.

Year 7 Long Term Plan	Départ	Unit 1	Unit 2	Unit 3	Unit 4	Unit 5	Unit 6
W1: Everyday words		L	R	R	R		
W2: High-frequency words		L	R		R		R
W3: Classroom words	L	R		R			
W4: Gender and plural	L	R			R	R	
W5: Verbs present (+ past)			L	R		R	R
W6: Letters and sounds		L	R	R			
W7: Learning about words		L	R	R		R	
W8: Finding meanings	L		R	R			
S1: Typical word order		L	R		R	R	
S2: Sentence gist			L		R	R	
S3: Adapting sentences	L	R	R			R	
S4: Basic questions		L	R	R			R
S5: Basic negatives		L	R			R	R
S6: Compound sentences				L	R	R	
S7: Time and tenses				L			R
S8: Punctuation	L	R				R	
S9: Using simple sentences		L	R		R	R	
T1: Reading using cues	L		R			R	R
T2: Reading aloud			L	R			R
T3: Checking before reading			L	R	R	R	
T4: Using resources		L	R			R	R
T5: Assembling text			L	R	R	R	R
T6: Texts as prompts for writing			L		R		R
T7: Improving written work		L				R	R
L1: Sound patterns	L	R	R	R		R	
L2: Following speech			L		R		R
L3: Gist and detail				L		R	R
L4: Classroom talk	L	R					
L5: Spontaneous talk	L		R			R	

The Long Term Plan shows that Framework objective 7W7 is specifically launched in Unit 1 and reinforced in Units 2, 3 and

The Medium Term Plan for Unit 1 provides the context and teaching focus to launch objective 7W7. The page cross-reference (in this case, Students' Book page 21) identifies precisely where 7W7 is launched.

CLIC! 1 STAR UNIT 1 MEDIUM TERM PLAN

About Unit 1, *Vive la France!* In this unit, students discover more about France and French-speaking countries, nouns and gender, learn how to record new vocabulary and how to use the reference sections in the Students' Book. Nasal sounds are practised, and reading, listening and comprehension skills are developed through a variety of texts, audio and video materials. Additional teaching and learning includes colours, numbers 1–10, the alphabet, places in town, jobs, nationalities and languages, and symbols of France (e.g. *la tour Eiffel*, *la Marseillaise*).

Framework objectives (launch)	Teaching and learning	Week-by-week overview (assuming 6 weeks' work or approximately 10–12.5 hours)
7W1: Everyday words	Learn how to record new language effectively and begin building own stock of words from Unit 1 (p. 21).	**Week 1 – Opening spread/1.1 C'est ça, la France!** Opening spread: introduction to unit themes and objectives, focusing on the geography of France and names of French towns (sound–spelling links) Spread 1.1: things associated with France, especially cultural aspects; numbers 1–10; gender of nouns
7W2: High-frequency words	Importance of knowing and remembering little words such as: *le/la/les*; *un/une/des*; *c'est/ce n'est pas…*; *il y a…*, *il n'y a pas de/d'…*; *je suis…*, *il/elle est…*; *oui, non.*	
7W6: Letters and sounds	Introduction to the alphabet and sounds (p. 14).	
7W7: Learning about words	Effective ways to record and learn new vocabulary (p. 21).	
7S1: Typical word order	Position of adjectives (p. 20).	
7S4: Basic questions	How to ask a basic question, e.g. *Tu t'appelles comment? C'est quoi, ton pays/ta nationalité? Tu parles quelles langues?*	
7S5: Basic negatives	*Ce n'est pas* (p. 13), *il n'y a pas de/d'* (p. 15).	**Week 2 – 1.2 En France** What there is/is not in a town; the alphabet; simple negatives (*il n'y a pas de…*)
7S9: Using simple sentences	Use simple model sentences to assist in producing own short text expressing basic information: *Salut! Je m'appelle… Mon pays, c'est…*, etc. (p. 17).	
7T4: Using resources	Familiarisation with the reference sections in the Students' Book (*Glossaire, Vocabulaire*, verb tables, etc.) (Workbook p. 17).	**Week 3 – 1.3 Ici, on parle français** Countries and languages; nationalities and agreements, e.g. *canadien(enne)*; colours
7T7: Improving written work	Awareness of common differences between French and English when writing, e.g. accents, agreement (Workbook p. 17).	
7C1: Geographical facts	Location of towns on a map of France (p. 11); French-speaking countries (p. 11, pp. 16–17).	
7C2: Everyday culture	Symbols of France, e.g. *la tour Eiffel, la pétanque* (p. 12, p. 25); French handwriting (p. 14 *l'alphabet*, p. 25 *La Marseillaise*).	**Week 4 – 1.4 Les langues des stars** Jobs and languages (two case studies)
7C3: Contact with native speakers	Video clip of native speakers talking about things that represent France (p. 13); video blog (p. 22).	
7C4: Stories and songs	Song about colours and flags (p. 27).	
Framework objectives (reinforce)	**Teaching and learning**	**Week 5 – Labo-langue** Nouns and gender; recording and learning new vocabulary; nasal sounds
7W3: Classroom words	Expand stock of words used in classroom situations via rubrics in French; grammar terms, e.g. what is a noun?, what is meant by gender? (p. 20).	
7W4: Gender and plural	Nouns and gender: determiners, masculine/feminine forms of job titles (*serveur, serveuse*), agreement of adjectives (p. 20, p. 27).	
7S3: Adapting sentences	Replace multiple-choice answers with own details to give information about self for a video blog (*Blog-notes*, p. 22).	**Week 6 – Blog-notes, Tu sais tout?, En plus, Clic.fr, On chante!, Lecture** Reinforcement and extension of the language of the unit; review of progress via the Checklist in the Workbook/on Copymaster; revision and assessment
7S8: Punctuation	Awareness that nationalities and languages are capitalised in English but not in French (p. 16); use of apostrophe before vowels and silent *h*, e.g. *il n'y pas d'hôtel* (p. 15), *l'Algérie* (p. 16).	
7L1: Sound patterns	Pronunciation: nasal sounds (p. 21).	

Départ Overview grid

Page reference	Contexts and objectives	Grammar	Language strategies and pronunciation	Key language	Framework	AT Level
6–7 **En français**	• Greetings • Recognising French (spoken and written)			*Bonjour!*	**L** – 7W8, 7S8, 7T1, 7L1, 7L6	
8–9 **Je parle français!**	• Names and nationalities • Classroom language	• *Je suis* • *Tu es…?* • Masculine and feminine agreement of nationality adjectives		*Bonjour! Salut! Je m'appelle…* *Tu es…? Je suis…* *Oui. Non.* *Les nationalités:* *français(e), sénégalais(e)* *anglais(e), écossais(e), gallois(e), irlandais(e)* *En classe:* *Asseyez-vous! Ouvrez vos livres.* *Faites l'activité trois. Silence!* *Je n'ai pas mon livre. Je ne comprends pas.* *C'est quelle page? Prête-moi ton crayon, s'il te plaît.* *J'ai fini! Je n'ai pas fini!* *Je peux aller aux toilettes, s'il vous plaît?*	**L** – 7W3, 7W4, 7S3, 7L4, 7L5, 7C5	1.1, 2.1, 3.1, 4.1

CLIC! 1 STAR DÉPART MEDIUM TERM PLAN

About the *Départ* unit: This initial unit introduces students to the French language and the French-speaking world while raising awareness of other languages and drawing on their existing knowledge and personal experiences. By the end of the unit, students will be able to recognise and say simple greetings, introduce themselves, and distinguish between texts in French and other languages. They search for cognates and are introduced to French accents. Some basic classroom language is presented and there is a gentle initiation to French grammar, including masculine and feminine nouns and verbs (*je suis, tu es*).

Framework objectives (launch)	Teaching and learning	Week-by-week overview (assuming 2 weeks' work or approximately 4 hours)
7W3: Classroom words	Classroom language and instructions, e.g. *Asseyez-vous, C'est quelle page?, J'ai fini* (p. 9).	**Week 1 – En français** Awareness of foreign languages, drawing on students' personal experiences and knowledge; the sounds and written appearance of different languages; recognising French (spoken and written); accents and other features of written French; cognates; a simple greeting in French: *Bonjour!*
7W4: Gender and plural	Masculine and feminine agreement of nationality adjectives (p. 8).	
7W8: Finding meanings	Look for cognates in newspaper cuttings (p. 7).	
7S3: Adapting sentences	Adapt a simple speech bubble to give own name and nationality (p. 8).	
7S8: Punctuation	Accents and other features (*accent aigu/grave/circonflexe, cédille, tréma* (p. 7).	
7T1: Reading using cues	Identify written cognates in newspaper cuttings (p. 7).	
7L1: Sound patterns	Introduction to the differences between English and French sounds (pp. 6–7); key pronunciation points, including vowels and accents, nasal sounds, silent consonants, etc. (Workbook pp. 4–5).	**Week 2 – Je parle français!** Nationalities, agreement of nationality adjectives; basic introductions and greetings, e.g. *Salut! Je m'appelle...; je suis, tu es; oui, non;* classroom language and instructions; *tu* and *vous*
7L4: Classroom talk	Classroom language and instructions (p. 9).	
7L5: Spontaneous talk	Greetings and classroom language (pp. 8–9).	
7L6: Improving speech	"Sound French!" (Workbook pp. 4–5) provides a reference source of key pronunciation points, designed for students to listen and practise repeating the sounds.	
7C5: Social conventions	Greetings; use of *tu* and *s'il te plaît* to a friend, use of *vous* and *s'il vous plaît* to an adult, e.g. a teacher.	

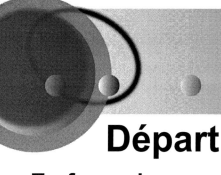

Départ

En français

Planner

> #### Objectives
> * Greetings
> * Recognising French (spoken and written)

> #### Resources
> Students' Book, pages 6–7
> Video clip 1
> *En solo* Workbook, pages 4–5;
> *En solo* CD, tracks 2–8

> #### Key language
> *Bonjour!*

> #### Framework reference
> L – 7W8, 7S8, 7T1, 7L1, 7L6

> #### Starters
> * In English, students name as many foreign languages as they can in 30 seconds.
> * Name a country; students tell you which languages they think are spoken there.

> #### Plenaries
> * Discuss students' linguistic experience, e.g. the languages they speak at home or when on holiday in other countries. How did they learn these languages? If English is their second language, how did they learn it? Why is it important to be able to speak different languages?
> * Try to connect the learning of French with other subjects on the school curriculum, e.g. students might learn about France in a geography or history lesson, or something they learn about in French grammar might help them with English grammar.

Differentiation in *Départ* and Units 1 and 2

In *Départ* and Units 1 and 2, the coursebook pages for **Clic! 1** *Star* and *Plus* are the same, to facilitate mixed group/class teaching to the end of term 1. To support individual practice, there are differentiated activities for higher/lower attainers in the *En solo* Workbooks (*Star* and *Plus*) and on the editable activity sheets on the Copymaster CD-ROM that comes with this Teacher's Resource Book.

Other suggestions for differentiation are given in the teaching notes that follow, but some general ideas for this early stage of language learning are:
* Try to provide opportunities for children with prior knowledge (e.g. those who have learned some French at primary school) to recycle what they already know.
* Absolute beginners can copy models provided, whereas others should be encouraged to be more independent, e.g. by extending activities using language of their own, researching vocabulary in the glossary, etc.

From the beginning of Unit 3 onwards, the coursebook activities in *Star* and *Plus* are tailored towards lower and higher attainers respectively.

1 Regarde.
* *Aim*: To raise awareness of languages; to enable students to draw on their existing knowledge of different languages.
* Students watch the video clip, in which a boy tries to tune in a radio. We hear snippets of different languages. Students pick out as many languages as they can.
* In English, discuss the general sound of the languages, e.g. are they hard, soft, flowing, choppy, etc.?

Answers: the languages heard are: English, Italian, German, Chinese, Russian, French

---

 Video clip 1   page 6, activité 1

– [Extract in English]
– [Extract in Italian]
– [Extract in German]
– [Extract in Chinese]
– [Extract in Russian]
– [Extract in French]

---

2 Relie.

- Students match the speech bubbles to the languages.

Answers: 1 Chinese; 2 Russian; 3 French; 4 English; 5 Italian; 6 German

Follow-up:

- Focus on the languages that use different scripts, and ask students if they know of any other languages that have different scripts, e.g. Urdu, Arabic.
- Do students see any similarities between English and German, French and Italian? (E.g. *Good morning* and *Guten Morgen* are very similar, as are *Bonjour* and *Buongiorno*.)

3 Explique.

- If any students know how to say "hello" (or anything else) in another language, ask them to tell the class.

4 Parle.

- Set up a Mexican Wave around the class: students say *Bonjour!* in turn.

Follow-up: If most of your students have not learned any French in primary school, repeat the Mexican Wave several times, prompting them to use different voices, e.g. speaking as monsters, ghosts, squeaky mice, etc.

5 Lis.

- *Aim*: To introduce students to features of written French.
- Students look at the magazine and newspaper cuttings in different languages and try to work out which ones are in French.

6 Combien?

- Students search the French texts for the accents listed in the information box.
- They begin by finding examples of words containing the *accent aigu*, *accent grave* and *accent circonflexe*, then follow this up with a hunt for any words containing the *cédille* and *tréma*.

Follow-up: Focus on other aspects of the languages in the texts, e.g. the use of capital letters for nouns in German, the umlaut in German.

 7 Traduis.

- *Aim*: To raise awareness of similarities between languages.
- Students search the texts for any words they understand, e.g. words that look similar to English words. They list these and compare with a partner.

W 4–5 Pages 4–5 of the *En solo* Workbook focus on key pronunciation points and could be used at any appropriate point during work on the *Départ* unit.

Je parle français!

Planner

> ### Objectives
> - Names and nationalities
> - Classroom language

> ### Resources
> Students' Book, pages 8–9
> CD 1, tracks 3–4

> ### Key language
> <u>*Les nationalités*</u>
> *français(e), sénégalais(e)*
> *anglais(e), écossais(e), gallois(e), irlandais(e)*
>
> *Bonjour! Salut!*
> *Je m'appelle...*
> *Tu es...? Je suis...*
> *Oui. Non.*
>
> <u>*En classe*</u>
> *Asseyez-vous! Ouvrez vos livres.*
> *Faites l'activité trois. Silence!*
> *Je n'ai pas mon livre. Je ne comprends pas.*
> *C'est quelle page? Prête-moi ton crayon, s'il te plaît.*
> *J'ai fini! Je n'ai pas fini!*
> *Je peux aller aux toilettes, s'il vous plaît?*

> ### Grammar
> *Je suis...*
> *Tu es...?*
> Masculine/Feminine agreement of nationality
> adjectives

> ### Framework reference
> **L** – 7W3, 7W4, 7S3, 7L4, 7L5, 7C5

> ### Starters
> - Bring in some photos of celebrities, taken from magazines or the Internet (or ask students to bring in some photos). Hold each one up in turn, with the image hidden, then slowly reveal the image. Students compete to be the first to recognise each celebrity. They say a greeting followed by the person's name in French, e.g. *Bonjour! Je m'appelle...*
> - Focus on the Senegalese teenagers on page 8 and point out that French is the official language of Senegal. Do students know of any other countries where French is spoken?

> ### Plenaries
> - Display a jumbled selection of celebrity photos (or pictures of cartoon characters) and masculine/feminine nationality adjectives from page 8: *français/française, anglais/anglaise, écossais/écossaise, gallois/galloise, irlandais/irlandaise.* If appropriate, add further nationalities, preferably cognates/near-cognates, e.g. *américain/américaine.* Each adjective must correspond with one of your celebrities in terms of nationality and gender. Students match the adjectives to the celebrities and write a couple of sentences: *Je m'appelle Orlando Bloom. Je suis anglais. Je m'appelle Victoria Beckham. Je suis anglaise.*
> - In pairs/groups, students take turns to mime the classroom language phrases for their partner or the rest of the group to guess.
> - In pairs/groups, students discuss why it is important to use French as much as possible for communication in class, e.g. it's fun, it helps you to learn more quickly, it gives you a real reason to use French. Pairs/Groups feed back their ideas to the class.

---

 1 Qui parle?

- *Aim*: To introduce the notion of gender and agreement; to raise awareness of French-speaking countries.
- Students read the speech bubbles while listening to the short exchanges. They work out who is being interviewed in each exchange.
- Point out the notes on masculine and feminine nationality adjectives. Ask students to consider how grammar knowledge such as this might sometimes help them to work out meanings.

Answers: 1 Kouakou; 2 Manon; 3 Adama; 4 Thomas

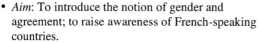 **CD 1, track 3**   page 8, activité 1

1 – Salut! Je m'appelle Manon.
   Je suis française.

2 – Salut! Je m'appelle Kouakou.
   Je suis sénéglais.

3 – Bonjour. Je suis sénégalaise.
   Je m'appelle Adama

4 – Bonjour! Je m'appelle Thomas.
   Je suis français!

AT 1.1

AT 1.1 | AT 3.1 **2 Réécoute.**

- Play the recording again. Students listen and read the speech bubbles, focusing on finding specific details.

Answers: a Bonjour! Salut!; b Je m'appelle…; c The differences are: *français* and *sénégalais* have silent endings, but in *française* and *sénégalaise* the endings are pronounced.

 AT 2.1 **3 Parle.**

- Set up a Mexican Wave around the class, with students each saying *Je m'appelle* + their own name.

 AT 2.1 **4 À deux. (A ➜ B)**

- Students take turns to pretend to be one of the four people from the photos. Their partner tries to find out who they are by asking questions, e.g.
Student A: *Tu es français?*
Student B: *Non.*
Student A: *Tu es française?*
Student B: *Oui.*
Student A: *Tu es Manon!*
Student B: *Oui, je suis Manon!*

AT 4.1 **5 Écris.**

- Students write a speech bubble stating their own name and nationality, illustrated with a photo or drawing of themselves. These could be used to make a class display.
- Point out the nationalites *anglais(e), écossais(e), gallois(e)* and *irlandais(e)*. If there are different ethnic groups within your class, you may need to prepare a list of the relevant nationalities in advance.

Follow-up:

- Throw a soft ball to someone in the class. They introduce themselves by saying *Bonjour!* or *Salut!* followed by *Je m'appelle…* and *Je suis* + nationality, before throwing the ball to someone else. Continue around the class, making sure that no one is left out.
- Students work their way around the class, introducing themselves as a celebrity or historical figure. Their classmates try to guess their nationality, e.g.
Student A: *Salut! Je m'appelle Zinédine Zidane.*
Student B: *Tu es français?*
Student A: *Oui, je suis français!*
Student B: *Je m'appelle Ewan McGregor.*
Student A: *Tu es écossais?*
You may need to provide a list of additional nationalites on the board or OHP for this activity.

AT 1.1 | AT 3.1 **6 Lis et écoute.**

- *Aim*: To introduce some basic classroom language.
- Students listen while reading the cartoon and try to work out the meaning of the phrases.
- Point out the information box on use of *tu* and *vous*.

 CD 1, track 4   page 9, activité 6

– Bonjour! Asseyez-vous!
– Bonjour, madame!

– Ouvrez vos livres.
– Oh! Je n'ai pas mon livre.
– C'est quelle page?

– Faites l'activité trois.
– Je ne comprends pas.

– Prête-moi ton crayon, s'il te plaît.
– Silence!

– J'ai fini!
– Je n'ai pas fini!

– Madame! Madame! S'il vous plaît… je peux aller aux toilettes?
– Oui!

 AT 3.1 **7 Relie**

- Students match the English phrases to the numbered French captions in the cartoon.

Answers: a 9; b 5; c 1; d 12; e 10; f 6; g 3; h 7; i 4; j 11; k 8

Follow-up: Discuss strategies for practising and remembering classroom language, e.g. display a "phrase of the week" somewhere in class and encourage students to use it as often as possible during that week – excluding *Je peux aller aux toilettes?* of course!

En solo Workbook

Pages 4–5   Sound French!

- This double-page spread focuses on key pronunciation points and could be used with pages 6–7 of the Students' Book.
- The activities are designed for students to listen to the French sounds and practise repeating them.
- In order to keep this section manageable for students, not all variations on spellings/sounds are included.

Vowels

1 French vowels are short and simple.

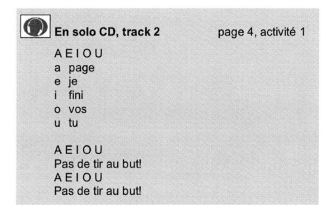

En solo CD, track 2 page 4, activité 1

A E I O U
a page
e je
i fini
o vos
u tu

A E I O U
Pas de tir au but!
A E I O U
Pas de tir au but!

2 Accents can change the sound of vowels.

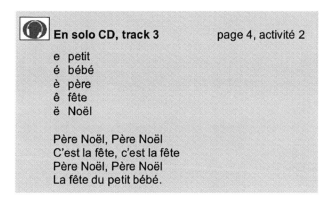

En solo CD, track 3 page 4, activité 2

e petit
é bébé
è père
ê fête
ë Noël

Père Noël, Père Noël
C'est la fête, c'est la fête
Père Noël, Père Noël
La fête du petit bébé.

3 Vowels together make up new sounds.

En solo CD, track 4 page 4, activité 3

ai   vrai, beige
au   faux, beau
eu   deux, bleu
oi   moi, trois
ou   vous, rouge
oui oui, Louis
ui   huit, lui

Deux pour moi
Trois pour toi
Huit pour lui.
Il est beau!
Vrai ou faux?

4 Vowels combine with *n* or *m* to make new sounds.

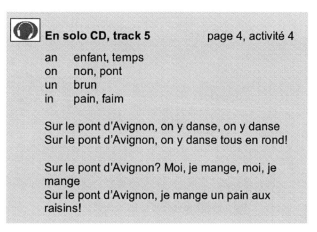

En solo CD, track 5 page 4, activité 4

an   enfant, temps
on   non, pont
un   brun
in   pain, faim

Sur le pont d'Avignon, on y danse, on y danse
Sur le pont d'Avignon, on y danse tous en rond!

Sur le pont d'Avignon? Moi, je mange, moi, je mange
Sur le pont d'Avignon, je mange un pain aux raisins!

Consonants

5 French and English consonants are mostly similar to each other, with a few differences.

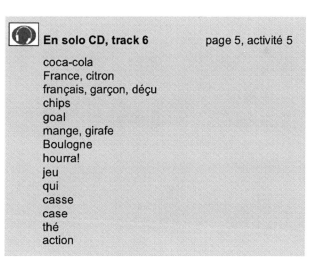

En solo CD, track 6 page 5, activité 5

coca-cola
France, citron
français, garçon, déçu
chips
goal
mange, girafe
Boulogne
hourra!
jeu
qui
casse
case
thé
action

6 Final consonants are usually silent in French.

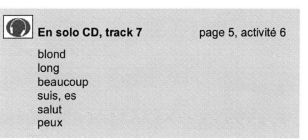

En solo CD, track 7 page 5, activité 6

blond
long
beaucoup
suis, es
salut
peux

7 A few final consonants are usually pronounced.

 En solo CD, track 8   page 5, activité 7

avec, anorak, cinq
bonjour, noir
sportif
avril

Qui est Simon?
C'est le garçon français, le sportif blond avec un anorak noir.

Unité 1: Vive la France! Overview grid

Page reference	Contexts and objectives	Grammar	Language strategies and pronunciation	Key language	Framework	AT Level
12–13 **1.1 C'est ça, la France!**	• Things that make you think of France • Numbers 1–10	• Gender: *le, la, les*		Numbers 1–10 *C'est quoi? C'est… Ce n'est pas…* *le jean, le parfum, le football, le TGV, le vélo, la baguette, la FNAC, la pétanque, les Carambars* *C'est la tour Eiffel? Oui. Non.*	**L** – 7S5, 7C2, 7C3	1.1, 2.1, 3.1
14–15 **1.2 En France**	• What there is/is not in a town • The alphabet	• *Il y a un/une/des…* • *Il n'y a pas de/d'…*		*Qu'est-ce qu'il y a? Il y a…* *un café-tabac, un camping, un cinéma, un hôtel, un restaurant, une école, une pharmacie, une rue, des toilettes/des WC* *Il n'y a pas de camping. Il n'y a pas d'hôtel.*	**L** – 7W6, 7S5 **R** – 7S8	1.1–2, 2.1–2, 3.1–2, 4.1–2
16–17 **1.3 Ici, on parle français**	• Your country and the languages you speak • Colours			*Tu t'appelles comment? Je m'appelle…* *C'est quoi, ton pays? Mon pays, c'est la France. C'est quoi, ta nationalité? Je suis français (e).* *l'Angleterre: anglais(e); l'Écosse: écossais(e); l'Irlande: irlandais(e); le pays de Galles: gallois(e); la France: français(e); la Belgique: belge; l'Algérie: algérien(enne); le Canada: canadien(enne); la Suisse: suisse; le Sénégal: sénégalais(e)* <u>*Les couleurs:*</u> *bleu, blanc, rouge, vert, noir, orange, jaune* *Le drapeau français est bleu, blanc et rouge.*	**L** – 7S4, 7S9 **R** – 7S8	1.1–2, 2.1, 3.1–2, 4.1–2
18–19 **1.4 Les langues des stars**	• Jobs • Languages			*Il/Elle s'appelle…* *Il est sportif. Elle est sportive. Il est acteur. Elle est actrice. Il est présentateur.* *Tu parles quelles langues? Je parle français, japonais, allemand, espagnol, italien, arabe, anglais, flamand.* *C'est important pour le travail/les voyages/la communication internationale.*	**L** – 7W2	1.2, 2.2, 3.2, 4.2
20–21 **Labo-langue**	• Grammar • Skills • Pronunciation	Nouns and gender: • Determiners • Masculine and feminine job titles • Agreement of nationality adjectives	• Recording new language • Nasal sounds **Workbook:** • Using reference materials • Differences between French and English		**L** – 7W1, 7W7, 7S1, 7T4, 7T7 **R** – 7W3, 7W4, 7L1	
22–25 **Blog-notes / Tu sais tout? / En plus / Clic.fr**	• End-of-unit summary and assessment • Extension • **Cultural focus:** symbols of France				**L** – 7C2, 7C3, 7C4 **R** – 7W4, 7S3	1.2–3, 2.1–2, 3.2, 4.2–3

CLIC! 1 STAR UNIT 1 MEDIUM TERM PLAN

About Unit 1, *Vive la France!* In this unit, students discover more about France and French-speaking countries, nouns and gender, learn how to record new vocabulary and how to use the reference sections in the Students' Book. Nasal sounds are practised, and reading, listening and comprehension skills are developed through a variety of texts, audio and video materials. Additional teaching and learning includes colours, numbers 1–10, the alphabet, places in town, jobs, nationalities and languages, and symbols of France (e.g. *la tour Eiffel, la Marseillaise*).

Framework objectives (launch)	Teaching and learning
7W1: Everyday words	Learn how to record new language effectively and begin building own stock of words from Unit 1 (p. 21).
7W2: High-frequency words	Importance of knowing and remembering little words such as: *le/le/les; un/une/des; c'est/ce n'est pas...; il y a...; il n'y a pas de/d'...; je suis... je suis... il/elle est...: oui, non.*
7W6: Letters and sounds	Introduction to the alphabet and sounds (p. 14).
7W7: Learning about words	Effective ways to record and learn new vocabulary (p. 21).
7S1: Typical word order	Position of adjectives (p. 20).
7S4: Basic questions	How to ask a basic question, e.g. *Tu t'appelles comment? C'est quoi, ton pays/ta nationalité? Tu parles quelles langues?*
7S5: Basic negatives	*Ce n'est pas* (p. 13), *il n'y a pas de/d'* (p. 15).
7S9: Using simple sentences	Use simple model sentences to assist in producing own short text expressing basic information: *Salut! Je m'appelle... Mon pays, c'est...* etc. (p. 17).
7T4: Using resources	Familiarisation with the reference sections in the Students' Book (*Glossaire, Vocabulaire*, verb tables, etc.) (Workbook p. 17).
7T7: Improving written work	Awareness of common differences between French and English when writing, e.g. accents, agreement (Workbook p. 17).
7C1: Geographical facts	Location of towns on a map of France (p. 11); French-speaking countries (p. 11, pp. 16–17).
7C2: Everyday culture	Symbols of France, e.g. *la tour Eiffel, la pétanque* (p. 12, p. 25); French handwriting (p. 14 *l'alphabet*, p. 25 *La Marseillaise*).
7C3: Contact with native speakers	Video clip of native speakers talking about things that represent France (p. 13); video blog (p. 22).
7C4: Stories and songs	Song about colours and flags (p. 27).
Framework objectives (reinforce)	**Teaching and learning**
7W3: Classroom words	Expand stock of words used in classroom situations via rubrics in French; grammar terms, e.g. what is a noun?, what is meant by gender? (p. 20).
7W4: Gender and plural	Nouns and gender: determiners; masculine/feminine forms of job titles (*serveur, serveuse*), agreement of adjectives (p. 20, p. 27).
7S3: Adapting sentences	Replace multiple-choice answers with own details to give information about self for a video blog (*Blog-notes*, p. 22).
7S8: Punctuation	Awareness that nationalities and languages are capitalised in English but not in French (p. 16); use of apostrophe before vowels and silent *h*, e.g. *il n'y pas d'hôtel* (p. 15), *l'Algérie* (p. 16).
7L1: Sound patterns	Pronunciation: nasal sounds (p. 21).

Week-by-week overview (assuming 6 weeks' work or approximately 10–12.5 hours)

Week 1 – Opening spread/1.1 C'est ça, la France!
Opening spread: introduction to unit themes and objectives, focusing on the geography of France and names of French towns (sound–spelling links)
Spread 1.1: things associated with France, especially cultural aspects; numbers 1–10; gender of nouns

Week 2 – 1.2 En France
What there is/is not in a town; the alphabet; simple negatives (*il n'y a pas de...*)

Week 3 – 1.3 Ici, on parle français
Countries and languages; nationalities and agreements; e.g. *canadien(enne)*; colours

Week 4 – 1.4 Les langues des stars
Jobs and languages (two case studies)

Week 5 – Labo-langue
Nouns and gender; recording and learning new vocabulary; nasal sounds

Week 6 – Blog-notes, Tu sais tout?, En plus, Clic.fr, On chante!, Lecture
Reinforcement and extension of the language of the unit; review of progress via the Checklist in the Workbook/on Copymaster; revision and assessment

1

Vive la France!

Unit objectives

Contexts: The French language; France and other countries
Grammar: Nouns and gender
Language learning: Recording new vocabulary
Pronunciation: Nasal sounds
Cultural focus: France and other French-speaking countries

Assessment opportunities

Reading: Students' Book, page 24, activity 2a
Writing: Students' Book, page 17, activity 4

See also **Clic! 1** OxBox Assessment CD-ROM

Differentiation in *Départ* and Units 1 and 2

See the beginning of the *Départ* teacher's notes (page 19) for general suggestions on differentiation in *Départ* and Units 1 and 2.

  1 Discute.

- *Aim*: To raise awareness of the French-speaking world; to promote the value of learning French; to develop powers of observation.
- Students discuss what the map of France tells them about France and the French. Ask them to share any prior knowledge they have of France.

 Follow-up: Students research the places and items illustrated and locate the French-speaking countries (listed in the information box) on a world map. This launches Framework Objective 7C1.

2 Écoute et répète.

- *Aim*: To familiarise students with French sounds and sound–spelling links through the names of French towns.
- Students listen, point to each town on the map and say the names silently to themselves. They listen again and repeat the names aloud.

Follow-up: Play the recording again and prompt students to repeat the names loudly/quietly/slowly/quickly, etc.

 CD 1, track 5 page 11, activité 2

- C'est... la France!
- Paris
- Dieppe
- Calais
- Boulogne
- Strasbourg
- Lille
- Nice
- Marseille
- Toulouse
- Bordeaux
- Brest
- Lyon
- Dijon
- Grenoble
- Nantes

 Follow-up: Provide a list of people's names. Students match them to the towns they rhyme with, e.g. *Arnaud habite à Bordeaux, Manon habite à Lyon, Alice habite à Nice, Marie habite à Paris.*

1.1   C'est ça, la France!

Planner

➤ Objectives
- Things that make you think of France
- Numbers 1–10

➤ Resources
Students' Book, pages 12–13
CD 1, track 7
Video clip 2
En solo Workbook, pages 6–7;
En solo CD, tracks 9–10
Copymasters 3, 5; CD 1, tracks 21–23

➤ Key language
Numbers 1–10
C'est quoi? C'est... Ce n'est pas...
le jean, le parfum, le football, le TGV, le vélo
la baguette, la FNAC, la pétanque
les Carambars
C'est la tour Eiffel?
Oui. Non.

➤ Grammar
Gender: *le, la, les*

➤ Framework reference
L – 7S5, 7C2, 7C3

➤ Starters
- Students name any famous French people or places they know, or suggest items (e.g. types of food) that make them think of France.
- Students do "number bonds" in pairs: student A says a number between one and ten, and their partner gives the number needed to make it up to ten:
  Student A: *Six!*
  Student B: *Quatre!... Un!*
  Student A: *Neuf!...*
- Copymaster 3 *À tes marques!* ex. 1.

➤ Plenaries
- In groups, students take turns to count from one to ten, and then backwards from ten down to one. The aim is to do this as quickly as possible but accurately and with good pronunciation. Students time/assess each other.
- Display the vocabulary items from the *Jeu-test* in two columns, with the words/phrases split into two and jumbled up, e.g.
  le foot / lo
  la tour / ball
  le vé / rix
  Asté / Eiffel
  Give students a time limit to match up the halves and copy out the list.
- Students tell their partner three things they have learned about France during this lesson and from the Unit 1 opening spread. Allow time for pairs to report back to the whole class.

AT 1.1 **1 Regarde.**

- *Aim*: To raise awareness of France and French culture.
- Students watch the video clip and identify the items mentioned.
- The *Jeu-test* and video clip provide an opportunity to dispel any stereotypical images that students may have of France.

Answers: a Astérix; c le football

 Video clip 2   page 13, activité 1

– Bonjour! Je m'appelle Julien. Je suis français. Aujourd'hui on va parler de la France. C'est quoi, la France? Regardez. C'est quoi pour toi la France?
– La France, c'est la baguette.
– La France, c'est Astérix.
– La France, c'est le parfum.
– La France, c'est quoi?... C'est le football!
– C'est quoi la France pour toi? C'est le football?

– Le football? Non... c'est le vélo.
– C'est quoi la France?
– C'est la tour Eiffel.
– La France, c'est quoi?... C'est la FNAC, non?
– La France pour moi, c'est le jean.
– C'est quoi la France?
– La France, c'est les Carambars.
– La France pour moi c'est le TGV.
– La France, c'est la pétanque. C'est typiquement français, ça!

AT 1.1 **2 Écoute et répète.**

AT 2.1

- Students listen and repeat the chant of numbers 1–10.

 CD 1, track 7   page 13, activité 2

– Un, deux,
– Trois, quatre,
– Cinq, six,
– Sept, huit,
– Neuf, dix.
– Encore une fois...

– Un, deux, trois, quatre,
– Cinq, six, sept, huit,
– Neuf, dix.
– Plus vite…
– Un, deux,
– Trois, quatre,
– Cinq, six,
– Sept, huit,
– Neuf, dix.
– Encore une fois…
– Un, deux, trois, quatre,
– Cinq, six, sept, huit,
– Neuf, dix.

C5 An additional listening activity on numbers 1–10 is provided on Copymaster 5 ex. 1.

AT 3.1 **3 Jeu-test: a ou b?**

• Students complete the *Jeu-test*.

Answers: 1 a; 2 b; 3 a; 4 b; 5 a; 6 a; 7 a; 8 b; 9 b; 10 a

4 Grammaire.

• Students read the grammar notes on *le*, *la* and *les*, then find the different forms of the definite article in the *Jeu-test*.

AT 2.1
AT 3.1 **5 À deux: parlez. (B → A)**

• Students take turns to name the items from the *Jeu-test*, e.g.
• Student A: *Trois… C'est quoi?*
• Student B: *C'est la baguette.*
• Student A: *Oui!*
• Student B: *Cinq… C'est quoi?*

Follow-up:

• Students do ex. 5 in reverse, e.g.
  Student A: *Le vélo… C'est quoi?*
  Student B: *Sept.*
  Emphasise the importance of using the correct form of the definite article.
• Students answer *Oui* or *Non* to questions about the *Jeu-test* items, e.g. *Le numéro un, c'est le football? Le numéro neuf, c'est le parfum?*
• Students make up similar questions to exchange with a partner.

AT 2.1
AT 3.1 **6a À deux: jouez à Ni oui, ni non.**

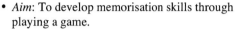

• Students play the *Ni oui, ni non* game, answering their partner's questions without saying the words *Oui* or *Non*, e.g.
  Student A: *Le numéro cinq, c'est le vélo?*
  Student B: *Ce n'est pas le vélo.*
• Note the use of *C'est* + plural noun (*C'est les Carambars*), as in familiar spoken French. Explain the apostrophes in *C'est* and *Ce n'est pas*.

AT 2.1 **6b À deux: test de mémoire. (B → A)**

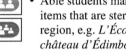

• *Aim*: To develop memorisation skills through playing a game.
• Students play *Ni oui, ni non* again. This time, the student answering the questions does so from memory, with the book closed; the student asking the questions has the book open, so that they can check whether their partner's answers are correct.
• Make this a competitive game by asking students to keep a tally of who has the most correct answers.

Follow-up:

• Able students make up their own *Jeu-test* using items that are stereotypical of your own country or region, e.g. *L'Écosse, c'est le haggis/les kilts/le château d'Édimbourg*. Provide access to dictionaries or a database of words to choose from. Students exchange their quiz with a partner or another group/class.
• Students who have visited France exchange simple experiences of France and the French, e.g.
  Student A: *Pour toi, la France, c'est quoi?*
  Student B: *C'est Paris!*
  Student C: *C'est les croissants!*

W6–7 Pages 6–7 of the *En solo* Workbook provide further activities to practise numbers 1–10 and the language from the *Jeu-test*.

1.2 En France

Planner

> **Objectives**
>   • What there is/is not in a town
>   • The alphabet

> **Resources**
> Students' Book, pages 14–15
> CD 1, tracks 8–10
> *En solo* Workbook, pages 8–9;
> *En solo* CD, track 11
> Copymasters 5, 6, 7; CD 1, tracks 21–23

> **Key language**
> *Qu'est-ce qu'il y a? Il y a...*
> *un café-tabac, un camping, un cinéma, un hôtel,*
> *un restaurant*
> *une école, une pharmacie, une rue*
> *des toilettes/des WC*
> *Il n'y a pas de camping. Il n'y a pas d'hôtel.*

> **Grammar**
> *il y a un/une/des...*
> *il n'y a pas de/d'...*

> **Framework reference**
> **L** – 7W6, 7S5; **R** – 7S8

> **Starters**
>   • Write six letters on the board or OHP.
>   Give students 30 seconds to put them into
>   alphabetical order. If they already know the
>   French alphabet (e.g. from primary school), ask
>   them to read the letters aloud. Repeat this with
>   other sets of letters.
>   • Play Hangman using the vocabulary for places
>   in town.

> **Plenaries**
>   • Spell out the names of some French towns
>   (from the Unit 1 opening spread) or famous
>   French people. Students note down the letters
>   and work out what the words spell.
>   • Students say the alphabet as a whole class, in a
>   Mexican Wave, with each student saying one
>   letter.
>   • Call out a word from the lesson, e.g. *Cinéma!*
>   Students supply the correct determiner
>   (*Un cinéma!*) or put the word into a sentence
>   (*Il y a un cinéma! C'est un cinéma!*)

---

 1 Écoute.

• *Aim*: To introduce the sounds of the French
  alphabet in a fun way and compare the sounds of
  English and French.
• Students listen out for any letters that are
  pronounced the same in French and English.
 • They compare their answers with a partner, then
  listen again to review their answers.

Answers: f, l, m, n and *s* are pronounced the same in
French and English

🔘 **CD 1, track 8**   page 14, activité 1

A B C D E F G H I J K L M N O P Q R S T U V W
X Y Z

On chante l'alphabet
L'ABC en français!
On chante l'alphabet en rap.
ABC
DEF
GHI
JKL
MNO
PQR
STU
VWX
YZ
[repeated]

Follow-up:
• Look at the pronunciation of groups of letters, e.g.
  the following groups are all pronounced using the
  same vowel sound:
  – *b, c, d, g, p, t, v*
  – *a, h, k*
  – *i, j, x*
  – *q, u*
• Look at the photo of the line of keys from a French
  computer keyboard. Ask students how it compares
  with an English keyboard. Why might the
  keyboards be set out differently? (Different
  keyboard layouts take account of common letter
  sequences in different languages, frequency of
  letters, any accented or special characters, etc.)

 2 Écoute, répète et continue.

• Students listen, repeat and say the next letter in the
  sequence.

Answers: 1 p; 2 t; 3 h; 4 d; 5 x; 6 j

🔘 **CD 1, track 9**   page 14, activité 2

  1 m, n, o... p
  2 q, r, s...
  3 e, f, g...
  4 a, b, c...
  5 u, v, w...
  6 g, h, i...

Follow-up:

- Students take turns to spell out words for each other, e.g.
  Student A: *B – A – G – U – E – T – T – E*
  Student B: *Baguette!*

- Memory test. Student A says a word from the current page or an earlier spread; student B spells it from memory, without looking at the book.

 C5
 C6
Further activities to practise the alphabet and spelling are provided on Copymaster 5 ex. 2 (listening) and Copymaster 6 ex. 1 (speaking).

Preparation:
- Look at the town signs on page 14. Not all of them are universal, e.g. *café-tabac*.
- Emphasise that although some of these words are cognates and may look like English words, they are not pronounced in the same way. Focus on sound–spelling links: ask students whether they can work out any pronunciation rules, e.g. silent *h*, nasal *am/an*, etc.

AT 3.1 **3 Relie.**

AT 4.1

This activity could replace task A or B in a Grade 1 Asset Languages teacher assessment.
- *Aim*: To introduce the different forms of the indefinite article via signs that you might see in a French town.
- Students match the words to the signs, and build sentences following the model.

Answers: 1 C'est une école. 2 C'est un hôtel. 3 C'est un camping. 4 C'est un cinéma. 5 C'est des toilettes/des WC. 6 C'est un restaurant. 7 C'est un café-tabac. 8 C'est une rue. 9 C'est une pharmacie.

AT 2.1 **4 À deux. (B → A)**

- Students spell out words for each other using the pictures on page 15 as prompts: student A begins spelling, and B tries to work out what the word is before A finishes.
- Encourage the use of full sentences using *C'est* + *un/une/des*, e.g.
  Student A: *C – I – N...*
  Student B: *C'est un cinéma!*

Follow-up: Students play spelling games using the vocabulary from this page or earlier spreads, e.g. I Spy: *un mot qui commence/finit par la lettre c* (or, to recycle numbers, *un mot de six lettres*).

AT 1.2 **5 Écoute.**
- Students hear Lola and Lucas discussing which places are/are not shown in *Poster 1* and *Poster 2*. In each case, they note who is correct.
- Make sure students understand the difference between *il y a un/une/des* and *il n'y a pas de/d'*.
- Point out the street sign. Explain that in France it is very common for streets to be named after famous people. (There will be more on this in Unit 5.)

Answers: 1 Lola; 2 Lola; 3 Lucas; 4 Lucas; 5 Lola; 6 Lola

 CD 1, track 10   page 15, activité 5
1 – Poster numéro un, il y a une école.
  – Non, il n'y a pas d'école.
2 – Poster numéro un, il y a un restaurant.
  – Non, il n'y a pas de restaurant.
3 – Poster numéro un, il y a un camping.
  – Non, il n'y a pas de camping.
4 – Poster numéro deux, il y a des toilettes.
  – Non, il n'y a pas de toilettes.
5 – Poster numéro deux, il y a une pharmacie.
  – Non, il n'y a pas de pharmacie.
6 – Poster numéro deux, il y a un hôtel.
  – Non, il n'y a pas d'hôtel.

AT 3.2 **6 Lis les phrases. Oui ou non?**

AT 4.2
- Students write sentences to say whether a–e are right or wrong, referring to the two pictures.
- Point out the grammar notes on *il n'y a pas de/d'*.

Answers: a Oui, il y a un cinéma. b Non, il n'y a pas de camping. c Oui, il y a des toilettes. d Oui, il y a une école. e Non, il n'y a pas de rue.

AT 4.2 **7 Jeu des différences. Résume.**
- Students write sentences to explain the differences between the two pictures.

Answers:
Poster numéro un, il y un restaurant. Poster numéro deux, il n'y a pas de restaurant.

Poster numéro un, il y a des toilettes/des WC. Poster numéro deux, il n'y a pas de toilettes/de WC.

Poster numéro un, il y a une rue. Poster numéro deux, il n'y a pas de rue.

Poster numéro un, il n'y a pas de pharmacie. Poster numéro deux, il y a une pharmacie.

Poster numéro un, il n'y a pas de camping. Poster numéro deux, il y a un camping.

Poster numéro un, il n'y a pas de café-tabac. Poster numéro deux, il y a un café-tabac.

8 Grammaire
- Students rewrite the sentences as negatives.

Answers: a Il n'y a pas de café-tabac. b Il n'y a pas de pharmacie. c Il n'y a pas de toilettes. d Il n'y a pas d'école.

AT 2.2 **9 Imagine.**

AT 4.2

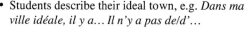

- Students describe their ideal town, e.g. *Dans ma ville idéale, il y a... Il n'y a pas de/d'...*
- They could do this first as an oral activity, then follow it up in writing.

Follow-up: *L'alphabet de la ville*. Students think of a place in town for each letter of the alphabet, e.g. *A – un aéroport, B – une boulangerie*. This allows those who have done some French at primary school to show off their knowledge. Provide dictionaries and encourage students to include the correct definite or indefinite articles.

C6
C7
Ex. 2 on Copymaster 6 is an additional speaking activity to practise *il y a un/une/des* and *il n'y a pas de/d'* with places in town. A reading/writing activity based on vocabulary from this and the previous spread is provided on Copymaster 7 ex. 3.

W8–9
Pages 8–9 of the *En solo* Workbook provide further activities to practise the language of this spread.

1.3   Ici, on parle français

Planner

> **Objectives**
> - Your country and the languages you speak
> - Colours

> **Resources**
> Students' Book, pages 16–17
> CD 1, tracks 11–12
> *En solo* Workbook, pages 10–11
> Copymasters 3, 4, 5, 7; CD 1, tracks 21–23

> **Key language**
> *Tu t'appelles comment?*
> *Je m'appelle…*
>
> *Les pays et les nationalités*
> *C'est quoi, ton pays? Mon pays, c'est la France.*
> *C'est quoi, ta nationalité? Je suis français(e).*
> *l'Angleterre: anglais(e)*
> *l'Écosse: écossais(e)*
> *l'Irlande: irlandais(e)*
> *le pays de Galles: gallois(e)*
> *la France: français(e)*
> *la Belgique: belge*
> *l'Algérie: algérien(enne)*
> *le Canada: canadien(enne)*
> *la Suisse: suisse*
> *le Sénégal: sénégalais(e)*
>
> *Les couleurs*
> *bleu, blanc, rouge, vert, noir, orange, jaune*
> *Le drapeau français est bleu, blanc et rouge.*

> **Framework reference**
> **L** – 7S4, 7S9; **R** – 7S8

> **Starters**
> - Can students name any countries or regions (apart from France) where French is spoken? They should remember some from the Unit 1 opening spread or from the *Départ* unit.
> - If students already know the colours (e.g. from primary school), point at items in the classroom and ask students to name the colours. Alternatively, call out colours in French and ask students to point to something of the corresponding colour in the classroom.
> - For a competitive game, divide the class into approximately four teams. Each team appoints a "runner". Call out a colour. Team members find an item of the appropriate colour (e.g. someone's pencil case, pen, bag, etc.) and give it to their runner, who brings it out to you. The first runner to hand you an item of the correct colour wins a point for their team.
> - Copymaster 3 *À tes marques!* ex. 2 and 3.

> **Plenaries**
> - Play Noughts and Crosses using colours. Prepare a three-by-three grid for use on the OHP or interactive whiteboard, with a different colour in each square. (In addition to the seven colours presented in the Students' Book, the colours *gris, rose* and *violet* are introduced on OxBox *Interactif* CD-ROM, so this gives you enough colours to fill the nine squares.) Divide the class into two teams. Team members name colours in an attempt to win three squares in a row.
> - Display some groups of words from the spread and ask students to choose an odd-one-out in each, e.g.
>   - *l'Écosse, la France, le Sénégal* (Senegal because it isn't in Europe, or Scotland because it isn't a French-speaking country)
>   - *français, sénégalais, suisse* (*suisse* because it doesn't have a masculine and feminine form, or *sénégalais* because it isn't European)
>   - *la Suisse, suisse, canadien* (*la Suisse* because it's a country, *canadien* because it doesn't relate to Europe)
>   - *sénégalais, française, algérien* (*française* because it's European/because it's feminine, *algérien* because it has a different ending to the other two)
> Explain that there is no single correct answer for any of these, but that students must be able to justify their choices.
> - Copymaster 4 *Bilan de leçon* ex. 2.

AT 1.2 | **1 Écoute, lis et trouve.**

AT 3.2
- *Aim*: To raise awareness of French-speaking countries and countries that have more than one language; to present masculine and feminine versions of nationality adjectives.
- Students listen while reading the three texts. They find three countries, three nationalities and four languages.

- Point out the note on the use of capital letters for countries but not for nationalities and languages.

Answers: a la France, le Sénégal, le Canada;
b français, sénégalaise, canadien; c français,
portugais, wolof, anglais

CD 1, track 11   page 16, activité 1

> **A** – Salut! Je m'appelle Nico.
> Mon pays, c'est la France.
> Je suis français.
> Je parle français et portugais.
> **B** – Salut! Je m'appelle Ana.
> Mon pays, c'est le Sénégal.
> Je suis sénégalaise.
> Je parle français et wolof.
> **C** – Salut! Je m'appelle Samuel.
> Mon pays, c'est le Canada.
> Je suis canadien.
> Je parle français et anglais.

AT 3.2

2 Réponds en anglais.

- Students answer questions in English about the texts.

Answers: a Samuel; b Nico; c Nico, Ana and Samuel

AT 4.2

3 Écris.

This activity could replace task A in a Grade 2 Asset Langauges teacher assessment.

- Students write three paragraphs to introduce three more teenagers, based on the information provided in the grid. They use the texts in ex. 1 as a model.

Answers:
Salut! Je m'appelle Laura. Mon pays, c'est la Belgique. Je suis belge. Je parle français et flamand.

Salut! Je m'appelle Omar. Mon pays, c'est l'Algérie. Je suis algérien. Je parle français et arabe.

Salut! Je m'appelle Christophe. Mon pays, c'est la Suisse. Je suis suisse. Je parle français et italien.

Follow-up: Students locate the countries from ex. 3, together with other French-speaking countries, on a world map. Talk about countries that have more than one official language.

AT 4.2

4 Écris et lis.

This activity would be suitable as part of preparation for external assessment at Breakthrough stage.

- Students write a short paragraph to introduce themselves, then read it aloud to the class.
- If there is a broad ethnic mix in your class, ask students to write their paragraphs omitting their names. Collect them in and read out a selection. The class guess who wrote each one. Plan for this if necessary by preparing a list of the countries and nationalities that your students are likely to need.

W 10–11

Pages 10–11 of the *En solo* Workbook provide further activities to practise countries and nationalities.

AT 3.1
AT 4.1

5 À deux: complétez.

- *Aim*: To introduce colours while revising some letters of the alphabet.
- Students compile a key to the colours of the flags.
- In addition to the colours introduced here, the digital flashcards on OxBox *Interactif* CD-ROM include three extra colours: *gris, rose* and *violet*.

Answers: a bleu; b blanc; c rouge; d vert; e jaune; f noir

AT 1.1

6 Écoute.

This activity would be suitable as part of preparation for external assessment at Breakthrough stage.

- Students listen and match each flag description to the corresponding picture.

Answers: 1 le Canada; 2 le Gabon; 3 l'Algérie; 4 le Tchad; 5 le Vanuatu

CD 1, track 12   page 17, activité 6

> – Numéro un: le drapeau est rouge et blanc.
> – Numéro deux: le drapeau est vert, jaune, bleu.
> – Numéro trois: le drapeau est vert, rouge, blanc.
> – Numéro quatre: le drapeau est bleu, jaune, rouge.
> – Numéro cinq: le drapeau est noir, jaune, rouge, vert.

AT 2.1

7 À deux: parlez. (B ➔ A)

- Students take turns to name the flag colours; their partner gives the corresponding country.
- Alternatively, students name a country and their partner gives the flag colours.

AT 4.1

8 Décris.

- Students name the colours of their own country's flag.
- They could add a drawing of the flag, with colours labelled in French.

C5
C7

Further activities to practise countries, flags and colours are provided on Copymaster 5 ex. 3 (listening) and Copymaster 7 ex. 1 and 2 (reading/writing).

1.4 Les langues des stars

Planner

> ### Objectives
> • Jobs
> • Languages

> ### Resources
> Students' Book, pages 18–19
> CD 1, tracks 13–15
> *En solo* Workbook, pages 12–13;
> *En solo* CD, track 12
> Copymasters 4, 8

> ### Key language
> *Mes idoles*
> *Il/Elle s'appelle...*
> *Il est sportif. Elle est sportive.*
> *Il est acteur. Elle est actrice.*
> *Il est présentateur.*
>
> *Les langues*
> *une langue étrangère*
> *Tu parles quelles langues?*
> *Je parle français, japonais, allemand, espagnol,*
> *italien, arabe, anglais, flamand.*
> *C'est important pour le travail/les voyages/la*
> *communication internationale.*

> ### Framework reference
> L – 7W2

> ### Starters
> • Before beginning work on spread 1.4, ask
>   students to note down/tell you everything they
>   already know about gender in French (e.g. *le/la,*
>   *un/une,* agreement of nationality adjectives),
>   with an example sentence to illustrate each
>   point, e.g. *le/la – C'est le jean. C'est la France.*
>   Continuing on the theme of gender, point out
>   that one of the topics of this spread is jobs.
>   Write the words "actor" and "actress" on the
>   board, together with *acteur* and *actrice* (both of

which will come up on this spread). Can
students identify the masculine and the
feminine form of *acteur/actrice*? Point out that
many French job titles have different masculine
and feminine forms. Can they think of any
other English jobs like this (e.g.
waiter/waitress)?
> • Brainstorm any languages that students have
>   already met in the *Départ* unit and earlier in
>   Unit 1, e.g. *français, sénégalais, anglais, arabe.*
> • Play an oral chain game around the class to
>   practise *je m'appelle* and *il/elle s'appelle,* as
>   follows:
>   Student A: *Bonjour, je m'appelle Anna.*
>   Student B: *Bonjour, je m'appelle Paul et elle*
>   *s'appelle Anna.*
>   Student C: *Bonjour, je m'appelle Jake, il*
>   *s'appelle Paul et elle s'appelle Anna...*

> ### Plenaries
> • To recap on the theme of reasons for learning
>   languages, students work in pairs/groups to
>   draw up a list of jobs with reasons why
>   knowing a foreign language might be relevant
>   for each job, e.g. doctor (to find out what is
>   wrong with a patient who doesn't speak
>   English), waiter/ waitress/shop assistant in a
>   popular tourist resort (to communicate with
>   foreign visitors). Students feed back their ideas
>   to the whole class.
> • Display some jumbled sentences halves and ask
>   students to match up the sentence beginnings to
>   their corresponding endings, e.g.
>   *Elle s'appelle / actrice.*
>   *Elle est / français, anglais et allemand.*
>   *Elle est / Audrey Tautou.*
>   *Elle parle / française.*
>
>   *Il s'appelle / anglais.*
>   *Il est / anglais et allemand.*
>   *Il est / Daniel Craig.*
>   *Il parle / acteur.*
> • Copymaster 4 *Bilan de leçon* ex. 1.

AT 3.2 **1a Lis.**

• *Aim:* To introduce *il/elle* and highlight
  masculine/feminine agreement of job titles and
  adjectives; to raise awareness of the value of
  learning languages.
• Students read the two texts about Gary Lineker
  and Charlize Theron. They fill in the gaps using
  the words provided.

Answers: 1 présentateur; 2 anglais; 3 parle;
4 actrice; 5 français; 6 communication

AT 1.2 **1b Écoute et vérifie.**

 • Students listen to check their answers to ex. 1a.

 CD 1, track 13 page 18, activité 1b

– Gary Lineker est <u>présentateur</u>. Il est ex-
  footballeur. Il est <u>anglais</u>.
  Il <u>parle</u> anglais, espagnol et japonais. Il dit:
  "Une langue étrangère, c'est important pour
  le travail."
– Charlize Theron est <u>actrice</u>. Elle est sud-
  africaine.
  Elle parle 28 langues: afrikaans, anglais,
  allemand, <u>français</u>, etc. Elle dit: "Une langue
  étrangère, c'est important pour la
  <u>communication</u>."

Follow-up: Focus on the *il/elle* information box and use it as an opportunity to recap on high-frequency words that students have met so far, e.g. *oui, non*; *je suis*; *c'est, ce n'est pas*; *il y a, il n'y a pas de/d'…*; *le/la/les*; *un/une/des*. Emphasise that although these words and phrases seem small and insignificant, it is particularly important to know them because they crop up so frequently. Compare these words with other vocabulary from the spread such as *présentateur, actrice, turc*, etc., and ask students which words they think they will meet most often.

 2 Lis et écoute.

- Students read and listen to texts about different celebrities. They work out who speaks the most languages.
- Point out the note about *je m'appelle…* and *il/elle s'appelle…*

Answers: Lucy Liu and Jay-Jay Okocha (they both speak four languages)

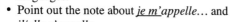 **CD 1, track 14**   page 19, activité 2

– Il s'appelle Johnny Depp. Il est acteur. Il est américain.
Il parle anglais et français. Il dit: "Une langue étrangère, c'est important pour la communication internationale."

– Elle s'appelle Lucy Liu. Elle est actrice. Elle est américaine.
Elle parle anglais, chinois, français et espagnol. Elle dit: "Une langue étrangère, c'est important pour le travail."

– Elle s'appelle Paula Radcliffe. Elle est sportive. Elle est anglaise.
Elle parle anglais, français et allemand. Elle dit: "Une langue étrangère, c'est important pour les voyages."

– Il s'appelle Jay-Jay Okocha. Il est sportif. Il est nigérien.
Il parle anglais, français, allemand et turc. Il dit: "Une langue étrangère, c'est important dans les clubs de football internationaux."

 Follow-up:

- Students search the texts for: six languages; three nationalities; two jobs; four masculine endings (*acteur, américain, sportif, nigérien*); four feminine endings (*actrice, américaine, sportive, anglaise*).
- Ask additional comprehension questions about the texts, either in French or English, e.g. *Elle parle trois langues. C'est…?* (Paula Radcliffe); Who thinks languages are important for work? (Lucy Liu)
- Focus on why the celebrities think it's important to learn languages. Do students agree? Can they think of any other reasons for learning languages?

 3 Écoute. C'est qui?

- Students listen to a series of statements about the four celebrities and work out who is being referred to in each case.
- Point out that in order to answer correctly, they will need to listen carefully for *il/elle* and the masculine and feminine endings.

Answers: 1 Paula Radcliffe; 2 Jay-Jay Okocha; 3 Lucy Liu; 4 Johnny Depp; 5 Johnny Depp; 6 Lucy Liu; 7 Lucy Liu; 8 Paula Radcliffe; 9 Johnny Depp; 10 Jay-Jay Okocha

 CD 1, track 15   page 19, activité 3

1 Elle est sportive. C'est qui?
2 Il est sportif. C'est qui?
3 Elle est actrice. C'est qui?
4 Il est acteur. C'est qui?
5 Il est américain. C'est qui?
6 Elle est américaine. C'est qui?
7 Elle parle anglais et chinois. C'est qui?
8 Elle parle français et allemand. C'est qui?
9 Il parle anglais et français. C'est qui?
10 Il parle allemand et turc. C'est qui?

4 Lis 1–4. Vrai ou faux?

- Students answer true/false questions about the four celebrities. They correct the false statements.
- Point out the note on the omission of *un* or *une* in French when talking about a person's job, e.g. *Il est acteur.*

Answers: 1 Faux, il est sportif. 2 Faux, il est américain. 3 Faux, elle est sportive. 4 Faux, elle parle anglais, chinois, français et espagnol.

5 À deux: vrai ou faux? (B ⟶ A)

- Students write true/false statements about the four celebrities.
- They read out their statements to their partner, who tries to respond from memory, with their book closed.

Défi!

This activity would be suitable as part of preparation for external assessment at Breakthrough stage.
- Students write their own text about an actor or sports star, stating their nationality and the languages they speak.

 See Copymaster 8 for additional reading/writing activities based on the language of this spread.

Pages 12–13 of the *En solo* Workbook provide further activities to practise third person singular descriptions, masculine/feminine agreement, jobs, nationalities and languages.

Labo-langue

Planner

▷ **Objectives**
- Nouns and gender
- Recording new vocabulary
- Nasal sounds

▷ **Resources**
Students' Book, pages 20–21
CD 1, tracks 16–17
En solo Workbook, pages 14–15, 17
Copymasters 9, 10, 11; CD 1, tracks 24–26

▷ **Framework reference**
L – 7W1, 7W7, 7S1, 7T4 (via Workbook), 7T7
(via Workbook); **R** – 7W3, 7W4, 7L1

Bien comprendre!
Nouns and gender

 1 Look up these words in the glossary at the back of the book. Are they masculine or feminine? Write them out starting with *le, la, l'* or *les*.

Answers: a la couleur (f); b l'Europe (f); c le paragraphe (m); d la date (f); e le football (m); f les invitations (f)

2 Copy the words and complete the missing letters.

Answers: chanteuse, vendeur, serveuse, mécanicienne

3 Choose the correct adjectives.
- Ask students what they notice about the adjectives in sentences a, b, d and f, apart from the adjective agreement. Students should notice that the adjectives follow the noun, whereas in English they would precede the noun. This will be dealt with fully in Unit 4.

Answers: a japonaise; b anglais; c hollandaise; d sénégalais; e française; f françaises

C9 See Copymaster 9 for further grammar practice focusing on nouns, genders and determiners.

W 14–15 Pages 14–15 of the *En solo* Workbook provide further activities based on these grammar points.

Bien apprendre!
Recording new vocabulary

This section suggests strategies to help students record and remember new language.

 1 Discuss the advantages and disadvantages of each suggestion.
- Point out that there is no right or wrong way to learn: what works well for one person may not work so well for another.

- Draw attention to tip a, which advises students to always record the gender of nouns, not just the noun itself. Ask students to suggest why it might be important to do this, given what they know about gender and the effect it has on other words.

2 Try the suggestions yourself and decide which works best for you.
- For homework, ask students to try out the strategies on some of the Unit 1 vocabulary. Pairs could test each other in a subsequent lesson to see how well they have remembered it.
- Ask students if they have any other ideas for ways to memorise new language, e.g. some students might find it helpful to record themselves reading aloud lists of words.

C10 Copymaster 10 provides further tips and activities focusing on recording and remembering new language.

W17 Further language learning strategies are provided on page 17 of the *En solo* Workbook, which could be used at any appropriate point during Unit 1:
- *Autonomous learning*: tips and activities to help students find their way around the reference sections in the Students' Book
- *Writing*: common differences between French and English that students need to take account of when writing in French

Bien parler!
Nasal sounds

1 Listen to these...

 CD 1, track 16   page 21, Bien parler! activité 1
- an...
- in...
- on...

2 Listen. Which word from each pair contains a nasal vowel sound? Repeat that word only.

Answers: a blanc; b cinq; c bonjour; d France; e les Carambars; f le camping

CD 1, track 17   page 21, Bien parler! activité 2

a bleu... blanc
b cinq... six
c bonjour... salut
d France... Canada
e les Carambars... les toilettes
f la pharmacie... le camping

3 Practise reading these phrases aloud. The nasal sounds are underlined.

- Give students time to have a go at the pronunciation first in pairs or small groups before you read the sentences together as a class.

C11 See Copymaster 11 for additional pronunciation practice of nasal sounds.

Blog-notes

Planner

> **Objectives**
> • To summarise the main points of the unit in context, in a format that is fun and familiar to students, i.e. a video blog
> • To provide a model enabling students to personalise the language of the unit
> • To provide opportunities for students to ask as well as answer questions
> • To provide extended listening practice recycling the language of the whole unit

> **Resources**
> Students' Book, page 22
> Video clip 3
> *En solo* Workbook, page 16;
> *En solo* CD, track 13
> Copymaster 2

> **Framework reference**
> **L** – 7C3; **R** – 7S3

AT 1.3 **1 Regarde le vidéo-blog. Choisis 1 ou 2.**

 • Students watch Thomas's video diary and choose 1 or 2 in answer to each question. Pause the video after each section to allow the students time to answer.

Answers: a 2; b 2; c 2; d 2; e 2; f 1; g 1; h 1

 Video clip 3   page 22, activité 1

10, 9, 8, 7, 6, 5, 4, 3, 2, 1... Salut! Bienvenue sur mon vidéo-blog!

a Je m'appelle Thomas, Thomas Garnier! G – A – R – N – I – E – R. Et toi, tu t'appelles comment? Voilà... ça, c'est moi – magnifique, hein!

b Mon pays, c'est la France. Tu vois, là, c'est écrit R – F, République française. Et toi, c'est quoi, ton pays?

c Moi, je suis français. C'est écrit là: nationalité française. Et toi, c'est quoi, ta nationalité?

d Je parle français et je parle aussi anglais... *a little bit English, not a big bit...!* Et toi, tu parles quelles langues? Pour moi, les langues, c'est très important pour la communication, pour les voyages et aussi important pour son travail! Surtout pour les pilotes, comme Sébastien Bourdais et Fernando Alonso.

e Sébastien Bourdais, c'est mon idole! Il est super super super super!

f Il est pilote de course. C'est un pilote super. Ton idole, c'est qui? Il ou elle est quoi?

g Magnifique, la photo, non! Ma couleur préférée, c'est le bleu! Le bleu, c'est super! C'est aussi la couleur des footballeurs français! Et c'est la couleur de cette belle voiture Renault! Magnifique, non!

h Pour moi, la France, c'est les voitures Renault. Elles sont super, les voitures Renault, hein! Et pour toi, c'est quoi, la France? Les voitures? Le parfum? Le fromage? Allez, ciao, à bientôt!

AT 4.2–3 **2 À toi de répondre!**

 • Students write their own answers to questions a–h.

Follow-up:

 • Students interview each other using questions a–h.
 • Students write their own blog, based on their answers to the interview questions.
 • If the appropriate technology is available, allow students to record their own video blogs and play them to the class.

C2
W16 A checklist summarising the language of the unit is provided on Copymaster 2 and on page 16 of the *En solo* Workbook. It could be used in tandem with the *Blog-notes* page or at an appropriate point towards the end of the unit. It provides an opportunity for students to review what they have learned and reflect on areas for improvement.

Tu sais tout?

Planner

> **Objectives**
> • To enable students to recap on the language and structures of the unit
> • To provide an opportunity for quick testing of all four skills

The page is divided into four sections: listening, speaking, reading and writing. Each section can be marked out of 5 to give a total score out of 20.

> **Resources**
> Students' Book, page 23
> CD 1, track 19

AT 1.2 **1 Listen and number. What are they speaking about?**

This activity could replace task C in a Grade 2 Asset Languages teacher assessment. This activity would be suitable as part of preparation for external assessment at Breakthrough stage.

Answers: 1 c; 2 a; 3 f; 4 b; 5 e; 6 d

 CD 1, track 19   page 23, activité 1

1 – Pour moi, c'est Orlando Bloom... il est acteur.
   – Moi, c'est David Beckham... il est footballeur.
2 – C'est quoi, ton pays?
   – Mon pays, c'est la France.
3 – C'est quoi, ta couleur préférée?
   – Hmm... c'est le bleu... ou... non, le rouge!
4 – Tu parles quelles langues?
   – Je parle français et anglais.
5 – Dans ma ville, il n'y a pas de cinéma.
   – Ah? Il n'y a pas de cinéma?
6 – Il y a un camping?
   – Oui, il y a un camping.

AT 1.2 **Défi!**

• Students listen again and note down extra details: a country, two colours, two languages and two places.

Answers: <u>country</u>: France; <u>colours</u>: blue, red; <u>languages</u>: French, English; <u>places</u>: cinema, campsite

AT 2.2 **2 A asks questions a–e. B looks at the pictures and answers in full sentences.**

Answers: a Oui, il y a un restaurant. b Non, il n'y a pas de toilettes. c Oui, il y a une école. d Oui, il y a une baguette. e Non, il n'y a pas de pharmacie.

AT 2.2 **Défi!**

• Students say their name and the languages they speak.

AT 3.2 **3 Read and choose the correct red word in each sentence.**

Answers: a Elle; b sportive; c française; d pays; e français; f le vert

AT 3.2 **Défi!**

• Students translate the ex. 3 sentences into English.

Answers: a Her name is Amélie Mauresmo. b She's a sportswoman. c She is French. d She lives in Switzerland at the moment. e She speaks French. f Her favourite colour is green.

AT 4.2 **4 Write answers to these questions in full sentences.**

This activity would be suitable as part of preparation for external assessment at Breakthrough stage.
• Students answer questions about their name, their country and nationality, and the languages they speak.

AT 4.2 **Défi!**

• Students write answers to 4a–d for a friend or family member, using the third person singular.
• Point out that the reading exercise on this page (ex. 3) uses the third person singular, so they could refer to it for a reminder of the third person forms.

En plus

Planner

> **Objectives**
> - To provide extension material for more able students who are confident with the core language of the unit, and to introduce new language where appropriate
> - To provide alternative class and homework material for students who finish other activities quickly

> **Resources**
> Students' Book, page 24

C'est moi!

1 À deux: dites vite!

- *Aim*: To reinforce numbers, the alphabet and colours in a fun way.
- Students say the items in each set as quickly and as accurately as they can, while another student times them. They may have several attempts at each set, gradually trying to improve their speed and accuracy.
- Teacher versus the class: alternatively, allow students to practise in pairs or small groups, then each group nominates their most successful player to challenge the teacher.

2a Relie.

This activity would be suitable as part of preparation for external assessment at Breakthrough stage.
- Students match the questions to the answers, then write out the interview in full.

Answers:
1e – Tu t'appelles comment?
  – Je m'appelle Glyn Davies.
2c – C'est quoi, ton pays?
  – Mon pays, c'est le pays de Galles.
3b – C'est quoi, ta nationalité?
  – Je suis gallois.
4a – Tu parles quelles langues?
  – Je parle anglais et gallois.
5d – Comment s'appelle ton idole?
  – Elle s'appelle Charlotte Church. Elle est chanteuse et actrice.

2b À deux: parlez.

- Students ask and answer questions 1–5, responding with their own details.

3 Lis et écris.

- Students choose two of the ID forms. They use the information on the forms as the basis for writing an interview with each person, modelled on the interview in ex. 2.

4 Write out a form with your own details.

- Students use the ID forms in ex. 3 as a framework for producing a similar form for themselves.

Clic.fr

Planner

> **Objectives**
> • To raise awareness of France and French culture
> • To promote intercultural understanding by providing opportunities to compare French culture with students' own culture

> **Resources**
> Students' Book, page 25
> Copymaster 12

> **Framework reference**
> **L – 7C2**

Les symboles de la France

AT 3.2 This page focuses on French national symbols: the logo and motto *Liberté, Égalité, Fraternité*, the initials RF (*République française*), the French flag, *la Marseillaise*, Marianne, the Gallic cockerel, and French euro coins.

Students answer questions in English about the text and describe their own national flag in French. They then list six things they have learned about France in Unit 1.

Answers: 1 République française; 2 euros

 Follow-up: Students write questions in English about the text to exchange with a partner.

C12 See Copymaster 12 for further activities focusing on symbols and images connected with France.

Vocabulaire

Planner

> **Objectives**
> * *Vocabulaire*: to provide a theme-based summary of the key language of the unit, which students can use as a reference or as an aid to learning
> * To develop language learning strategies
> * *On chante!*: to reinforce the language of the unit in a fun way

> **Resources**
> Students' Book, pages 26–27
> CD 1, track 20
> *En solo* Workbook, pages 18–19;
> *En solo* CD, track 14
> Copymaster 1

> **Framework reference**
> **L** – 7C4; **R** – 7W4

C1
W 18–19
A list of key language from the unit, with associated activities, is also provided on Copymaster 1 and on pages 18–19 of the *En solo* Workbook.

Get to grips with gender!

* *Aim*: To focus on the importance of knowing the gender of nouns; to encourage students to note down genders when recording new vocabulary.

* In pairs, students test each other on the gender of nouns they have learned in Unit 1. Student A says a noun from the vocabulary list; student B tries to remember the gender.

On chante!

AT 1.2
AT 3.2
1 Écoute et lis.

* Students listen to the song and read the lyrics. They match the pictures of flags to the countries/colours described in the song.

Answers: flags left to right: Belgium, France, Brazil, China

 CD 1, track 20　　　　　　　**page 27, activité 1**

Vive les couleurs!

Refrain:

Vive les couleurs! Vive les couleurs!
Bleu, blanc, rouge,
Noir, jaune, vert.

Vive la France! Vive la France!
Bleu, blanc, rouge,
Bleu, blanc, rouge.

Refrain

Vive la Chine! Vive la Chine!
Rouge et jaune,
Rouge et jaune.

Refrain

Vive la Belgique! Vive la Belgique!
Noir, jaune, rouge,
Noir, jaune, rouge.

Refrain

Vive le Brésil! Vive le Brésil!
Vert, jaune, bleu,
Vert, jaune, bleu.

Follow-up: Students draw and colour in flags of the countries mentioned in the song. They can wave these at appropriate points when they sing the song in ex. 2.

AT 2.2
2 Chante.

* Students join in with the song.

AT 4.2

3 Invente d'autres couplets.

* Students write additional verses for the song.

Follow-up: Arrange for students to perform the song to other classes, and/or record their performance on audio or video.

Lecture

Planner

> **Objectives**
> - To encourage independent reading and develop reading strategies
> - To provide alternative class and homework material for students who finish other activities quickly

The texts and activities on *Lecture A* should be suitable for all; *Lecture B* is more challenging and may be suitable for more able students only.

> **Resources**
> Students' Book, pages 118–119

Lecture A

Les mascottes de la Coupe du Monde de football

AT 3.2 **1 Read and find the French for...**

Answers: a la Coupe du Monde; b année; c briques; d un chien; e un bec; f marron; g avec

Follow-up:
- Talk about the strategies students used when doing ex. 1, e.g. looking for cognates and near-cognates, focusing on pictures to help with understanding, using context to help them make educated guesses. Point out that these are all useful reading strategies that can be applied to any text.
- Discuss high-frequency words from the texts that are likely to crop up often and are therefore worth learning, e.g. point out that students probably won't meet *un bec* very often, but they can expect to come across *avec* in all sorts of situations.

AT 3.2 **2 Choose the mascot you like best and write a paragraph about it in English.**
- Point out that the bold headings on the ID cards will help them to structure their paragraph.

AT 4.2 **Défi!**
- Students design their own World Cup mascot and write an ID card for it.

Lecture B

Les Jeux Olympiques

AT 3.3 **1 Read and find out what is France's connection with the Olympic Games.**

Answer: In 1896, a Frenchman called Pierre de Coubertin organised the first modern version of the Olympic Games. French is one of the official languages of the Olympic Games.

AT 3.3 **2 Answer the questions in English.**

Answers: a J.O.; b Greece; c a Frenchman who organised the first modern version of the Olympic Games in 1896; d English and French; e Europe

Follow-up:
- Ask further comprehension questions about the text.
- Ask students to translate the fact boxes into English. To revise colours, identify the fact boxes by their colours.

- Students write questions for each other in English about the text.
- Using the initials *J.O.* (*Jeux Olympiques*) from the text as a starting point, ask students to suggest the initials for other international organisations. Revise the alphabet by providing the French for these, e.g. *ONU* (*Organisation des Nations unis*), *UE* (*Union européenne*), *USA*, *GB* (*Grande-Bretagne*).

Copymasters

Feuille 1 Vocabulaire

A list of key language from the unit is provided here as well as on pages 26–27 of the Students' Book and pages 18–19 of the *En solo* Workbook.

Feuille 2 Je sais…

Use this checklist with *Blog-notes* (Students' Book page 22) or towards the end of the unit. It provides an opportunity for students to review what they have learned and reflect on areas for improvement. This checklist is also provided on page 16 of the *En solo* Workbook.

Feuille 3 À vos marques!

These starter activities are intended for use with the following Students' Book pages:
- Use ex. 1 with pages 12–13.
- Use ex. 2 and 3 with pages 16–17.

1a Quels chiffres entre 1 et 10 trouves-tu dans le serpent?
- Students search in the word snake for numbers between one and ten.

Answers: neuf, quatre, huit, un, six, trois

1b Quels chiffres ne sont pas dans le serpent?
- Students work out which numbers between one and ten do not appear in the word snake.

Answers: deux, cinq, sept, dix

2 Mets les couleurs dans la grille.
- Students fit the colour vocabulary provided into the crossword grid.

Answers:

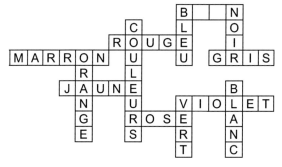

3 Relie.
- Students match up the English and French words for countries and nationalities.

Answers: Belgium – *Belgique*; Ireland – *Irlande*; Senegal – *Sénégal*; Switzerland – *Suisse*; Wales – *pays de Galles*

Algerian – *algérien(ne)*; Belgian – *belge*; English – *anglais(e)*; French – *français(e)*; Scottish – *écossais(e)*

Feuille 4 Bilan de leçon

These plenary activities are intended for use with the following Students' Book pages:
- Use ex. 1 with pages 18–19.
- Use ex. 2 with pages 16–17.

1 Oh là là! Regarde le mail! Il faut le corriger!
- Students rearrange the words of each sentence into the correct order.

Answers: Je m'appelle Noah. Mon pays, c'est la Belgique. Je suis belge. Je parle français et flamand. Mon idole s'appelle Patrick Vieira. Il est sportif. Il est sénégalais. Il parle français, anglais et italien.

2a Choisis un pays francophone. Trouve les détails et remplis le tableau.
- Students choose a French-speaking country and find out the following details: its name in French, the colours of its flag, its capital city, the languages spoken, and its currency.
- They note down the details in grid form.

2b Présente le pays à la classe.
- Students present the information about their chosen country (ex. 2a) to the class, and/or design a poster.
- Key phrases are provided as a framework.

Feuille 5 Écouter
- Use ex. 1 with Students' Book pages 12–13.
- Use ex. 2 with Students' Book pages 14–15.
- Use ex. 3 with Students' Book pages 16–17.

AT 1.1 **1 Écoute et note les numéros.**
- Students listen to a list of numbers. They note down each number they hear inside the shapes provided.

Answers: see transcript

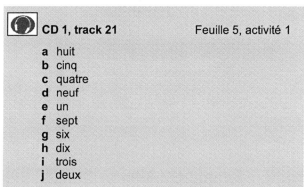

CD 1, track 21   Feuille 5, activité 1
a huit
b cinq
c quatre
d neuf
e un
f sept
g six
h dix
i trois
j deux

AT 1.1 **2 Comment s'appellent-ils? Écoute et écris.**

- Students listen to six people introducing themselves and spelling out their names. They note down each person's name.

Answers: 1 Paul; 2 Manon; 3 Louis; 4 Laure; 5 Marie; 6 Hugo

 CD 1, track 22   Feuille 5, activité 2

1 Je m'appelle Paul. P – A – U – L.
2 Je m'appelle Manon. M – A – N – O – N.
3 Je m'appelle Louis. L – O – U – I – S.
4 Je m'appelle Laure. L – A – U – R – E.
5 Je m'appelle Marie. M – A – R – I – E.
6 Je m'appelle Hugo. H – U – G – O.

AT 1.1 **3 Écoute. C'est quel pays? Note la bonne lettre.**

- Students listen and note down the letter of each country's flag.

Answers: 1 b; 2 e; 3 a; 4 f; 5 d; 6 c

 CD 1, track 23   Feuille 5, activité 3

1 Mon pays, c'est le pays de Galles.
2 Mon pays, c'est la France.
3 Mon pays, c'est l'Algérie.
4 Mon pays, c'est la Suisse.
5 Mon pays, c'est le Sénégal.
6 Mon pays, c'est le Canada.

Feuille 6   Parler

- Use with Students' Book pages 14–15.

 AT 1.1 AT 2.1 **1a Écoute ton/ta partenaire et écris les prénoms.**

 1b Épelle les autres prénoms pour ton/ta partenaire.

- In this information-gap speaking activity, students take turns to spell out names for each other to complete a list of ten French names.

 AT 1.1 AT 2.1 **2a Décris Alphaville. Dis à ton/ta partenaire ce qu'il y a et ce qu'il n'y a pas.**

 2b Écoute ton/ta partenaire. Note les détails pour Bétaville.

- This is another paired information-gap activity. Each partner has two sets of tourist information symbols relating to two towns: for one town (Alphaville), the symbols are ticked/crossed to show what facilities there are; for the other town (Bétaville), no information is given.
- Students take turns to tell each other which places their town does and doesn't have; the partner listens and fills in the details accordingly.

Feuille 7   Lire et écrire 1

- Use ex. 1 and 2 with Students' Book pages 16–17.
- Use ex. 3 with Students' Book pages 14–15.

AT 3.1 AT 4.1 **1 Fais le calcul des couleurs!**

- Students work out the "colour maths" and fill in the names of the colours in French.

Answers: 1 vert; 2 rose; 3 orange; 4 gris; 5 marron; 6 violet; 7 rouge; 8 bleu; 9 jaune; 10 noir

AT 4.1 **2 C'est quel pays? Écris les voyelles et écris l'anglais.**

- Students fill in the missing letters to make a list of countries in French, then add each country's name in English.

Answers: a *l'Algérie* – Algeria; b *l'Angleterre* – England; c *l'Écosse* – Scotland; d *l'Irlande* – Ireland; e *la Belgique* – Belgium; f *le Canada* – Canada; g *le pays de Galles* – Wales; h *le Sénégal* – Senegal; i *la France* – France; j *la Suisse* – Switzerland

AT 3.1 AT 4.2 **3 C'est quoi? Réponds aux questions.**

- Students write short sentences stating what the pictured items are.

Answers: a C'est une école. b C'est une baguette. c C'est le parfum. d C'est un jean. e C'est une rue. f C'est la pétanque.

Feuille 8   Lire et écrire 2

- Use with Students' Book pages 18–19.

AT 4.2 **1 Lis et écris des phrases.**

- Students write sentences following the model provided, stating the name, country and nationality of the people pictured.

Answers:

a Je m'appelle Julien. Mon pays, c'est la France. Je parle français.

b Je m'appelle Niamh. Mon pays, c'est l'Irlande. Je parle anglais.

c Je m'appelle Robert. Mon pays, c'est le pays de Galles. Je parle gallois et anglais.

d Je m'appelle Souleymane. Mon pays, c'est le Sénégal. Je parle français.

e Je m'appelle Céline. Mon pays, c'est la Suisse. Je parle français, allemand et italien.

AT 3.2 **2 Lis la lettre. Lis les phrases a–f: vrai ou faux?**

- Students read the letter and work out whether the statements listed are true or false.
- Ask them to correct the false statements.
- As a follow-up, students could write a reply, copying out Antoine's letter and replacing his details with their own.

Answers: a vrai; b faux (c'est le Sénégal); c vrai;
d faux (il est acteur); e faux (il parle danois, anglais,
français et espagnol); f faux (c'est le bleu)

Feuille 9   Labo-langue

• Use with Students' Book page 20.

1 Encercle les six noms.

• Students identify the six nouns in a jumble of
words.

Answers: cahier, école, euros, footballeur, paquet,
pétanque, sœur

2 Complète le tableau avec les noms de l'activité 1.

• Students fill in the grid with details of the nouns
they identified in ex. 1.

Answers:

anglais	français	le	la	l'	les	un	une	des
exercise book	cahier	✓				✓		
school	école			✓			✓	
euros	euros				✓			✓
footballer	footballeur	✓				✓		
language	langue		✓				✓	
packet	paquet	✓				✓		

3 Complète le tableau.

• Students fill in the grid of masculine and feminine
forms of job titles.

Answers:

English	masculine noun (for men)	feminine noun (for women)
singer	chanteur	chanteuse
shop assistant	vendeur	vendeuse
waiter/waitress	serveur	serveuse
mechanic	mécanicien	mécanicienne
electrician	électricien	électricienne
hairdresser	coiffeur	coiffeuse

Feuille 10   Bien apprendre!

• Use with *Bien apprendre!* on Students' Book
page 21.

1a Mets les mots dans l'ordre alphabétique, puis écris l'anglais.

• Students put the list of words into alphabetical
order and write the English beside the French.

Answers:

c'est	it is
elle	she
la France	France
gallois	Welsh
il y a	there is/are
noir	black
oui	yes
le parfum	perfume
le pays	country
la pharmacie	chemist
quoi	what
sept	seven
le sportif	sportsman
les toilettes (f)	toilets

1b Trouve les noms et écris *le, la ou les*.

• Students identify the nouns in ex. 1a and fill in the
genders.

Answers: see grid in ex. 1a

2 Organise les mots en groupes.

• Students organise the words into groups.

Possible answers:

les pays: Algérie, Belgique, pays de Galles, Suisse
les nationalités et les adjectifs: allemand, anglaise,
flamand, japonais, étrangère
les couleurs: blanc, brun, rouge, violet
les symboles de la France: Carambars, vélo
les numéros: dix, huit, trois
les prénoms: Nicole, Patrice
les expressions pour s'introduire: je m'appelle
autres expressions: c'est, elle est, il y a

Feuille 11   Bien parler!

• Use with *Bien parler!* on Students' Book page 21.

1a Read the pairs of words below. Which word in each pair will contain a nasal sound? Underline it.

1b Listen and check your underlining.

1c Listen again and repeat only the word with a nasal sound.

Answers: a un; b parfum; c ton; d un; e vin;
f canadien; g grand; h ange

CD 1, track 24   Feuille 11, activité 1

a une ... un
b parfum ... parfumerie
c tonique ... ton
d un ... unité
e vin ... vinaigre
f canadien ... canadienne
g granite ... grand
h âne ... ange

2 Practise saying these words. Check your pronunciation by listening and repeating.

 CD 1, track 25   Feuille 11, activité 2

1 un
2 bonjour
3 français
4 comment?
5 cinq
6 non
7 important
8 parfum
9 restaurant
10 canadien

3 Tongue-twisters: listen and practise!

 CD 1, track 26   Feuille 11, activité 3

– Son chat chante sa chanson.
– Dans ta tente, ta tante t'attend.
– Combien sont ces six saucissons?

Feuille 12   Culture

• Use with Students' Book page 25.

1 Relie les images et les mots.

• Students match the pictures representing various symbols of France to the corresponding words.

Answers: 1 h; 2 e; 3 b; 4 i; 5 g; 6 d; 7 a; 8 c; 9 f

2 Écris les légendes.

• Students label some additional images connected with France. They choose from the words and phrases provided.

Answers: 1 des escargots; 2 le 14 juillet; 3 le champagne; 4 Napoléon; 5 un croissant; 6 le TGV

En solo Workbook

Pages 6–7 1.1 C'est ça, la France!

- Use with Students' Book pages 12–13.

 1 Which players have not turned up for training? Listen and write the numbers on the right list.

Answers: présents: 5, 9, 1, 6, 3; absents: 2, 4, 7, 10, 8

En solo CD, track 9   page 6, activité 1

Alors… présents: Numéro cinq… numéro neuf… numéro un… numéro six… et… numéro trois.
Absents: numéro deux… numéro quatre… numéro sept… numéro dix… et numéro huit.

AT 3.1
AT 4.1
2 Write in the missing vowels to spell numbers one to ten. Then find the same words in the wordsquare.

Answers: un, deux, trois, quatre, cinq, six, sept, huit, neuf, dix

Q	U	A	T	R	E
D	N	B	O	C	N
E	T	R	O	I	S
U	S	I	X	N	E
X	D	I	X	Q	P
J	O	H	U	I	T
N	E	U	F	U	R

AT 3.1 **3 The remaining letters in the grid spell out a French word. What is it?**

Answer: bonjour

AT 2.1 **Défi!**

- Students practise counting backwards from ten down to one, as quickly and accurately as they can.
- Pairs could compete against each other, trying to beat each other's time.

AT 3.1
AT 4.1
4a Use the words in the box below to label the pictures.

Answers: see transcript for ex. 4b

AT 1.1 **4b Listen to check your answers.**

En solo CD, track 10   page 7, activité 4b

- Numéro un, c'est le football.
- Numéro deux, c'est le jean.
- Numéro trois, c'est la baguette.
- Numéro quatre, c'est la pétanque.
- Numéro cinq, c'est le parfum.
- Numéro six, c'est le vélo.

AT 4.1 **5 One object named in the box in activity 4a was not illustrated. Draw it and write a caption.**

Answer: C'est la tour Eiffel.

Pages 8–9 1.2 En France

- Use with Students' Book pages 14–15.

AT 3.1 **1 Underline the words for places in a town. Leave the other words as they are.**

Answers: masculine: un cinéma, un café-tabac; feminine: une pharmacie, une école; plural: des toilettes, des rues

AT 4.1 **2 Rearrange the letters to make the names of three more places in a town.**

Answers: a un hôtel; b un camping; c un restaurant

AT 1.2 **3 Listen and tick to show what there is in Sophie's part of town. Put a cross by the places that she says aren't there.**

Answers: ✓ une rue, des toilettes, un café-tabac, un restaurant, un cinéma, un hôtel, une pharmacie; ✗ une école, un camping

---

En solo CD, track 11   page 9, activité 3

Salut! Ici, il y a… un cinéma… il y a un restaurant… il y a un hôtel… et il y a une pharmacie. Il y a un café-tabac. Il y a une rue, bien sûr – c'est ma rue!... et il y a des toilettes. Mais il n'y a pas de camping… et il n'y a pas d'école.

AT 4.2 **4 Write captions under the pictures above.**

Answers: une rue, des toilettes, un café-tabac, un restaurant, une école, un cinéma, un camping, un hôtel, une pharmacie

AT 2.2 **Follow-up:**

- Students play Noughts and Crosses or Three-in-a-Row using the grid of pictures.
- For Three-in-a-Row, they will need small objects as "markers", e.g. coins, pencil sharpener, rubber, etc. They take turns to describe the pictures (*Il y a un/une/des…* or *Il n'y a pas de/d'…*), and place one of their markers on each square that they describe correctly. Three correct squares in a row wins.

Pages 10–11   1.3 Ici, on parle français

• Use with Students' Book pages 16–17.

 AT 3.2 **1 Tick a or b to show the correct meaning.**

Answers: 1 a; 2 b; 3 b; 4 b

AT 3.2
AT 4.2 **2 Choose from sentences 1–4 in activity 1 to write in the speech bubbles.**

• Ask students to exchange their work with a partner, who checks to make sure they have copied out the sentences correctly. This encourages accuracy and attention to detail in written work.

Answers: a Je m'appelle Nina. b Je suis française. c Mon pays, c'est la France.

AT 2.2
AT 4.2 **Défi!**

• Students interview each other using the questions from ex. 2, then write up their interviews.

AT 4.2 **3 Write a word from the box to show where each person lives and their nationality.**

• This task provides extra practice with talking about areas of the UK.

Answers: <u>Ben</u>: Mon pays, c'est l'Angleterre. Je suis anglais. <u>David</u>: Mon pays, c'est le pays de Galles. Je suis gallois. <u>Janine</u>: Mon pays, c'est l'Irlande. Je suis irlandaise. <u>Daniel</u>: Mon pays, c'est la France. Je suis français.

AT 4.2 **4 Write your own country and nationality.**

• Students use the texts in ex. 3 as a model to help them write a couple of sentences about themselves.

Pages 12–13   1.4 Les langues des stars

• Use with Students' Book pages 18–19.

AT 3.1 **1 Sort the words in the cloud into masculine and feminine words. Write them into the correct column.**

Answers: <u>masculin</u>: il, un acteur, sportif, français, le sport, mon pays; <u>féminin</u>: elle, la communication, une actrice, française, sportive, une langue

Défi!

• Students add more masculine and feminine words to ex. 1.

AT 3.2 **2 Read about Véronique Mang and answer the questions.**

Answers: a French and English; b French; c Cameroon, in Africa; d an athlete

AT 1.2 **3 Listen to the interview and write the missing words in the gaps.**

Answers: see underlining in transcript

 En solo CD, track 12   page 13, activité 3

– Ton idole, c'est qui?
– Il s'appelle David Beckham.
– Il est quoi?
– Il est footballeur.
– C'est quoi, sa nationalité?
– Il est anglais.
– Il parle quelles langues?
– Il parle anglais et espagnol.
– Très bien. Merci.

AT 4.2 **Défi!**

• Students write a paragraph about David Beckham, modelled on the text about Véronique Mang.

Pages 14–15   Labo-langue

• Use with Students' Book pages 20–21.

1 Do the quiz on gender. Circle a, b or c. Explain your choices.

Answers: 1 b (it isn't a noun); 2 c (*le* is the masculine word for "the"); 3 b (*une* is the feminine word for "a"); 4 c (the other two have the feminine *e* ending); 5 a (*Elle est* means "She is" so the only possible answer is *française* because it has the feminine *e* ending); 6 c (*est* is the third person singular form, and Madonna is female, so the only possible answer is *elle*); 7 c (because the adjectives must agree with the pronoun)

2 Underline the masculine words and circle the feminine words.

Answers: <u>masculine</u>: il, un vélo, le parfum, américain, un animal; <u>feminine</u>: la rue, une baguette, elle, écossaise, une question

3 Fill in the correct word for "the" (*l'*, *le*, *la* or *les*).

Answers: a la; b le, la; c l'; d les, les

4 After *il n'y a pas…*, the determiners *un/une/des* change to *de* (or *d'*). Make these sentences negative, to say "there isn't…" or "there aren't…".

Answers: a Il n'y a pas de camping. b Il n'y a pas de restaurant. c Il n'y a pas de pharmacie. d Il n'y a pas de toilettes. e Il n'y a pas d'hôtel.

5 Choose the right words in the description of Médor. Cross out the wrong words.

Answers: Il s'appelle Médor. Il est acteur. Il est américain. Il parle anglais.

Défi!

- Students write a similar description for a female dog, Lulu.

Answers: Elle s'appelle Lulu. Elle est actrice. Elle est américaine. Elle parle anglais.

Page 16 Checklist

- Use with *Blog-notes* (Students' Book page 22) or towards the end of the unit.

The checklist, recording and follow-up activities provide opportunities for students to review what they have learned, test themselves orally on key language and reflect on areas for improvement.

 En solo CD, track 13   page 16, activité 2

1 four [*beep*] quatre
2 X Y Z [*beep*] X Y Z
3 cycling [*beep*] le vélo
4 There's a restaurant. [*beep*] Il y a un restaurant.
5 There isn't a campsite. [*beep*] Il n'y a pas de camping.
6 I'm from France. [*beep*] Mon pays, c'est la France.
7 I'm French. [*beep*] Je suis français. Je suis française.
8 I speak French and Spanish. [*beep*] Je parle français et espagnol.
9 black [*beep*] noir
10 She's an actress. [*beep*] Elle est actrice.
11 His name is Robert. [*beep*] Il s'appelle Robert.
12 Paul is Welsh. [*beep*] Paul est gallois.
13 She speaks English and Arabic. [beep] Elle parle anglais et arabe.
14 No... yes! [*beep*] Non... oui!
15 He is English, she is English. [*beep*] Il est anglais, elle est anglaise

Follow-up: Encourage students to draw up their own individual action plan of steps they could take to help them improve. Provide a checklist of suggestions for them to choose from, e.g. try harder to learn vocabulary, read the grammar notes again and make sure they understand them/ask for help if they don't understand, check written work carefully for mistakes, etc.

Page 17 Top tips and strategies

Autonomous learning

This section helps to familiarise students with the different types of reference material in the Students' Book. It can be used at any appropriate point during Unit 1.

1a Here are the titles of reference sections in *Clic! 1* **Students' Book. Match them up with definitions a–e.**

Answers: a Glossaire; b Vocabulaire; c Grammaire; d Expressions utiles; e Verb tables

 1b How quickly can you note the page numbers those reference sections start on? Race against a partner.

Answers: Glossaire: p. 144; Vocabulaire: end of each unit; Grammaire: p. 130; Expressions utiles: p. 143; Verb tables: p. 137–138

 Follow-up: Students discuss what specifically they might use the different reference sections for and when they might find them useful, then report back their ideas to the class. To give them some ideas, provide a list of typical activities that they might find themselves doing in a French class and ask them to suggest where they would look for help, e.g. if they're writing something and want to check that they've put the correct ending on a verb, if they've lost their pen and want to ask if they can borrow one, if they are reading something and find a word that they don't understand, if they want to find out whether a word is *le* or *la*.

Writing

This section focuses on some common differences between French and English that students need to take account of when writing. It can be used at any appropriate point during Unit 1.

2 Add accents to make these words French.

- Once students have added the accents, read aloud the list of words, emphasising the different sound of the French and the English. Ask the class to repeat.

Answers: cinema: *cinéma*; president: *président*; hotel: *hôtel*; elephant: *éléphant*; Senegal: *Sénégal*

Follow-up: Extend this activity by adding further cognates, e.g. television (*télévision*), telephone (*téléphone*), gateau (*gâteau*), which students look up in the glossary or a bilingual dictionary.

Pages 18–19 Vocabulaire

- Use with Students' Book pages 26–27.

A list of key language from the unit is provided here as well as in the Students' Book and on Copymaster 1.

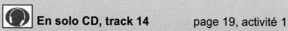

1 Listen and tick the phrases you hear.

> ⊙ **En solo CD, track 14**   page 19, activité 1
>
> C'est la tour Eiffel?
> Il y a... un café-tabac.
> Il n'y a pas d'hôtel.
> Elle s'appelle Manon.
> Mon pays, c'est la France.
> Je suis française.
> Tu parles quelles langues?
> Je parle français.
> Il est sportif.
> Elle est actrice.
> Le drapeau français est bleu, blanc, rouge.

2 Underline in coloured pencil...

- Students search the list for key language items.

3 What's your favourite word or phrase in this unit?

- Challenge students to make up a sentence using their favourite word/phrase.

Unité 2: Moi, j'aime!   Overview grid

Page reference	Contexts and objectives	Grammar	Language strategies and pronunciation	Key language	Framework	AT Level
30–31 **2.1 Mes passions**	• Things you like and don't like • Pets	• j'aime, tu aimes, il/elle aime • j'ai, tu as, il/elle a • je n'aime pas de/d'…		Tu aimes…? J'aime…/Je n'aime pas… la musique, le sport, les ordinateurs, les films (d'action), les jeux vidéo, les animaux Je n'aime pas ça! J'aime ça! Tu as un animal? J'ai un chat. Je n'ai pas d'animal. un chien, un lapin, un oiseau, un poisson	L – 7T3	1.2–3, 2.2, 3.1, 3.3, 4.2
32–33 **2.2 Mes fêtes préférées**	• Special occasions • Dates, age, birthday	• mon, ma, mes • ton, ta, tes		Numbers 11–31 janvier, février, mars, avril, mai, juin, juillet, août, septembre, octobre, novembre, décembre le Nouvel An, la Chandeleur, Pâques, le premier avril, la fête des Mères, la fête des Pères, la Fête Nationale, la Toussaint, Noël, la fête, l'anniversaire Ma fête préférée, c'est… Tu as quel âge? J'ai… ans. C'est quand, ton anniversaire? Mon anniversaire, c'est… Quelle est la date aujourd'hui? C'est le premier mai.	L – 7S2, 7T2 R – 7S3, 7S4	1.1–2, 2.1–3, 3.1–2, 4.2–3
34–35 **2.3 C'est le week-end!**	• Weekend activities you like or dislike	• j'aime/je déteste + infinitive • 1st/2nd person singular of regular -er verbs • je fais, tu fais		Qu'est-ce que tu aimes faire le week-end? J'aime bien…/J'adore… Je n'aime pas beaucoup…/Je déteste… faire mes devoirs, faire du sport, jouer avec mon chien, regarder la télé, visiter des sites Internet, visiter des musées, jouer sur l'ordinateur, écouter des CD, ranger ma chambre Je fais mes devoirs. Je fais du sport. Je range ma chambre. Je visite des sites Internet. Je regarde la télé. Je joue avec mon chat. Super! Youpi! Génial! Bof! Nul! Beurk!	L – 7W5	1.2–3, 2.2–3, 3.2, 4.2–3
36–37 **2.4 Copains-copines**	• You and your friends	• son, sa, ses • il/elle fait • 3rd person singular present tense of regular -er verbs		Comment est ton copain idéal/ta copine idéale? mon/ton copain idéal, ma/ta copine idéale Il/Elle aime regarder la télé. Le week-end, il/elle fait ses devoirs. Sa passion, c'est la musique. Son animal préféré, c'est le chien.	L – 7T6	1.3, 3.3, 4.2–3
38–39 **Labo-langue**	• Grammar • Skills • Pronunciation	French verbs (1): • The infinitive • Subject pronouns je/tu/il/elle • 1st/2nd/3rd person singular of regular -er verbs • ne… pas	• Using a bilingual dictionary • Silent letters **Workbook:** • Listening strategies • High-frequency words **Copymaster:** • Cognates, false friends		L – 7W5, 7L2 R – 7W2, 7W6, 7W7, 7W8, 7S1, 7S5, 7T1, 7T4, 7L1	
40–43 **Blog-notes / Tu sais tout? / En plus / Clic.fr**	• End-of-unit summary and assessment • Extension • **Cultural focus:** French festivals				R – 7W7, 7S9, 7C2, 7C3, 7C4	1.2–3, 2.2–3, 3.1–3, 4.2–3

CLIC! 1 STAR UNIT 2 MEDIUM TERM PLAN

About Unit 2, *Moi, j'aime!* This unit focuses on everyday themes such as favourite things, likes and dislikes, pets, special occasions, dates, age and birthdays, weekend activities and friends. Grammar coverage includes: basic high-frequency present tense verbs; *j'aime* + infinitive; *ne… pas; mon/ma/mes, ton/ta/tes, son/sa/ses*. Students learn how to use bilingual dictionaries and practise pronunciation of silent letters. Additional teaching and learning includes numbers 11–31 and considers French and other international festivals, drawing in students' personal experiences.

Framework objectives (launch)	Teaching and learning	Week-by-week overview (assuming 6 weeks' work or approximately 10–12.5 hours)
7W5: Verbs present (+ past)	Present tense first/second/third person singular of regular -er verbs (p. 38); *j'ai, tu as, il/elle a* (p. 31); *je fais, tu fais* (p. 35); *j'aime/je déteste* + infinitive (p. 35).	**Week 1 – Opening spread/2.1 Mes passions** Opening spread: introduction to unit themes and objectives, including pets and favourite hobbies
7S2: Sentence gist	Comparison of English "I am eleven years old" with French *J'ai onze ans* (p. 33).	Spread 2.1: interests, hobbies, likes and dislikes; pets
7T2: Reading aloud	Read aloud an interview about name, age, birthday, favourite festivals (p. 33 ex. 8).	
7T3: Checking before reading	Use pictures and key words to help understand the gist of a survey about animals and hobbies/interests (*Sondage*, p. 31).	**Week 2 – 2.2 Mes fêtes préférées** Special occasions, dates, age and birthday; numbers 11–31
7T6: Texts as prompts for writing	Adapt a model text to write a paragraph about a friend; adapt a multiple-choice quiz to write own quiz about a friend (p. 37).	
7L2: Following speech	Listening strategies (Workbook p. 31).	**Week 3 – 2.3 C'est le weekend!** Weekend activities you like or dislike
Framework objectives (reinforce)	**Teaching and learning**	
7W1: Everyday words	Build own stock of vocabulary relating to likes/dislikes (p. 29 ex. 2), re-applying vocabulary from Unit 1 where possible.	**Week 4 – 2.4 Copains–copines** All about friends (third person singular forms)
7W2: High-frequency words	Importance of knowing high-frequency words (Workbook p. 31).	
7W6: Letters and sounds	Pronunciation: silent letters (p. 39).	**Week 5 – Labo-langue** French verbs (the infinitive, subject pronouns, first/second/third person singular of regular -er verbs, *ne… pas*); using a bilingual dictionary; pronunciation of silent letters
7W7: Learning about words	Using a bilingual dictionary (p. 39); using similarities between French and English words to help remember vocabulary (p. 45).	
7W8: Finding meanings	Using a bilingual dictionary (p. 39); cognates and false friends (Copymaster 22).	
7S1: Typical word order	Position of *ne… pas* around the verb (p. 38).	**Week 6 – Blog-notes, Tu sais tout?, En plus, Clic.fr, On chante!, Lecture** Reinforcement and extension of the language of the unit; review of progress via the Checklist in the Workbook/on Copymaster; revision and assessment
7S3: Adapting sentences	Adapt a conversation to give personal information, including name, age, birthday, favourite festivals (p. 33 ex. 8).	
7S4: Basic questions	Different question forms: *Tu aimes…? Tu as…?* (pp. 30–31); *Tu as <u>quel âge?</u> C'est <u>quand</u> ton anniversaire?* (pp. 32–33); *Qu'est-ce que tu aimes faire?* (pp. 34–35).	
7S5: Basic negatives	How to form a negative: *ne… pas* (p. 38).	
7S9: Using simple sentences	Understand and produce simple sentences about likes and dislikes, age and birthday, weekend activities and friends.	
7T1: Reading using cues	Cognates and false friends (Copymaster 22).	
7T4: Using resources	Using a bilingual dictionary (p. 39).	
7L1: Sound patterns	Pronunciation: silent letters (p. 39).	
7C2: Everyday culture	French festivals (p. 43); popular sports in France (p. 120).	
7C3: Contact with native speakers	Video clip of native speakers talking about hobbies and interests (p. 30); video blog (p. 40).	
7C4: Stories and songs	Rap about hobbies and interests (p. 45).	

2 Moi, j'aime!

Unit objectives

Context: My favourite things
Grammar: Verbs (1)
Language learning: Using a bilingual dictionary
Pronunciation: Silent letters
Cultural focus: French festivals

Assessment opportunities

Listening: Students' Book, page 31, activity 6
Speaking: Students' Book, page 33, activity 8b (if done as an oral activity)

See also **Clic! 1** OxBox Assessment CD-ROM

Differentiation in *Départ* and Units 1 and 2

See the beginning of the *Départ* teacher's notes (page 19) for general suggestions on differentiation in *Départ* and Units 1 and 2.

 1 C'est quoi?

 This activity could replace task B in a Grade 1 Asset Languages teacher assessment.

- Students match the photos to the correct letters/words.

  Answers: 1 I – c'est l'iPod; 2 C – c'est le cheval;
  3 B – c'est le basket; 4 G – c'est le gâteau au chocolat; 5 F – c'est le football

Follow-up:

- Use the A–Z to revise the alphabet and spellings.
- Use the photos to recycle *C'est/Ce n'est pas le/le/les...* and *Il y a un/une/des, Il n'y a pas de/d'...* from Unit 1.
- Ask more able students to close their books, then question them about the photos, e.g. *La photo numéro 5, c'est le football ou le basket?*

 2 Défi! Fais l'ABC des passions de la classe.

- *Aim*: To introduce students to using a glossary or bilingual dictionary to start building their own personal stock of words for use in different contexts. This reinforces Framework Objective 7W1.
- Students make their own A–Z of the class's favourite things, using the glossary or a dictionary to help them. Point out that they can name favourite people or places as well as objects.

Follow-up:

- Students illustrate their class A–Z list to make a display. Use this as the basis for class discussion, to recycle some of the language of Unit 1, e.g. *Il y a un/une/des* and *Il n'y a pas de/d'*:
  Teacher (pointing to the list): *Il y a un vélo?*
  Student: *Oui, il y a un vélo.*
- Students who have learned some French already at primary school may be able to express their likes and dislikes, e.g. *J'aime/Je n'aime pas...*

- Students discuss the cultural information about pets and hobbies in France. How does this compare with the situation in the UK? What are the most popular pets here? Which sports and hobbies are popular here?

2.1 Mes passions

Planner

> **Objectives**
- Things you like and don't like

> **Resources**
Students' Book, pages 30–31
CD 1, track 28
Video clip 4
En solo Workbook, pages 20–21;
En solo CD, tracks 15–16
Copymaster 17; CD 1, tracks 41–43

> **Key language**
Mes passions
Tu aimes…?
J'aime…/Je n'aime pas…
la musique, le sport, les ordinateurs,
les films (d'action), les jeux vidéo,
les animaux
Je n'aime pas ça! J'aime ça!

Tu as un animal?
J'ai un chat. Je n'ai pas de chat.
un chien, un lapin, un oiseau, un poisson
Je n'ai pas d'animal.

> **Grammar**
j'aime, tu aimes, il/elle aime
j'ai, tu as, il/elle a
je n'ai pas de/d'…

> **Framework reference**
L – 7T3

> **Starters**
- Before matching the words to the pictures in ex. 1 (page 30), ask students to look at the pictures and guess what the mystery picture 6 might be. They check whether they were correct by doing ex. 1 and watching the video.

- Students compete to solve anagrams of the key leisure activities and animal vocabulary.
- Students work in groups using dictionaries to find extra animal vocabulary. Limit each group to finding only two or three extra words, and suggest a different category of animals for each group, e.g. pets, farm animals, British wild animals, wild animals of other countries, animals that spend a lot of time in water, insects and reptiles, etc. Collect in the words and write them on the board, pronouncing each one and asking the class to repeat.

> **Plenaries**
- Students choose the odd-one-out from sets of words/phrases from the spread, giving a reason for each one, e.g.
  - *j'ai, j'aime, tu as* (*j'aime* because it isn't a part of *avoir*, or *tu as* because it isn't the first person singular)
  - *il aime, elle a, elle n'aime pas* (*elle a* because it isn't a part of *aimer*, or *il aime* because it is masculine, or *elle n'aime pas* because it is negative)
  - *oiseau, poisson, chat* (*chat* because it's a land animal, *oiseau* because it's the only one that is preceded by *l'* or because it's the only one that can fly)
  - *les films d'action, les jeux vidéo, le sport* (*le sport* because it's the only one that involves physical activity, or because it's singular)
- Remind students of the strategies for recording/remembering new language suggested in the Unit 1 *Bien apprendre!* section (Students' Book page 21). Ask them to try these out with the key leisure activities and animal vocabulary. In a subsequent lesson, pairs could test each other on how well they have remembered the vocabulary.

AT 1.2
AT 3.1

1 Relie. Le numéro 6, c'est quoi?
- Students match the words to the corresponding pictures. They work out by a process of elimination what the picture for number 6 would be.
- They then watch the video clip to check their answers. At this stage, they focus only on checking their answers, and disregard any other details given.

Answers: 1 d; 2 a; 3 c; 4 e; 5 f; 6 b

 Video clip 4   page 30, activité 1

1 – Aujourd'hui, on parle de vos passions! Quelles sont tes passions? Tu aimes quoi? Tu aimes les ordinateurs?
  – Oui, j'aime les ordinateurs.
  – Et les animaux, tu aimes les animaux?
  – Les animaux, non, je n'aime pas les animaux!
2 – Salut! Tu aimes la musique?
  – Comment?
  – Tu aimes la musique?
  – Ah oui, j'aime la musique.
  – Et les ordinateurs? Tu aimes les ordinateurs?
  – Non, je n'aime pas les ordinateurs.

3 – Salut! Tu aimes les films?
– Oui, j'aime les films d'action… Jackie Chan!
– Et la musique, tu aimes la musique?
Comme le rap?
– Euh. Non! Je n'aime pas trop le rap.
4 – Ah! Salut! Tu as une console?
– Oui, j'aime les jeux vidéo!
– Et les films, tu aimes? Les films d'action?
– Les films d'action? Non, je n'aime pas ça!
5 – Salut! Tu aimes les animaux?
– Oui! J'aime bien les animaux, surtout les chevaux!
– Et les jeux vidéo, tu aimes?
– Non, je n'aime pas ça.
6 – Salut! Tu aimes le sport?
– Ah le sport, j'aime ça! J'adore le sport!
J'aime le tennis, le badminton, le judo.
– Oui… OK! Et le cricket, tu aimes le cricket?
– Le cricket? Je ne connais pas! On ne joue pas au cricket en France.
Moi j'aime le rugby, j'aime le football, j'aime le basket…
– Oui, bon, très bien, merci…!

AT 1.3 **2 Fais des phrases.**

AT 4.2
- Play the video clip again. This time, students make a note of what each person likes and dislikes. Ask them to note the letter of each hobby (a–f) with a tick beside it if the person likes it or a cross if they don't like it.
- Students then use these notes to help them write a couple of sentences for each person, summarising what they like and dislike.
- In addition to *j'aime* and *je n'aime pas*, number 6 on the video clip also uses *j'adore*. Ask students to listen out for this, then encourage higher attainers to extend their range of language by using all the phrases. They could also listen out for the full list of sports mentioned by number 6.
- Point out the note on *je* and *j'*. Ask students where they have met this sort of thing before, i.e. letter *e* replaced by apostrophe (e.g. *c'est, ce n'est pas, il n'y a pas*).

Answers: 1 J'aime les ordinateurs. Je n'aime pas les animaux. 2 J'aime la musique. Je n'aime pas les ordinateurs. 3 J'aime les films d'action. Je n'aime pas la musique rap/le rap. 4 J'aime les jeux vidéo. Je n'aime pas les films d'action. 5 J'aime les animaux. Je n'aime pas les jeux vidéo. 6 J'aime le sport (le tennis, le badminton, le judo, le rugby, le football, le basket). Je n'aime pas le cricket.

AT 2.2 **3 À deux. (B ➔ A)**

- In pairs, students ask each other questions about likes and dislikes, e.g.
Student A: *Tu aimes la musique?*
Student B: *Oui, j'aime ça/la musique. Tu aimes les ordinateurs?*
Student A: *Non, je n'aime pas ça/les ordinateurs. Tu aimes…?*
- Point out the notes on the conjugation of *aimer*. Emphasise that *aime* and *aimes* sound the same.

AT 4.2 **4 Choisis deux correspondants.**

- Students choose two ideal penfriends from the young people in the video clip, giving a reason for their choice, e.g. *Je choisis le numéro 3. Il aime les films d'action.*
- Encourage more able students to use *parce que* to build a more complex sentence, e.g. *Je choisis le numéro 3 parce qu'il aime les films d'action.* Point out that they can base their choices on what the people don't like as well as on what they like, e.g. *Je choisis le numéro 6 parce qu'il déteste le cricket.*

Follow-up:
- Extend the list of sports and hobbies for more able students to include all the sports mentioned on the video clip plus any others they are interested in.
- Hold a class discussion about "desert island (*île déserte*) hobbies": which hobbies or sports would students not be able to live without on a desert island?

AT 3.3 **5 Relie.**

- Students read teenagers' answers to the survey questions A–D. They match the questions to the answers.
- Use this as an opportunity to show students how visuals and other clues can help them to understand texts. Point out that in order to find a match for question A (*Tu as un animal?*), they don't actually need to read any of the texts at all – all they need to do is to look for a photo with an animal in it. This is likely to be the answer they are looking for, so they can read the text to confirm.

Answers: A Manon; B Thomas; C Mehdi; D Diane

AT 1.2 **6 C'est quelle question (A, B, C ou D)?**

This activity could replace task B or C in a Grade 1 Asset Languages teacher assessment.
- Students listen to ten people talking about likes and dislikes, and what they do and don't have. They match each speaker to the corresponding survey question (see ex. 5).

Answers: 1 A; 2 C; 3 C; 4 A; 5 B; 6 D; 7 A; 8 D; 9 B; 10 A

 CD 1, track 28   page 31, activité 6

1 Moi, j'ai un chien. Il s'appelle Gréco.
2 J'ai une Nintendo DS. C'est super!
3 Je n'ai pas de console. Je n'aime pas ça.
4 Je n'ai pas d'animal. Maman n'aime pas les animaux!
5 Je n'ai pas d'ordinateur. Je n'aime pas beaucoup ça!
6 Moi, j'ai un portable! Il est génial!
7 J'ai un lapin et un poisson. J'adore les animaux.
8 Non, moi, je n'ai pas de portable. Papa n'aime pas ça.
9 Moi, j'ai un ordinateur. J'adore communiquer avec mes amis par MSN!
10 Moi, j'ai trois oiseaux, Tic, Tac et Toc. J'adore les oiseaux!

Follow-up:

- For more able students, play the recording again. Students note down in English the details given by the speakers. Alternatively, provide specific questions for students to listen out for, e.g. Who is Gréco? Why doesn't number 4 have any pets?

 7 À deux: vrai ou faux? (B ➞ A)

- Students ask and answer questions about what they do and don't have. They may tell the truth or give a false answer, and their partner tries to guess whether it is true or not, e.g.
  Student A: *Tu as un animal?*
  Student B: *Non, je n'ai pas d'animal.*
  Student A: *C'est vrai?*
  Student B: *Oui, c'est vrai! Tu as un portable?*
  Student A: *Oui,…*

 8 Grammaire: complète.

- Students copy out and complete the sentences with the correct pronoun or part of *avoir*. Less able students could focus on a–c only.
- Look at the grammar notes on the conjugation of *avoir*. Ask students what they notice about the pronunciation of the forms *as* and *a*, and refer them back to the note about the pronunciation of *aime* and *aimes* on page 30 of the Students' Book.

Answers: a as; b ai; c je; d a; e tu; f il/elle

 Follow-up: More able students make up their own gap-fill sentences to practise *avoir* and *aimer*, which they exchange with a partner. Encourage them to recycle previously learned vocabulary instead of limiting themselves to the language of this spread, e.g. *Tu aimes la France? Tu as un vélo?*

 See Copymaster 17 ex. 2 for an additional listening activity on animals.

 Pages 20–21 of the *En solo* Workbook provide further activities focusing on animals.

2.2 Mes fêtes préférées

Planner

> ### Objectives
> - Special occasions
> - Dates, age, birthday

> ### Resources
> Students' Book, pages 32–33
> CD 1, tracks 29–31
> *En solo* Workbook, pages 22–23;
> *En solo* CD, track 17
> Copymasters 15, 16, 17, 19, 20; CD 1, tracks 41–43

> ### Key language
> Numbers 11–31
>
> *Mois de l'année*
> *janvier, février, mars, avril, mai, juin, juillet, août,*
> *septembre, octobre, novembre, décembre*
>
> *Les fêtes*
> *le Nouvel An, la Chandeleur, Pâques, le premier*
> *avril, la fête des Mères, la fête des Pères, la Fête*
> *Nationale, la Toussaint, Noël*
> *la fête, l'anniversaire*
> *Ma fête préférée, c'est…*
>
> *Tu as quel âge?*
> *J'ai… ans.*
> *C'est quand, ton anniversaire?*
> *Mon anniversaire, c'est…*
> *Quelle est la date aujourd'hui?*
> *C'est le premier mai.*

> ### Grammar
> *mon/ma/mes, ton/ta/tes*

> ### Framework reference
> L – 7S2, 7T2; R 7S3, 7S4

> ### Starters
> - To revise numbers one to ten (introduced in Unit 1), set some simple sums for students to do against the clock, or students make up sums for a partner to solve, e.g.
>   *quatre – trois = …*
>   *cinq + … = sept*
> - In pairs or groups, students play a version of Fizz-Buzz, counting alternate numbers from one to 31 and replacing every multiple of a certain number (e.g. five, three) with an agreed word or phrase in French (e.g. *Bonne fête!*).
> - Using the OHP or interactive whiteboard, display the months of the year in jumbled order, with all the vowels missing, e.g. j _ _ l l _ t, j _ n v _ _ r, etc. Students compete to fill in the missing letters and rearrange the months into the correct sequence.
> - Copymaster 15 *À tes marques!* ex. 1 and 2.

> ### Plenaries
> - *Contre la montre: du plus vieux au plus jeune!* Working as a class or in groups, students say their age and birthday and organise themselves into a row in order of age, ranging from the oldest to the youngest. When they are standing in line, they each say their age and birthday again, to check whether they are in the correct order.
> - Show (or call out) a word from the lesson. Students respond with a question or answer containing the word, e.g.
>   Teacher: *Vingt-cinq!*
>   Student: *Noël, c'est le vingt-cinq décembre.*
> - Students tell each other three similarities or differences between French and English festivals that they have learned about during work on this spread.
> - Copymaster 16 *Bilan de leçon* ex. 1.

---

1 C'est quel mois?

- Students listen while looking at the calendar in the Students' Book. As each month is mentioned, they point to it on the calendar.
- Tell them to focus on the months only and ignore the dates at this point.

CD 1, track 29   page 32, activité 1

– Quelle est la date aujourd'hui?
– le onze janvier
– le dix-sept mai
– le trente octobre

– Quelle est la date aujourd'hui?
– le douze août

– le quatorze novembre
– le vingt-deux juillet
– le trente et un mars

– Quelle est la date aujourd'hui?
– le treize février
– le quinze décembre
– le seize avril
– le dix-huit juin
– le dix-neuf… non!… le vingt… non!… le vingt et un septembre
– Quelle est la date aujourd'hui?

2 Réécoute et note.

- Play the recording from ex. 1 again. Students note down the numbers, then work out which numbers between 11 and 31 are missing.
- Alternatively, students sketch out a rough Bingo-style grid containing all the numbers between 11 and 31. Play the recording. Students tick off the numbers as they hear them.

Answers: 11, 17, 30, 12, 14, 22, 31, 13, 15, 16, 18, 19, 20, 21 (numbers 23–29 are missing)

Follow-up:

- Play Bingo. Students draw out a grid containing their own choice of ten numbers between 11 and 31. Call out a list of numbers. Students tick them off as they hear them.
- Focus on the structure of the numbers, e.g.
  - the *-ze* ending in *onze, douze, treize, quatorze, quinze, seize*
  - *dix* + number in *dix-sept, dix-huit, dix-neuf*
  - *vingt et un, trente et un*
  - *vingt* + hyphen + number, e.g. *vingt-deux, vingt-trois*, etc.
  - *trois, treize, trente*
- If appropriate, explain how to say the year in French, e.g. 2007 = *deux mille sept*.

 3 À deux: parlez. (B 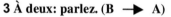 **A)**

- Students say dates in French for their partner to translate as quickly as possible into English, e.g.
  Student A: *Le premier juin!*
  Student B: 1st June! *Le vingt août!*
  Student A: 20th August!

 4 Louis parle de fêtes. C'est quoi en anglais?

- *Aim*: To raise awareness of French festivals and provide opportunities for comparison with festivals celebrated by other cultures.
- Students listen to a teenage boy talking about French festivals and look at the illustrated calendar in the Students' Book. They work out the English equivalent of each occasion.

Answers:
le Nouvel An: New Year's Day, 1st January
la Chandeleur: Candlemas, 2nd February (equivalent of Pancake Day)
Pâques: Easter, in March
le Poisson d'avril: April Fool's Day, 1st April
la fête des Mères: Mother's Day, in May
la fête des Pères: Father's Day, in June
la Fête Nationale: Bastille Day/National Day, 14th July
la Saint-Louis: St Louis' Day (Saint's Day), 25th August
mon anniversaire: my birthday, 21st September
Halloween: Halloween, 31st October
la Toussaint: All Saints' Day, 1st November
Noël: Christmas, 25th December

 CD 1, track 30   page 32, activité 4

Alors, le premier janvier, c'est le Nouvel An.
Le 2 février, c'est la Chandeleur (hmmm, j'adore les crêpes!).
En mars, il y a Pâques.
Le 1er avril, c'est le Poisson d'avril.
En mai, il y a la fête des Mères. Bonne fête, maman!
En juin, c'est la fête des Pères. Bonne fête, papa!
Le 14 juillet, c'est la Fête Nationale.
Le 25 août, c'est ma fête, la Saint-Louis!
Le 21 septembre, c'est mon anniversaire.
Le 31 octobre, c'est Halloween.
Le 1 novembre, c'est la Toussaint. Je n'aime pas la Toussaint.
Et le 25 décembre, c'est Noël. Joyeux Noël!

Follow-up:

- Exploit the recording further for the benefit of more able students by asking them to listen out for any additional comments, e.g. *Joyeux Noël, J'adore les crêpes, Bonne fête, maman.*
- Students test each other on the festivals shown in the Students' Book: they hide the words and try to name each festival by looking at the pictures only.

 5 Fais un calendrier. Écris tes fêtes préférées.

- Students create a calendar showing their own notable dates and favourite festivals. Provide dictionaries so that they can research the names of other festivals, e.g. *Aïd-el-Fitr, Ramadan, Hanoukka*.
- Students note down what their favourite festival is. More able students explain why: *Ma fête préférée, c'est Pâques parce que j'adore le chocolat!* Encourage them to add what their favourite birthday or Christmas present is, e.g. *Mon cadeau d'anniversaire/de Noël préféré, c'est…*

 6 À deux. (B A)

- Students interview each other about their age and the date of their birthday.
- They begin by referring to the details on the party invitation and asking/answering as if they are Louis, then progress to giving details about themselves.
- Point out the notes on English "I am 11" compared with French "I have 11 years".

 7 Lis *Interview Express*.

- Students read and listen to the interview with Thomas.
- Point out the notes on *mon/ma/mes* and *ton/ta/tes*.

CD 1, track 31   page 33, activité 7

 – Bonjour! Tu t'appelles comment?
 – Je m'appelle Thomas.
 – Tu as quel âge?
 – J'ai 12 ans.
 – C'est quand, ton anniversaire?
 – Mon anniversaire, c'est le 18 mars.
 – C'est quoi, tes fêtes préférées?
 – Mes fêtes préférées, c'est Noël et mon anniversaire. J'adore les cadeaux!

C17
C19 Ex. 1 on Copymaster 17 is an additional listening activity on birthdays. Copymaster 19 provides reading/writing activities on age and birthday.

C20 On Copymaster 20, ex. 1 and 2 are reading/writing activities to practise questions and answers from this and the previous spread.

W 22–23 Pages 22–23 of the *En solo* Workbook provide further activities to practise the language of this spread.

AT 2.2–3
AT 4.2–3

8 À deux: a) lisez la conversation. b) adaptez. (A ➔ B, B ➔ A)

This activity would be suitable as part of preparation for external assessment at Breakthrough stage.

• Students read aloud the interview, then adapt it to give their own answers to the questions.

• Encourage able students to extend the interview by recycling previously learned language, e.g. additional questions (all from Unit 1) might be: *C'est quoi, ton pays? C'est quoi, ta nationalité? Tu parles quelles langues? C'est quoi, ta couleur préférée?*

• Able students could rewrite the interview in the third person singular. To enable them to do this, remind them of *Il/Elle s'appelle…* from Unit 1 and provide *son/sa/ses*.

Follow-up:

• To practise asking and saying ages, set up a Mexican Wave around the class, encouraging students to go faster and faster:
Teacher: *Tu as quel âge?*
Student 1: *J'ai douze ans. Tu as quel âge?*
Student 2: *J'ai onze ans. Tu as quel âge?*
Student 3: *J'ai…*

• To increase the challenge of the Mexican Wave, write different numbers on the board, point to them and ask students to say them instead of their real age. To make this even more challenging, replace the numbers with maths sums, e.g. 3 x 10, 23 + 4, 4^2, etc.

• *Sondage: le pic des naissances!* Students carry out a survey on birthdays, asking each other *C'est quand, ton anniversaire?* They create a bar chart to show the results, and find out which is the most common month of birth in the class.

• *Fais une invitation originale pour ton anniversaire.* Students create an original design for a birthday party invitation. Encourage them to recycle previously learned language instead of copying the invitation in the Students' Book.

• *Sondage: c'est quoi, ta fête préférée?* Students do a survey in class about favourite festivals, and show the results in the form of a bar chart.

2.3 C'est le week-end!

pages 34–35

Planner

> ### Objectives
> - Weekend activities you like or dislike

> ### Resources
> Students' Book, pages 34–35
> CD 1, tracks 32–33
> *En solo* Workbook, pages 24–25;
> *En solo* CD, track 18
> Copymasters 15, 16, 17, 18, 20; CD 1, tracks 41–43

> ### Key language
> *Qu'est-ce que tu aimes faire le week-end?*
> *J'aime bien…/J'adore…*
> *Je n'aime pas beaucoup…/Je déteste…*
> *faire mes devoirs, faire du sport, jouer avec mon chien, regarder la télé, visiter des sites Internet, visiter des musées, jouer sur l'ordinateur, écouter des CD, ranger ma chambre*
>
> *Qu'est-ce ce que tu fais?*
> *Je fais mes devoirs. Je fais du sport. Je range ma chambre. Je visite des sites Internet. Je regarde la télé. Je joue avec mon chat.*
>
> *Super! Youpi! Génial! Bof! Nul! Beurk!*

> ### Grammar
> *j'aime/je déteste* + infinitive
> First/Second person singular present tense of regular -er verbs
> *je fais, tu fais*

> ### Framework reference
> L – 7W5

> ### Starters
> - Before beginning work on this spread, recap quickly on likes and dislikes. Call out the names of celebrities (or hold up photos of them) and ask students to invent appropriate sentences about their likes and dislikes, using different persons of the verb, e.g. Bill Gates: *J'adore les ordinateurs*; Arnold Schwarzenegger: *Il adore les films d'action.* Students will need to imagine things that the celebrities don't like, e.g. Thierry Henry: *Je n'aime pas le cricket.*
> - Use a variety of props (e.g. magazine pictures/advertisements, CDs, TV listings, tennis ball/football, a school exercise book, etc.) to prompt students to form sentences, e.g. *J'aime faire du sport, J'aime regarder la télé, Je n'aime pas faire mes devoirs.*
> - Copymaster 15 *À tes marques!* ex. 3.

> ### Plenaries
> - In pairs, groups or as a whole class, students play Word Tennis to practise likes and dislikes, e.g.
>   Student A: *J'aime…*
>   Student B: *faire…*
>   Student A: *du sport. C'est…*
>   Student B: *génial!*
> - Call out an infinitive from the spread. Students put it into the *je* or *tu* form and build it into a sentence, e.g. Teacher: *Écouter!*
>   Student: *J'écoute des CD.*
> - Give students some sentences using *j'aime/je n'aime pas/j'adore/je déteste* + infinitive and ask them to rephrase them using *je/tu* present tense forms followed by an exclamation of like or dislike, e.g.
>   Teacher: *Je n'aime pas faire mes devoirs.*
>   Students: *Je fais mes devoirs. Bof!*
>   Give them some examples in reverse, e.g.
>   Teacher: *Je joue avec mon chien. Youpi!*
>   Students: *J'adore jouer avec mon chien.*
> - Copymaster 16 *Bilan de leçon* ex. 2.

AT 1.2

1 C'est quel numéro?

- Students listen to a radio phone-in, in which teenagers say what they like and don't like doing at the weekend.
- They choose a picture in the grid to represent each speaker.

Answers: 1 b; 2 c; 3 h; 4 f; 5 g; 6 e; 7 i; 8 d; 9 a

 CD 1, track 32   page 34, activité 1

- Bienvenue sur Clic! radio. Le sondage aujourd'hui: Qu'est-ce que tu aimes faire le week-end? Alors, on écoute les messages…
1 Le week-end, j'aime bien faire du sport.
2 Le week-end, j'adore jouer avec mon chien.
3 Moi, j'adore jouer sur l'ordinateur.
4 J'aime bien visiter des sites Internet.
5 Moi, le week-end, j'aime bien écouter mes CD.

- Et qu'est-ce que tu n'aimes pas faire le week-end? On écoute…
6 Le week-end, je n'aime pas beaucoup regarder la télé.
7 Le week-end, je déteste ranger ma chambre.
8 Moi, je n'aime pas beaucoup visiter des musées.
9 Je déteste faire mes devoirs le week-end!
- Voilà! Et toi, qu'est-ce que tu aimes faire le week-end? Qu'est-ce que tu n'aimes pas faire?

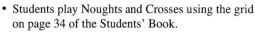

 2 Compte.

- Play the recording from ex. 1 again. Students note how many times they hear the key phrases.

Answers: J'aime bien: 3; J'adore: 2; Je n'aime pas beaucoup: 2; Je déteste: 2

 3 Complète pour toi.

- Students build sentences about their own likes and dislikes.
- Point out the grammar notes on pronoun + verb + infinitive.

 4 À deux. (B ➔ A)

- Students ask and answer questions about what they like and dislike doing.
- Encourage students who have learned French at primary school to suggest other ways to express likes and dislikes, e.g. *J'aime un peu…, Je n'aime pas du tout…, J'aime beaucoup…*

Follow-up:

- For higher attainers: students try to find someone who shares the same likes and dislikes as them. To do this, they will need to ask lots of questions and pay close attention to the answers.
- Students play Battleships. They prepare grids in advance: along the top row, they need a series of activities (in words or simple pictures); down the left-hand column, they list expressions of like/dislike (again, in words or using the heart symbols from the Students' Book). Each student ticks a few squares of the grid, and their partner tries to find out where the ticks are by asking questions.
- To practise negatives, students play a game of Contradictions. Student A says something they like or don't like, and B says the opposite, e.g.
  A: *J'aime bien regarder la télé.*
  B: *Ah non, moi, je n'aime pas beaucoup regarder la télé.*

 5 Qui dit a–f: Alex ou Yasmina?

- Students look at the pictures of Alex and Yasmina and work out, from their facial expressions, whether they had a good or a bad weekend.
- They match each positive and negative statement (a–f) to either Alex or Yasmina.

Answers: Alex: b, d, f; Yasmina: a, c, e

AT 1.3 **6 Vérifie. Note les symboles.**

- Students listen to the recording to check their answers to ex. 5.
- They note down a heart symbol (from ex. 2) to represent what Yasmina and Alex say about each activity.
- Able students could note down the actual phrases used, instead of the heart symbols.

Answers: a Yasmina ✖✖ (je déteste); b Alex ♥♥ (j'adore); c Yasmina ✖ (je n'aime pas beaucoup); d Alex ♥ (j'aime bien); e Yasmina ✖ (je n'aime pas beaucoup); f Alex ♥ (j'aime bien)

 CD 1, track 33 page 35, activité 6

- Tu fais tes devoirs le week-end?
- Oui, je fais me devoirs. Beurk! Je déteste ça! Tu fais du sport?
- Oui, le week-end, je fais du sport. Génial! J'adore ça. Tu ranges ta chambre?
- Oui, le week-end, je range ma chambre. Bof! Je n'aime pas beaucoup ça. Tu visites des sites Internet le week-end?
- Moi, le week-end, je visite des sites Internet. Youpi! J'aime bien ça. Tu regardes la télé le week-end?
- Pfff… oui, le week-end, je regarde la télé. Nul! Je n'aime pas beaucoup ça. Le week-end, tu joues avec ton chat?
- Oui! Le week-end, je joue avec mon chat. Super! J'aime bien ça.

 7 À deux. (B ➔ A)

- Students interview each other about weekend activities, e.g. *Tu fais du sport?* They respond with an opinion and a suitable exclamation, e.g. *Oui, j'aime bien ça! Youpi!*
- Point out the key verb patterns: *Je/Tu fais…, Je visite/Tu visites…, Je joue/Tu joues…*, etc. Encourage more able students to research other activities to go with each of the verbs, e.g. *Tu fais… la cuisine? Tu visites… un château? Tu joues… avec tes copains? Tu regardes… des DVD? Tu ranges… la maison?*

 8 Écris.

- Students write down three things they do at the weekend, including one that is not true. The partner tries to guess what the invented activity is.
- Less able students use the examples provided on the page.
- To challenge more able students, encourage them to write in greater detail, adding their likes and dislikes, e.g. *Je fais du sport. J'adore le football et le tennis.* Award bonus points for any expressions of like/dislike.

 9 Grammaire. À deux: le morpion.

- Students play Noughts and Crosses using the grid on page 34 of the Students' Book.
- To win a square, they write down a correct sentence describing the activity shown in the square, e.g. square 1: *Je fais mes devoirs* or *Tu fais tes devoirs.*
- Increase the challenge for more able students by asking them to add an opinion to each activity, e.g. square 2: *Je fais du sport. J'adore ça, c'est génial!*

- This exercise is best done in groups of three: two students play the game while the third monitors their written sentences to make sure the spelling is completely accurate. They then swap roles so that everyone has a turn at playing the game and being the monitor.

Follow-up:

- Challenge students to find additional weekend activities in a dictionary and to incorporate them into sentences.
- Refer them to the Unit 2 *Labo-langue* spread for advice on using a bilingual dictionary. Make sure students realise that verbs are listed in a dictionary in their infinitive form, and need to be changed into the correct person of the verb.

| C17 |
| C18 |
| C20 |

Ex. 3 on Copymaster 17 is a listening activity on likes/dislikes. Copymaster 18 provides additional speaking practice on likes/dislikes. Further reading/writing practice on this topic is provided on Copymaster 20, ex. 3 and 4.

| W |
| 24–25 |

Pages 24–25 of the *En solo* Workbook provide further activities to practise the language of this spread.

2.4 Copains–copines

Planner

> ### Objectives
> - You and your friends

> ### Resources
> Students' Book, pages 36–37
> CD 1, track 34
> *En solo* Workbook, pages 26–27;
> *En solo* CD, track 19
> Copymaster 16

> ### Key language
> *Comment est ton copain idéal/ta copine idéale?*
> *mon/ton copain idéal*
> *ma/ta copine idéale*
> *Il/Elle aime regarder la télé.*
> *Le week-end, il/elle fait ses devoirs.*
> *Sa passion, c'est la musique.*
> *Son animal préféré, c'est le chien.*

> ### Grammar
> *son/sa/ses*
> *il/elle fait*
> Third person singular present tense of
> regular -*er* verbs

> ### Framework reference
> **L** – 7T6

> ### Starters
> - Before beginning work on this spread, revise language from the previous spread by asking students general questions about their likes and dislikes of items in the quiz, e.g. *Tu aimes la musique? – Oui, j'adore écouter des CD. Le week-end, tu fais tes devoirs? – Oui, je fais mes devoirs. Beurk!*
> - Students answer the register by saying something they like/dislike, something they do at the weekend, or their favourite animal/festival/colour, etc.

> ### Plenaries
> - Give students a word from the spread. Students think of a sentence containing the word, e.g. *animal – Mon animal préféré, c'est le lapin.* More able students could be asked to provide both a question and an answer for each word.
> - In groups, students brainstorm all the words and phrases they have met so far connected with likes and dislikes, sports, hobbies and weekend activities. Allow time for them to feed back to the class.
> - Students write gap-fill sentences to exchange with a partner, to practise the language of Unit 2, e.g. *mon/ma/mes, ton/ta/tes, son/sa/ses,* present tense verbs and infinitives, *ne... pas.* Alternatively, set them some gap-fill sentences to complete within a time limit.
> - Copymaster 16 *Bilan de leçon* ex. 3.

AT 3.3 **1 Lis.**

- Students read and complete the quiz about the ideal boyfriend/girlfriend.
- Point out the notes on *son/sa/ses*.

AT 1.3 **2 Note les réponses de Yasmina.**

- Students listen and note down Yasmina's answers to the quiz.
- The Students' Book version of the quiz is in the third person (e.g. *Sa passion, c'est...*, *Il/Elle aime...*), but the recording is done in question-and-answer format, in the first and second person singular (e.g. *Ta passion, c'est quoi? Qu'est-ce que tu aimes faire? J'adore...*).

Answers: 1 b; 2 a; 3 a; 4 b; 5 a; 6 b; 7 a; 8 a

 CD 1, track 34   page 37, activité 2

– Numéro 1: Ta passion, c'est quoi?
  a: la musique?
  b: le cinéma?
– C'est le cinéma.

– Numéro 2: Ton animal préféré, c'est quoi?
  a: le chien?
  b: le rat?
– C'est le chien!

– Numéro 3: Tes fêtes préférées, c'est quoi?
  a: Noël et Halloween?
  b: Pâques et la Chandeleur?
– C'est Noël et Halloween!

– Numéro 4: Qu'est-ce que tu aimes faire?
  a: regarder la télé?
  b: jouer sur ta console?
– J'adore jouer sur ma console!

– Numéro 5: Qu'est-ce que tu détestes faire?
  a: ranger ta chambre?
  b: faire du shopping?
– Je déteste ranger ma chambre!

– Numéro 6: Le week-end, qu'est-ce que tu regardes?
  a: la télé?
  b: des DVD?
– Le week-end, je regarde des DVD.

– Numéro 7: Le week-end, qu'est-ce que tu
  fais?
  a: tes devoirs?
  b: du sport?
– Le week-end, je fais mes devoirs!

– Numéro 8: Le week-end, qu'est-ce que tu
  préfères?
  a: retrouver des copains?
  b: rester au lit?
– Le week-end, je préfère retrouver des
  copains! N'est-ce pas, Alex!

3 Yasmina, c'est la copine idéale de Alex?

- Students compare Yasmina's quiz answers with those of Alex (shown in the Students' Book). They decide whether Yasmina is Alex's ideal girlfriend.

Answers: Five (out of a possible eight) of Yasmina's answers are the same as the answers given by Alex, so although they wouldn't be the ideal couple they would probably be reasonably compatible!

Follow-up:

- Able students do the quiz together as an interview, asking the questions and answering, exactly as Alex and Yasmina do on the recording. To do this, they will need to change all the third person singular forms used in the Students' Book quiz into questions and answers in the second and first person singular, e.g. *Ta passion, c'est quoi? Qu'est-ce que tu aimes faire? J'adore… Je déteste…*

- Students try to guess their partner's answers to the quiz. First, they each do the quiz separately, keeping their answers hidden from their partner. They then ask questions to guess their partner's answers.

AT 4.2 ### 4 Grammaire: complète.

- Students copy out the email message and fill in the correct forms of the verbs.
- The infinitives are provided, but students will need to change them into the correct third person singular forms. Point out the notes on *il/elle* forms.

Answers: Ma copine s'appelle Yasmina. Elle a 13 ans. Sa passion, c'est le cinéma. Elle adore les films d'action. Elle déteste faire ses devoirs. Elle n'aime pas beaucoup regarder la télé. Le week-end, elle préfère retrouver des copains!

Follow-up: To encourage students to think about language patterns, challenge them to use their knowledge of verbs to help them work out the first, second and third person singular forms of *préférer* and *retrouver*.

 ### 5 Écris six choses sur ton copain/ta copine.

 This activity would be suitable as part of preparation for external assessment at Breakthrough stage.
- Students write at least six things about one of their friends.
- Less able students may limit themselves to adapting the models provided in the Students' Book.
- Encourage able students to write a longer text, recycling previously learned language, e.g. *Il/Elle est* + nationality, *Il/Elle parle* + languages.

AT 4.3 ### 6 Invente un quiz sur ton copain/ta copine!

- Students make up their own multiple-choice quiz about a friend. This could be done in pairs or groups and exchanged with other pairs/groups.

W 26–27 Pages 26–27 of the *En solo* Workbook provide further activities to practise the language of this spread.

Labo-langue

Planner

> **Objectives**
> • French verbs (1)
> • Using a bilingual dictionary
> • Silent letters

> **Resources**
> Students' Book, pages 38–39
> CD 1, tracks 35–37
> *En solo* Workbook, pages 28–29, 31;
> *En solo* CD, track 21
> Copymasters 21, 22, 23; CD 1, tracks 44–45

> **Framework reference**
> **L** – 7W5, 7L2 (via Workbook); **R** – 7W2 (via
> Workbook), 7W6, 7W7, 7W8, 7S1, 7S5, 7T1 (via
> Copymaster), 7T4, 7L1

Bien comprendre!

French verbs (1)

These grammar notes focus on different aspects of verbs, including the infinitive, subject pronouns *je, tu* and *il/elle*, the present tense of regular verbs (first, second and third person singular) and *ne... pas*. After working through the grammar explanations, students complete ex. 1 and 2.

1 Put the words in order.

• The words are colour-coded to correspond with the grammar explanations: subject pronouns are pink, verbs are green, negative expressions are blue.

Answers: a Elle regarde un DVD. b Je ne joue pas. c Elle adore écouter des CD. d Tu n'aimes pas regarder la télé?

2 Fill in the gaps with the correct form of the verb.

Answers: a aime; b regardes; c adore; d déteste

 See Copymaster 21 for additional grammar practice focusing on subject pronouns and verbs.

 Pages 28–29 of the *En solo* Workbook provide further activities to practise these grammar points.

Bien apprendre!

Using a bilingual dictionary

This section aims to familiarise students with the general layout of a bilingual dictionary and the way in which information is presented at dictionary entries.

1 Look at a bilingual dictionary. On which pages will you find…?

Answers: will depend on which particular dictionaries are used

2 Look at the extract from the dictionary. Where does it say…?

Answers: a 1; b 3; c 4; d 2

3 Use the dictionary to translate.

Answers: a J'adore danser. b J'aime regarder la télé. c Is it my turn? d I'd like to have dinner with you.

4 In what form are verbs listed in the dictionary?

• This reminds students that in a dictionary verbs are listed in the infinitive.

C22 Copymaster 22 focuses on recognising cognates and false friends, and could be used at any point towards the end of Unit 2.

W31 Further language learning strategies are provided on page 31 of the *En solo* Workbook:

• *Listening*: tips and activities to help students develop listening strategies
• *Vocabulary*: the importance of knowing and recognising high-frequency words in French

This Workbook page features language and vocabulary from pages 30–35 of the Students' Book (age, birthday, weekend activities), so it would be best used towards the end of Unit 2 once students are familiar with this language.

Bien parler!

Silent letters

1 Look and listen. What's the main difference between the French and the English versions of these words?

- Each word is pronounced twice on the recording, first in English and then in French. Students should spot that in French the final letter of each word is not pronounced.

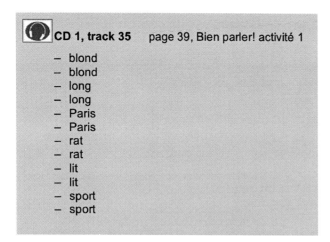

CD 1, track 35   page 39, Bien parler! activité 1

- blond
- blond
- long
- long
- Paris
- Paris
- rat
- rat
- lit
- lit
- sport
- sport

2 Listen carefully. Which words have silent final consonants?

Answers: see underlining in transcript

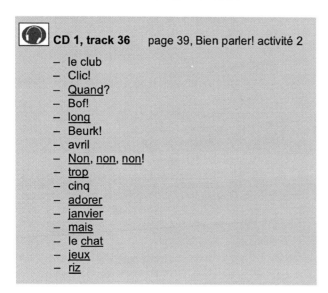

CD 1, track 36   page 39, Bien parler! activité 2

- le club
- Clic!
- Quand?
- Bof!
- long
- Beurk!
- avril
- Non, non, non!
- trop
- cinq
- adorer
- janvier
- mais
- le chat
- jeux
- riz

3 Say these phrases aloud. Listen to check!

- Give students time to work on the pronunciation for themselves in pairs, before playing the recording and reading aloud as a whole class.

CD 1, track 37   page 39, Bien parler! activité 3

- Salut, les copains!
- Tu as des cadeaux?
- Non! C'est faux!
- En janvier, en juin ou en juillet?
- Tu as beaucoup trop de devoirs!

C23 Copymaster 23 provides further pronunciation activities focusing on silent letters.

Blog-notes

Planner

> ### Objectives
> * To summarise the main points of the unit in context, in a format that is fun and familiar to students, i.e. a video blog
> * To provide a model enabling students to personalise the language of the unit
> * To provide opportunities for students to ask as well as answer questions
> * To provide extended listening practice recycling the language of the whole unit

> ### Resources
> Students' Book, page 40
> Video clip 5
> *En solo* Workbook, page 30;
> *En solo* CD, track 20
> Copymaster 14

> ### Framework reference
> **R** – 7S9, 7C3

AT 1.3 | **1 Regarde le vidéo-blog. Choisis 1 ou 2.**

* Students watch Alex's video diary and choose 1 or 2 in answer to each question. Pause the video after each section to allow students time to answers.

Answers: a 1; b 1; c 2; d 2; e 2; f 1; g 2; h 2

 Video clip 5   page 40, activité 1

Salut! Bienvenue sur mon vidéo-blog!
Je m'appelle Alex! Je suis français. Je suis à Nantes.
a J'ai 12 ans. Et toi, tu as quel âge?
b Mon anniversaire, c'est le 31 mars...
c Euh... Quel jour sommes nous aujourd'hui? Nous sommes le 21 septembre..., octobre, novembre, décembre, janvier, février, mars... Ah! Encore six mois attendre! Et toi? C'est quand ton anniversaire?
d Moi, ma passion, c'est la Chine! Mon rêve, ce serait de visiter la Chine! Moi, ma fête préférée, c'est le Nouvel An chinois. C'est génial! C'est quoi, ta fête préférée? Mon signe du calendrier chinois, c'est le rat! Je déteste les rats! Beurk!
e Moi, mon animal préféré, c'est le panda. J'adore les pandas! Il y a des pandas en Chine! Et toi, c'est quoi, ton animal préféré?...
f Tu as un animal? Moi, j'ai un chat! Le voilà Il s'appelle Jet! J'aime beaucoup Jet Li! Il a deux ans. Il est super!
g Qu'est-ce que tu aimes faire, le week-end? Moi, je n'aime pas beaucoup le sport mais j'aime bien l'aikido. Regarde.
h Moi, le week-end, je retrouve mes copains. Ma copine idéale déteste faire du shopping et adore le foot! Euh... je n'ai pas de copine! Et toi, comment est ton copain idéal? Comme moi? Allez, salut! Zài jiàn.

AT 4.3 | **2 À toi de répondre!**

* Students write their own answers to questions a–h.

Follow-up:

* Students interview each other using questions a–h.
* Students write their own blog, based on their answers to the interview questions. Suggest a limit of 100 words.
* If the appropriate technology is available, allow students to record their own video blogs and play them to the class.

C14
W30
A checklist summarising the language of the unit is provided on Copymaster 14 and on page 30 of the *En solo* Workbook. It could be used in tandem with the *Blog-notes* page or at an appropriate point towards the end of the unit. It provides an opportunity for students to review what they have learned and reflect on areas for improvement.

Tu sais tout?

Planner

> **Objectives**
> • To enable students to recap on the language and structures of the unit
> • To provide an opportunity for quick testing of all four skills

The page is divided into four sections: listening, speaking, reading and writing. Each section can be marked out of 5 to give a total score out of 20.

> **Resources**
> Students' Book, page 41
> CD 1, track 39

| AT 1.2 | **1 Listen (1–6) and note. Who speaks about…?**

This activity could replace task C in a Grade 2 Asset Languages teacher assessment.

Answers: 1 d; 2 a; 3 f; 4 e; 5 c; 6 b

 CD 1, track 39   page 41, activité 1

1 – Tu as un animal, toi?
– Oui, j'ai un chat et un lapin.
2 – Tu as quel âge?
– J'ai 13 ans.
3 – Quelle est la date aujourd'hui?
– Aujourd'hui? C'est le 21 octobre.
4 – C'est quoi, ta fête préférée?
– Hum… Ma fête préférée, c'est Noël pour les cadeaux!
5 – Tu as un copain?
– Oui, j'ai un copain. Il s'appelle Clément.
6 – C'est quoi ton animal préféré?
– Mon animal préféré, c'est le chien.

| AT 1.3 | **Défi!**

• Students listen again for extra details.

Answers: 1 chat, lapin; 2 âge = 13 ans; 3 date = 21 octobre; 4 fête préférée = Noël (cadeaux); 5 copain = Clément; 6 animal préféré = chien

---

| AT 3.2 | **2 Read and find.**

This activity would be suitable as part of preparation for external assessment at Breakthrough stage.

Answers: a he's 12; b music; c football; d rugby; e Étienne; f video games

---

| AT 3.3 | **Défi!**

• Students note down extra details from Bruno's text.

Answers: birthday is on 28th July; Étienne is 13; Bruno doesn't like video games very much

---

| AT 4.2 | **3 Copy the sentences in the correct order.**

Answers: a J'ai un chien. b J'aime regarder la télé. c Mon anniversaire, c'est le 8 juin. d Je range ma chambre le week-end. e Je n'aime pas beaucoup le football. f Ma copine idéale aime visiter des musées.

| AT 4.3 | **Défi!**

• Students adapt sentences a–f to give information about themselves.

| AT 2.2 | **4 Mini-interview. Look at the photo. Imagine how he might answer the questions.**

Answers: a J'ai quinze ans. b Mon anniversaire, c'est le onze juillet. c Mon animal préféré, c'est le chien. d J'ai un chien. e J'adore le football.

| AT 2.3 | **Défi!**

• Students interview each other using the questions from ex. 4.

En plus

Planner

> **Objectives**
> * To provide extension material for more able students who are confident with the core language of the unit, and to introduce new language where appropriate
> * To provide alternative class and homework material for students who finish other activities quickly

> **Resources**
> Students' Book, page 42

Je n'ai pas d'animal!

AT 3.2 **1 Lis.**

* Students compare the picture of an animal shelter with the speech bubbles, which describe the pets that people have adopted from the shelter.
* They use this information to work out which animals haven't yet been adopted.

Answers: poisson, rat, souris

 AT 2.2–3 **2 À deux.**

* Students use the animal shelter to play Noughts and Crosses. To win a square, they make up a sentence featuring the animal in the square.
* Students may model their sentences on a–e in ex. 1, but encourage more able students to say as much as they can.

AT 3.2 **3 Relie. Qui n'a pas d'animal?**

* Students read four teenagers' opinions of animals.
* They try to match each teenager to an animal from the three that haven't yet been adopted (*poisson, rat, souris*). Which person is left without an animal?
* Point out the reminder about the difference between *j'ai* and *j'aime*. Ex. 1 uses *J'ai…*, whereas ex. 3 uses *J'aime…*: students often confuse these two verb forms.

Answer: Lola n'a pas d'animal (Lili and Loulou take the mouse and the rat respectively, because these are their favourite animals; the only animal remaining is the fish, but Lola doesn't like fish. Lulu therefore takes the fish, and Lola is left without an animal.)

 Follow-up: Students invent their own animal-based puzzles for another pair to solve.

AT 2.2–3 **4 Parle.**

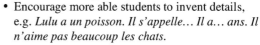
* Students make up sentences to say which pet each person has, using third person singular verbs.
* Encourage more able students to invent details, e.g. *Lulu a un poisson. Il s'appelle… Il a… ans. Il n'aime pas beaucoup les chats.*

71

Clic.fr

Planner

> **Objectives**
> * To raise awareness of France and French culture
> * To promote intercultural understanding by providing opportunities to compare French culture with students' own culture

> **Resources**
> Students' Book, page 43
> Copymaster 24

> **Framework reference**
> **R** – 7C2

Fêtes à la française

AT 3.1	This page describes in English how some festivals are celebrated in France.

1 Relie les bulles aux bonnes fêtes.

* Students match the French speech bubbles to the dates/occasions.

Answers: 1 Bastille Day; 2 saint's day; 3 Christmas and New Year; 4 April Fool's Day

2 Which *fête* would you like to celebrate the French way? Why?

* Students explain their favourite French festival.

C24	Further activities on the theme of French festivals are provided on Copymaster 24.

Vocabulaire

Planner

> ### Objectives
> * *Vocabulaire*: to provide a theme-based summary of the key language of the unit, which students can use as a reference or as an aid to learning
> * To develop language learning strategies
> * *On chante!*: to reinforce the language of the unit in a fun way

> ### Resources
> Students' Book, pages 44–45
> CD 1, track 40
> *En solo* Workbook, pages 32–33;
> *En solo* CD, track 23
> Copymaster 13

> ### Framework reference
> **R** – 7W7, 7C4

C13
W
32–33

A list of key language from the unit, with associated activities, is also provided on Copymaster 13 and on pages 32–33 of the *En solo* Workbook.

Use English to remember French!

* *Aim*: To show that similarities between English and French words can make them easier to remember; to show that although some words might look the same, it is important to remember any differences in spelling.
* Students find in the vocabulary list a sequence of 12 words that look very similar to their English equivalents.
* They note one main difference between the French and the English.

Answers: A the months of the year; B they don't start with a capital letter in French

On chante!

AT 3.1	**1 C'est dans quel ordre?**

* Students search the song lyrics for the list of English hobbies. They note down the order in which they are mentioned.

Answers: e, d, c, a, b

AT 1.2	**2 Rappe avec le CD!**

AT 2.2

AT 3.2

The rap song could replace the text of task A in a Grade 1 Asset Languages teacher assessment.
* Students listen and follow the words. Encourage them to join in.

🎧 **CD 1, track 40**   page 45, activité 1

– Yo! Qu'est-ce que tu aimes faire?
– J'aime faire du sport.
– Le sport, super! J'adore le sport!

– Yo! Qu'est-ce que tu aimes faire?
– J'aime faire du ski.
– Le ski, youpi! J'adore le ski!

– Yo! Qu'est-ce que tu aimes faire?
– J'aime faire du cheval!
– Le cheval, génial! J'adore le cheval!

– Yo! Qu'est-ce que tu aimes faire?
– Moi, j'aime danser!
– Danser, le pied! J'adore danser!

– Yo! Qu'est-ce que tu aimes faire?
– J'aime faire du rap!
– Le rap, c'est cool! Moi, je kiffe le rap!

– Je kiffe le rap!
– Tu kiffes le rap!
– Il kiffe le rap!
– Elle kiffe le rap!
– On kiffe le rap!

AT 4.2	**3 Invente un couplet!**

* Students write an additional verse for the song.

Lecture

Planner

> **Objectives**
> • To encourage independent reading and develop reading strategies
> • To provide alternative class and homework material for students who finish other activities quickly
>
> The texts and activities on *Lecture A* should be suitable for all; *Lecture B* is more challenging and may be suitable for more able students only.

> **Resources**
> Students' Book, pages 120–121

> **Framework reference**
> **R** – 7C2

Lecture A

En France, on aime le sport!

This page provides reading material about sports and activities that are popular in different regions of France.

AT 3.3 **1 Read and find the French for…**
• Remind students of the reading strategies discussed in Unit 1 (see teaching notes for Unit 1 *Lecture A* on page 44 of this book), e.g. pictures, cognates, context.

Answers: a l'escalade; b une course; c le cyclisme; d la pétanque, des boules; e on aime; f on joue

AT 3.3 **2 Read and work out…**

Answers: a Tour de France; b horse riding; c in June, it lasts 24 hours; d in *pétanque*, the bowls are made of metal; e about 3,500 km; f it is named after the Basque region, where it is very popular (the *pelote* is the ball itself)

Lecture B

Joyeux anniversaire!

This text is designed as an Internet forum. A teenage girl asks for ideas on how to celebrate her birthday and receives a number of replies to her message.

AT 3.3 **1 Explain in English: a) Liliput's problem; b) the ideas suggested on the forum.**

Answer: Lili's birthday is on 14th March but she doesn't have any ideas about how to celebrate it. The suggestions are: Maya: play games and have cakes and sweets; Minimiss: listen to music and dance with her friends; Al3x: invite friends round, play video games and watch DVDs; Charlie31: go to the cinema with friends to watch horror films, eat pizza and cake

AT 4.2–3 **2 Whose party would you prefer to go to? Why?**
• Provide students with a framework, if necessary, as support, e.g. *Je préfère l'anniversaire de… parce que j'aime beaucoup…*

AT 4.2–3 **Défi!**
• Students write their own forum message in reply to Lili.

Copymasters

Feuille 13   Vocabulaire

A list of key language from the unit is provided here as well as on pages 44–45 of the Students' Book and pages 32–33 of the *En solo* Workbook.

Feuille 14   Je sais…

Use this checklist with *Blog-notes* (Students' Book page 40) or towards the end of the unit. It provides an opportunity for students to review what they have learned and reflect on areas for improvement. This checklist is also provided on page 30 of the *En solo* Workbook.

Feuille 15   À vos marques!

These starter activities are intended for use with the following Students' Book pages:

- Use ex. 1 and 2 with pages 32–33.
- Use ex. 3 with pages 34–35.

1 Dans la grille, trouve les noms des six mois de l'encadré.

- Students find six months in the wordsearch grid.

Answers:

U	O	C	I	U	S	E	J	J
J	A	N	V	I	E	R	U	U
H	V	S	L	E	P	T	I	G
N	R	E	Y	U	T	M	L	A
T	I	B	K	S	E	E	L	O
G	L	P	A	L	M	D	E	U
Q	F	E	I	V	B	E	T	T
O	C	T	O	B	R	E	L	W
J	R	H	E	F	E	O	R	E

2 Complète les additions.

- Students calculate the sums and fill in the answers, choosing from the words provided.

Answers: a quatorze; b vingt-trois; c trente et un; d vingt-deux; e dix; f dix-neuf

3 Relie les phrases.

- Students match the French sentences to their English translations.

Answers: a 4; b 1; c 2; d 3; e 6; f 5

Feuille 16   Bilan de leçon

These plenary activities are intended for use with the following Students' Book pages:

- Use ex. 1 with pages 32–33.
- Use ex. 2 with pages 34–35.
- Use ex. 3 with pages 36–37.

1 Remplis les blancs, puis écris le bon chiffre.

- Students fill in the missing letters and write the corresponding figures in the boxes.

Answers: a quinze (15); b vingt (20); c vingt-quatre (24); d quatorze (14); e douze (12); f trente et un (31)

2 Relie les questions aux réponses.

- Students match the questions to the answers.

Answers: 1 e; 2 f; 3 d; 4 a; 5 c; 6 b

3 Écris la bonne phrase.

- Students follow the lines to link the subject pronouns to the verbs, then write out the phrases.

Answers: a je visite; b tu aimes; c il range; d elle aime; e je fais; f j'ai; g tu as; h il fait

Feuille 17   Écouter

- Use ex. 1 with Students' Book pages 32–33.
- Use ex. 2 with Students' Book pages 30–31.
- Use ex. 3 with Students' Book pages 34–35.

AT 1.2 **1 Écoute. Vrai ou faux?**

- Students listen while reading statements a–f giving the dates of six people's birthdays.
- They note whether each statement is true or false, and correct the false statements.

Answers: a vrai; b faux (le 23 mai); c faux (le 17 août); d vrai; e faux (le 30 octobre); f vrai

 CD 1, track 41   Feuille 17, activité 1

- a Laurent: Mon anniversaire, c'est le neuf janvier.
- b Aimée: Mon anniversaire, c'est le vingt-trois mai.
- c Noémie: Mon anniversaire, c'est le dix-sept août.
- d Benoît: Mon anniversaire, c'est le quinze juillet.
- e Élise: Mon anniversaire, c'est le trente octobre.
- f Léo: Mon anniversaire, c'est le seize mars.

AT 1.2 **2 Écoute. Mets le bon numéro dans la case.**

- Students listen and number the animals in the order they hear them mentioned.

Answers: a 3; b 5; c 1; d 4; e 6; f 2

 CD 1, track 42   Feuille 17, activité 2

- – Tu as un animal?
- 1 Oui, j'ai un chien.
- 2 Oui, j'ai un oiseau.
- 3 Oui, j'ai un poisson.
- 4 Non, je n'ai pas d'animal.

5 J'ai un chat.
6 Oui, j'ai deux lapins.

 3 Écoute. Coche la bonne image.

- Students listen and tick the activities/interests mentioned.

Answers: a football; b museum; c tidying bedroom; d dog; e TV; f computer

CD 1, track 43   Feuille 17, activité 3

  a Moi, j'aime le sport. Le football, c'est ma passion!
  b J'adore visiter des musées. Génial!
  c Je déteste ranger ma chambre. C'est nul.
  d J'ai beaucoup d'animaux. J'adore jouer avec mon chien.
  e Je n'aime pas regarder la télé.
  f J'ai un ordinateur. J'adore visiter des sites Internet.

Feuille 18   Parler

- Use with Students' Book pages 34–35.

AT 2.1   **1 Donne ton opinion à ton/ta partenaire.**

   • In response to the picture prompts, students take turns to tell their partner what they like and dislike.

AT 1.2   **2 Décris tes préférences à ton/ta partenaire.**

AT 2.2   **3 Écoute ton/ta partenaire. Coche les activités mentionnées.**

   • Ex. 2 and 3 are done together as a paired information-gap activity. Student A reads out a text about preferred hobbies and interests, replacing the pictures with words. Student B listens and ticks the symbols/activities that are mentioned.
- The pair then exchange roles.

Feuille 19   Lire et écrire 1

- Use with Students' Book pages 32–33.

AT 3.2   **1 Écris une bulle pour chaque personne.**

AT 4.2   • Students complete a speech bubble for each person, using the details provided.

Answers:

b Je m'appelle Lucas. J'ai douze ans. Mon anniversaire, c'est le premier mai.

c Je m'appelle Thomas. J'ai treize ans. Mon anniversaire, c'est le vingt-trois décembre.

AT 4.2   **2 Écris une carte et une bulle pour toi.**

- Students write an identity card and a speech bubble for themselves, similar to those in ex. 1.

Feuille 20   Lire et écrire 2

- Use ex. 1 and 2 with Students' Book pages 32–33.
- Use ex. 3 and 4 with Students' Book pages 34–35.

AT 3.2   **1 Relie les questions aux réponses.**

- Students match the questions to the answers.

Answers: 1 c; 2 a; 3 d; 4 b

AT 4.2   **2 Réponds aux questions de l'activité 1.**

- Students write their own answers to the ex. 1 questions.

AT 3.2   **3 Regarde l'image et souligne la bonne phrase.**

- Students replace the pictures with words in a gap-fill text about likes and dislikes. There is a choice of two words or phrases for each gap.

Answers: Moi, le week-end, j'aime <u>faire du sport</u>. J'adore le tennis.

J'adore jouer sur l'ordinateur. Je visite <u>des sites Internet</u> aussi. Génial!

Je n'aime pas <u>regarder la télé</u> et je déteste ranger ma chambre. <u>Beurk!</u>

AT 4.2–3   **4 Écris un paragraphe pour toi: "Moi, le week-end, je…"**

- Students write a paragraph describing what they like and dislike doing at the weekend.

Feuille 21   Labo-langue

- Use with Students' Book page 38.

1a Écris le sujet.

- Students fill in the correct subject pronoun in each sentence.

Answers: a je; b il; c elle; d tu

1b Encercle le sujet.

- Students circle the subject in each sentence.

Answers: a je; b tu; c Luc; d le chien

1c Souligne le verbe.

- Students underline the verb in each sentence in ex. 1a and 1b.

Answers:

Ex. 1a: a regarde; b préfère; c fait; d aimes
Ex. 1b: a fais; b as; c aime; d est

2 Choisis et encercle la bonne forme du verbe.

- Students circle the correct form of the verb in each sentence.

Answers: a aime; b écoutes; c adore; d joue; e déteste; f regarde

Feuille 22   Bien apprendre!

- This skills copymaster focuses on recognising cognates and false friends. It could be used at any point towards the end of Unit 2.

1 Read the text and underline all the cognates.

Answers: six, novembre, préférée, célèbre, parents, cousins, grands-parents, adore, gâteau, super, cinéma, film, romantiques

2a Find these three false friends in the text and circle them.

2b Look them up in a dictionary. Write their meanings.

Answers: la journée (*day*), sympathiques (*nice*), restent (*stay*)

3 Are there any words in the text that you don't understand? Look them up in a dictionary and write their meanings in the box below.

4 Look back at Unit 2 in the *Clic! 1* Students' Book or *En solo* and see if you can find other examples of cognates and false friends.

Feuille 23   Bien parler!

- Use with *Bien parler!* on Students' Book page 39.

 1a In pairs, read these words aloud and decide whether the final letter is silent or not. Circle the letter that you think is silent.

Answers: all the final letters are silent apart from in: 2 un cheval; 6 un animal; 8 le cinéma; 9 le rap

1b Listen to check.

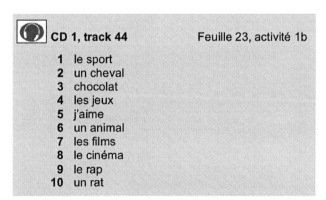

CD 1, track 44   Feuille 23, activité 1b

1 le sport
2 un cheval
3 chocolat
4 les jeux
5 j'aime
6 un animal
7 les films
8 le cinéma
9 le rap
10 un rat

 2a Now read these sentences aloud with your partner. Check that you are pronouncing the words in bold correctly.

2b Listen to check.

CD 1, track 45   Feuille 23, activité 2b

1 J'aime le chocolat.
2 J'ai un animal.
3 Je fais du sport.
4 Je n'aime pas les films.

Feuille 24   Culture

- Use with Students' Book page 43.

1 Lis les descriptions des fêtes.

- Students read the descriptions of French festivals and underline any new words they recognise as being similar to English words.

2 Relie le français à l'anglais.

- Students match the French to the English words and phrases.

Answers: 1 c; 2 d; 3 a; 4 f; 5 b; 6 e

3 Vrai ou faux?

- Students decide whether each statement about French festivals is true or false.

Answers: a faux; b faux; c vrai; d faux; e vrai; f faux

En solo Workbook

Pages 20–21   2.1 Mes passions

- Use with Students' Book pages 30–31.

AT 1.1 **1 Listen and number the animals 1–5.**

Answers: un chat 1; un chien 4; un oiseau 5; un poisson 2; un lapin 3

 En solo CD, track 15   page 20, activité 1

numéro 1... un chat
numéro 2... un poisson
numéro 3... un lapin
numéro 4... un chien
numéro 5... un oiseau

AT 4.1 **2 Fill in the bubbles with *J'ai...* + a word for a pet. Who will say: *Je n'ai pas d'animal*?**

Answers: 1 J'ai un chat. 2 J'ai un poisson. 3 J'ai un lapin. 4 J'ai un chien. 5 J'ai un oiseau. 6 Je n'ai pas d'animal.

AT 1.1
AT 3.1 **3a Listen to the conversation. Circle the animals you hear mentioned.**

Answers: cat, rabbit and dog are mentioned

 En solo CD, track 16   page 21, activité 3a

– Tu <u>aimes</u> les animaux?
– Oui, <u>j'aime</u> bien les animaux.
– Tu <u>as</u> un animal?
– Oui, j'ai <u>un chat</u> et <u>un lapin</u>. Et toi?
– Moi, j'ai <u>un chien</u>.

AT 1.2 **3b Listen again and fill the gaps using the words in the box.**

- Although the missing words are provided, students need to use their knowledge of verb endings to work out where to put *aime* and *aimes*, since both sound the same.

Answers: see underlining in transcript for 3a

Pages 22–23   2.2 Mes fêtes préférées

- Use with Students' Book pages 32–33.

AT 3.1 **1 Find the twelve months in the letter sequence.**

Answers: janvier, février, mars, avril, mai, juin, juillet, août, septembre, octobre, novembre, décembre

AT 4.1 **2 Write the names of the months into the correct spaces.**

Answers: <u>spring</u>: mars, avril, mai; <u>summer</u>: juin, juillet, août; <u>autumn</u>: septembre, octobre, novembre; <u>winter</u>: décembre, janvier, février

3 Can you think of other ways of grouping the months of the year?

- *Aim*: To encourage students to develop their own learning strategies.
- Emphasise that students will find it easier to learn the vocabulary if they organise it in a way that they find logical or meaningful, e.g. words that have similar endings, the four seasons, words that look similar to English words, etc.

AT 3.2 **4a Read and circle the correct answer so that Toto's interview makes sense.**

Answers: see transcript for 4b

AT 1.2 **4b Listen to check your answers.**

 En solo CD, track 17   page 23, activité 4b

– Tu as quel âge?
– J'ai douze ans.
– C'est quand, ton anniversaire?
– C'est le 11 juin.
– C'est quoi, ta fête préférée?
– C'est ma fête!... La Saint-Toto!

AT 2.2
AT 4.2 **4c Write down your own answers to the interview questions.**

- As a follow-up, students interview each other in pairs.

Pages 24–25   2.3 C'est le week-end!

- Use with Students' Book pages 34–35.

AT 1.2 **1 Listen and draw the correct symbol by each picture.**

Answers: 1 ✖; 2 ♥♥; 3 ✖✖; 4 ✖; 5 ♥; 6 ♥

 En solo CD, track 18   page 24, activité 1

1 – Tu aimes faire du sport?
     – Non, je n'aime pas beaucoup ça.
2 – Tu aimes jouer avec ton chien?
     – Ah oui, j'adore ça!
3 – Tu aimes ranger ta chambre?
     – Non, beurk, je déteste ça!
4 – Tu aimes visiter un musée?
     – Non, je n'aime pas beaucoup ça.

5 – Tu aimes écouter des CD?
  – Oui, j'aime bien ça.
6 – Tu aimes regarder la télé?
  – Oui, j'aime bien ça.

AT 4.2 | **2a** *Qu'est-ce que tu aimes faire?* **Make sentences about your likes and dislikes. Include a lie!**

• Students write four sentences corresponding to the heart symbols (*j'aime bien, j'adore, je n'aime pas beaucoup, je déteste*).

AT 2.2 | **2b Read out your sentences for your partner to spot the lie if they can.**

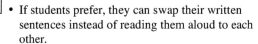

• If students prefer, they can swap their written sentences instead of reading them aloud to each other.

AT 3.2 | **3 Choose a verb from the box to complete each sentence.**

Answers: 1 je fais; 2 j'écoute; 3 je range; 4 je visite; 5 je joue; 6 je regarde; 7 je joue; 8 je fais

AT 4.2 | **4 Write down two serious sentences and two silly ones!**

• Students use the sentences from ex. 3 as prompts to write two serious sentences and two silly ones, e.g. *Je range ma chambre. Je visite ma chambre!*

Pages 26–27 2.4 Copains–copines

• Use with Students' Book pages 36–37.

AT 3.3 | **1 Read the text about Laura and fill in the form.**

Answers: <u>Nom</u>: Laura; <u>Âge</u>: 13 ans; <u>Anniversaire</u>: le 11 novembre; <u>Fête préférée</u>: son anniversaire; <u>Animal préféré</u>: le chien; <u>Adore</u>: regarder la télévision; <u>Déteste</u>: ranger sa chambre

AT 3.3 | **2 Read the form and complete the text for Julien.**

Answers: Il s'appelle <u>Julien</u>. Il a <u>12</u> ans. Son anniversaire, c'est le <u>21 octobre</u>. Sa fête préférée, c'est <u>Noël</u>. Son animal préféré, c'est <u>le chat</u>. Il adore <u>faire du sport</u>. Il déteste <u>faire ses devoirs</u>.

AT 1.2 | **3 Listen and circle the girl's details.**

Answers: <u>Nom</u>: Lucie; <u>Âge</u>: 11 ans; <u>Anniversaire</u>: le 16 juin; <u>Fête préférée</u>: Halloween; <u>Animal préféré</u>: le lapin; <u>Adore</u>: écouter ses CD; <u>Déteste</u>: les ordinateurs

 En solo CD, track 19   page 27, activité 3

Elle s'appelle Lucie. Elle a onze ans. Son anniversaire, c'est le 16 juin. Sa fête préférée, c'est Halloween. Son animal préféré, c'est le lapin. Elle adore écouter ses CD. Elle déteste les ordinateurs.

AT 4.2 | **4 Would you choose Laura, Julien or the last girl as your penpal? Why?**

• A framework is provided as support: *Je choisis… parce qu'il/elle…*

AT 4.2–3 | **Défi!**

• Students write a paragraph about a famous person of their own choice.

Pages 28–29 Labo-langue

• Use with Students' Book pages 38–39.

1 Do the quiz on verbs. Circle a, b or c. Explain your choices.

Answers: 1 a (it isn't a verb); 2 b (it's the *je* or *il/elle* form of *regarder*); 3 b (it's the *je* form of the verb *faire*); 4 c (it's the correct person of the verb to go with *aime*, and it has to be *j'* because of the following vowel); 5 c (it's the *je* ending); 6 c (it's the infinitive); 7 a (*ne… pas* is negative); 8 b (because the *je* and *tu* forms of *faire* are the same in the present tense)

2 Circle the verbs that are in the infinitive.

Answers: parler, faire, choisir, ranger, adorer

3 Underline the eight verbs in this letter.

Answers: m'appelle, aime, ai, est, s'appelle, joue, aimes, as

4 Fill the gaps with the correct verb endings.

Answers: a joues; b joue; c joue; d parles, parle; e parle

5 Write the opposite! Use *ne… pas* or *n'… pas*.

Answers: a Je ne suis pas français. b Je n'ai pas 11 ans. c Je n'aime pas visiter des sites Internet.

Défi!

• Students write three sentences about their partner, using third person singular verb forms.

Page 30 Checklist

• Use with *Blog-notes* (Students' Book page 40) or towards the end of the unit.

The checklist, recording and follow-up activities provide opportunities for students to review what they have learned, test themselves orally on key language and reflect on areas for improvement.

En solo CD, track 20   page 30, activité 2

1   thirteen *[beep]* treize
2   August *[beep]* août
3   Mother's Day *[beep]* la fête des Mères
4   Today's the 30th of June. *[beep]* Aujourd'hui, c'est le 30 juin.
5   I'm eleven years old. *[beep]* J'ai onze ans.
6   My birthday is the 21st of April. *[beep]* Mon anniversaire, c'est le 21 avril.
7   My favourite special occasion is New Year. *[beep]* Ma fête préférée, c'est le Nouvel An.
8   My favourite animal's the cat. *[beep]* Mon animal préféré, c'est le chat.
9   Do you have a pet? *[beep]* Tu as un animal?
10 Do you like sport? *[beep]* Tu aimes le sport?
11 I love music and I hate sport! *[beep]* J'adore la musique et je déteste le sport!
12 I like watching TV. *[beep]* J'aime bien regarder la télé.
13 I hate tidying my room. *[beep]* Je déteste ranger ma chambre.
14 At the weekend, I listen to CDs. *[beep]* Le week-end, j'écoute des CD.
15 She likes visiting museums. *[beep]* Elle aime visiter des musées.

Follow-up: Encourage students to draw up their own individual action plan of steps they could take to help them improve. Provide a checklist of suggestions for them to choose from, e.g. try harder to learn vocabulary, read the grammar notes again and make sure they understand them/ask for help if they don't understand, check written work carefully for mistakes, etc.

Page 31   Top tips and strategies

Listening

This section focuses on strategies to help students cope with listening activities, e.g. staying calm and focused, reading the questions before listening, being aware that information is usually given in the same order as the questions. It features language and vocabulary introduced on pages 30–35 of the Students' Book (age, birthday, weekend activities), so would be best used towards the end of Unit 2.

1a Listen to an interview with Marie and answer these questions in English.

Answers: a 11; b September; c sport, watches TV; d doing homework

En solo CD, track 21   page 31, activité 1a

– Tu t'appelles comment?
– Je m'appelle Marie Ferrand.
– Tu as quel âge?
– J'ai 11 ans.
– C'est quoi, ta nationalité?
– Je suis française.

– C'est quand, ton anniversaire?
– Mon anniversaire, c'est le trois septembre.
– Qu'est-ce que tu aimes faire le week-end?
– Le week-end, c'est relax! Je fais du sport ou je regarde la télé. Super! Mais je déteste faire mes devoirs... non, je n'aime pas ça!

1b Listen to Marie talking without the interviewer. Answer questions a–d again. Did you find it easier to understand with or without the interview questions? Why? (Be prepared for all kinds of listening situations!)

• This recording gives the same information as in ex. 1a, but here the information is presented as a monologue and there are no interview questions.
• Students will probably find ex. 1a easier, because the interview questions provide hints as to what is coming next, prompting them to focus their attention on the specific details they need to listen for.

En solo CD, track 22   page 31, activité 1b

Salut! Je m'appelle Marie Ferrand. J'ai 11 ans. Je suis française. Mon anniversaire, c'est le trois septembre. Le week-end, c'est relax! Je fais du sport ou je regarde la télé. Super! Mais je déteste faire mes devoirs... non, je n'aime pas ça!

Vocabulary

This section focuses on the importance of knowing high-frequency words. It can be used at any appropriate point during Unit 2, perhaps as a follow-up to the section on using a bilingual dictionary on Students' Book page 39.

2a Circle the word in each line that you think is used most frequently in everyday conversation.

Answers: a je; b j'ai; c oui; d un chien; e et

2b Compare your choices in activity 2a with a partner's.

• Emphasise that if students instantly recognise little words like *et, mais, j'ai, mon/ma/mes*, etc., they will save a lot of time by not having to look them up in a dictionary.

Pages 32–33 Vocabulaire

• Use with Students' Book pages 44–45.

A list of key language from the unit is provided here as well as in the Students' Book and on Copymaster 13.

1 Listen and tick the phrases you hear.

 En solo CD, track 23   page 33, activité 1

Tu aimes... les ordinateurs?
Je n'aime pas ça.
J'aime... les jeux vidéo.
J'ai un lapin.
Tu as quel âge?
J'ai onze ans.
C'est quand, ton anniversaire?
C'est le premier mai.
J'aime bien... faire du sport.
Je fais mes devoirs.
Génial!
Nul!

2 Underline in coloured pencil...

• Students search the list for key language items.

3 Note 3 key words/phrases to remember.

• Encourage students to try writing some sentences using these words.

Follow-up: Challenge students to write a sentence containing the correct form of an *-er* verb, a masculine noun and a plural noun. Ask them to set a similar challenge for their partner.

Unité 3: Au collège Overview grid

Page reference	Contexts and objectives	Grammar	Language strategies and pronunciation	Key language	Framework	AT Level
48–49 **3.1 Les matières: top ou flop?**	• Subjects you like and don't like			*l'anglais, le dessin, l'EPS, le français, la géographie, l'histoire, les mathématiques, la musique, les sciences, la technologie* *Tu aimes quelles matières?* *J'adore, j'aime (bien), je n'aime pas (beaucoup)* *Ta matière préférée, c'est quoi? Ma matière préférée, c'est…* *C'est super/bien/intéressant/nul.*	**L** – 7S6, 7T5, 7L3 **R** – 7W1, 7S4	1.2–3, 2.2–3, 3.1–2, 4.2
50–51 **3.2 Quelle heure est-il?**	• Numbers up to 60 and how to tell the time			Numbers up to 60 *Quelle heure est-il? Il est (deux) heures. Il est (quatre) heures cinq. Il est (sept) heures dix. Il est (dix) heures quinze. Il est (trois) heures vingt. Il est (huit) heures vingt-cinq. Il est (neuf) heures trente. Il est (cinq) heures trente-cinq. Il est (quatre) heures quarante. Il est (six) heures quarante-cinq. Il est (une) heure cinquante. Il est (onze) heures cinquante-cinq. Il est midi/minuit.*	**R** – 7C5	1.1–2, 2.1, 3.1–2, 4.1
52–53 **3.3 Mon emploi du temps**	• Talk about your school timetable	• *on* + 3rd person singular		*Le lundi, à onze heures, j'ai français. Le mardi, à neuf heures, on a EPS.* *C'est bien/nul.* *le déjeuner* *lundi, mardi, mercredi, jeudi, vendredi, samedi, dimanche*	**L** – 7S7 **R** – 7T2, 7C5	1.2–3, 2.2, 3.1–3, 4.2
54–55 **3.4 Bien équipés!**	• School objects	• Full present tense conjugation of *avoir* and *être*		*un bâton de colle, un cahier, une calculatrice, un cartable, un classeur, une clé USB, un crayon, une gomme, un livre, une règle, un stylo, une trousse, une chaise, un ordinateur, un poster, une table, un tableau noir/blanc*	**R** – 7W3, 7T3, 7L4, 7L5	1.2, 2.1–2, 3.1–2, 4.2
56–57 **Labo-langue**	• Grammar • Skills • Pronunciation	French verbs (2): • *-er, -ir, -re* verbs • Introduction to irregular verbs • 1st/2nd/3rd person plural of *-er* verbs • *avoir* and *être*	• Learning vocabulary • The *é* sound **Workbook:** • How to sound French • Cognates, false friends		**R** – 7W5, 7W6, 7W7, 7W8, 7L1, 7L6	
58–61 **Blog-notes / Tu sais tout? / En plus / Clic.fr**	• End-of-unit summary and assessment • Extension • **Cultural focus:** school life in France	**En plus:** • Introduction to the perfect tense of regular *-er* verbs with *avoir*		**En plus:** *Je n'ai pas terminé mes devoirs. J'ai commencé mais je n'ai pas terminé. J'ai cassé mon stylo. J'ai oublié mon cahier. On a volé ma règle. Mon hamster a mangé mes devoirs.* *Euh…*	**L** – 7S7 **R** – 7W3, 7W5, 7L4, 7L5, 7C2, 7C3, 7C4	1.2–3, 2.2, 3.2, 4.2–3

CLIC! 1 STAR UNIT 3 MEDIUM TERM PLAN

About Unit 3, *Au collège*: In this unit, students work in the context of school. They express opinions of school subjects and learn vocabulary for schoolbag items and school facilities. They develop their knowledge of regular *-er* verbs in the present tense, and are introduced to irregular verbs, focusing on *avoir* and *être*. There is also an opportunity for able students to begin using the perfect tense to explain problems and excuses. Students learn days of the week, numbers up to 60 and how to tell the time, and practise pronunciation of the *é* sound. There are opportunities to compare the French and British education systems, and students are given a glimpse into school life in Burkina Faso.

Framework objectives (launch)	Teaching and learning
7S6: Compound sentences	Focus on use of *et* and *mais* in the domino phrases on p. 49: *J'aime bien les sciences et l'anglais mais ma matière préférée, c'est...* Point out the importance of using linking words to build more complex sentences.
7S7: Time and tenses	Understand and give information about timetables, e.g. *Le mardi, à dix heures, on a anglais* (pp. 52–53); introduction to the perfect tense in the context of explaining problems, e.g. *On a volé ma règle* (p. 60).
7T5: Assembling text	Build a paragraph about school and subjects by arranging domino phrases into the correct sequence, then use the text as a model to construct own similar paragraph (p. 49).
7L3: Gist and detail	Watch video and note the order in which school subjects are mentioned, then watch again and note down opinions of the subjects (p. 48).

Framework objectives (reinforce)	Teaching and learning
7W1: Everyday words	Re-apply phrases from Unit 2 (*j'aime, je n'aime pas,* etc.) to express likes and dislikes of school subjects.
7W3: Classroom words	Expand stock of classroom vocabulary, e.g. *Tu as un crayon/livre?* etc. (p. 54); classroom facilities, e.g. *un tableau noir/blanc* (p. 55); problems and excuses, e.g. *j'ai cassé mon stylo* (p. 60).
7W5: Verbs present (+ past)	Present tense first/second/third person plural of regular *-er* verbs, *avoir* and *être*, introduction to irregular verbs such as *avoir* (p. 63).
7W6: Letters and sounds	Pronunciation: the *é* sound (p. 57).
7W7: Learning about words	Techniques to learn vocabulary (p. 57).
7W8: Finding meanings	Cognates and false friends (Workbook p. 45).
7S4: Basic questions	Conduct a survey about school subjects (p. 49).
7T2: Reading aloud	Listen to and read aloud a conversation about school timetables, imitating pronunciation and intonation (p. 53 ex. 6–7).
7T3: Checking before reading	Before reading a text comparing schools in France and Burkina Faso (p. 55), predict what facilities each school might have, then find key words in the text and work out English meanings.
7L1: Sound patterns	Pronunciation: *é* (p. 57).
7L4: Classroom talk	Ask for things in class, e.g. *Tu as/Vous avez une règle?* (p. 54); explain problems, e.g. *Où sont tes devoirs? – J'ai oublié mon cahier* (p. 60).
7L5: Spontaneous talk	Ask for things/Explain problems in class (see 7L4); use hesitation words, e.g. *euh, alors* (p. 60 ex. 2 recording).
7L6: Improving speech	How to sound more like a French person (Workbook p. 45).
7C2: Everyday culture	School life in France compared with the UK.
7C3: Contact with native speakers	Video clip of French students discussing school subjects (p. 48); video blog (p. 58).
7C4: Stories and songs	Song about school (p. 63); cartoon story about school (p. 123).
7C5: Social conventions	Use of polite *vous* and *monsieur/madame* when addressing a teacher, e.g. *Excusez-moi, monsieur,* contrasted with informal *tu* (p. 50); use of *on* + third person singular to mean "we" in informal contexts (p. 53).

Week-by-week overview (assuming 6 weeks' work or approximately 10–12.5 hours)

Week	Overview
Week 1 – Opening spread/3.1 Les matières: top ou flop?	Opening spread: introduction to unit themes and objectives, including aspects of school life in France. Spread 3.1: school subjects; likes and dislikes
Week 2 – 3.2 Quelle heure est-il?	Numbers up to 60; telling the time
Week 3 – 3.3 Mon emploi du temps	School timetables; days of the week; *on* + third person singular
Week 4 – 3.4 Bien équipés!	School objects, including items in a schoolbag and classroom equipment; school life in France and Burkina Faso
Week 5 – Labo-langue	French verbs (first/second/third person plural of regular *-er* verbs, introduction to irregular verbs, full present tense of *avoir* and *être*); learning vocabulary; pronunciation of *é*
Week 6 – Blog-notes, Tu sais tout?, En plus, Clic.fr, On chante!, Lecture	Reinforcement and extension of the language of the unit; review of progress via the Checklist in the Workbook/on Copymaster; revision and assessment

3 Au collège

Unit objectives

Contexts: School
Grammar: Verbs (2)
Language learning: Learning vocabulary
Pronunciation: The *é* sound
Cultural focus: School life in France

Assessment opportunities

Listening: Students' Book, page 51, activity 4a
Speaking: Students' Book, page 48, activity 5

See also **Clic! 1** OxBox Assessment CD-ROM

---

1 Regarde les photos. C'est en France ou en Grande-Bretagne?

- *Aim*: To promote intercultural awareness and develop powers of observation.
- Students work out whether the school photos are in France or the UK.

Answer: The left-hand photo is in France, the right-hand photo is in the UK. Point out that school uniform is not worn in French schools.

2 Avantages et désavantages.

- *Aim*: To promote intercultural awareness.
- Discuss in English the two information panels. Compare the subjects studied in a *collège* with the subjects in your school.
- Look at the second information panel and compare the details given about France and the UK. Discuss the advantages and disadvantages of school life in each country.

3.1 Les matières: top ou flop?

pages 48–49

Planner

> ### Objectives
> - Subjects you like and don't like

> ### Resources
> Students' Book, pages 48–49
> Video clip 6
> *En solo* Workbook, pages 34–35;
> *En solo* CD, track 24
> Copymaster 28

> ### Key language
> *Les matières*
> *l'anglais, le dessin, l'EPS (l'éducation physique et sportive), le français, la géographie (la géo), l'histoire, les mathématiques (les maths), la musique, les sciences, la technologie*
>
> *Tu aimes quelles matières?*
> *j'adore, j'aime (bien)*
> *je déteste, je n'aime pas (beaucoup)*
> *Ta matière préférée, c'est quoi?*
> *Ma matière préférée, c'est...*
> *C'est super/bien/intéressant/nul.*

> ### Framework reference
> L – 7S6, 7T5, 7L3; R – 7W1, 7S4

> ### Starters
> - Display groups of three subjects on the board, OHP or interactive whiteboard. Students identify the odd-one-out in each, e.g. *le français, l'anglais, la musique* (*la musique* because it's feminine, or because it isn't a language, or because it doesn't end in *-ais*).

- To revise *j'aime/je n'aime pas*, etc., hold a quick question-and-answer session asking students about their likes and dislikes of school subjects.
- Display some mixed-up subject words. Set students a time limit to work them out and list them with the correct determiners. For example:
  hist-ématiques, math-oire (= l'histoire, les mathématiques)
  franç-ique, mus-ais (= le français, la musique)
  angl-aphie, géogr-ais (= l'anglais, la géographie)
  tech-in, dess-nologie (= la technologie, le dessin)

> ### Plenaries
> - Students organise the school subjects into different groups, to try to make learning them easier. Students themselves decide on the groupings, e.g. masculine and feminine, or by type of subject (all science and maths subjects together, all languages together, all practical subjects together). Discuss students' ideas as a whole class.
> - Students have 30 seconds to list from memory as many subjects as they can. Give them an extra 30 seconds to add an opinion to each subject in their list. They then check their lists with a partner for spellings and genders.
> - Copymaster 28 *Bilan de leçon* ex. 1.

Preparation:
- Present and practise the school subjects using the visuals on OxBox *Interactif* CD-ROM.
- For further oral practice, set up a memory chain around the class, e.g.
  Student A: *J'aime le dessin.*
  Student B: *J'aime le dessin et le français.*
  Student C: *J'aime le dessin, le français et la musique.*
  Student D: *J'aime le dessin, le français, la musique et...*

| AT 3.1 | **1 Regarde. C'est quelle matière?**

- Students look at the three stills from the video clip and find the school subjects (in the key language list) represented by the symbols.

Answers: la géographie, la musique, le dessin

| AT 1.2 | **2 Regarde. Note les matières.**

- Play the first half of the video clip. Students note down the letters/names of the subjects from the key language list.
- Tell them to leave a space beside each subject so that they can add an opinion when they do ex. 3.

Answers: 1 e (la géographie), f (l'histoire); 2 g (les maths), a (l'anglais); 3 c (l'EPS), j (la technologie); 4 i (les sciences), h (la musique); 5 b (le dessin), d (le français)

 Video clip 6   pages 48–49, activités 2, 3 et 6

– Aujourd'hui on parle du collège. Le collège, c'est super... non? Et toi, tu aimes quelles matières?
1 – Au collège, j'aime la géographie et l'histoire.

2 – J'aime les maths... et l'anglais... j'adore l'anglais.

3 – Et toi? Au collège, tu aimes quelles matières?
– J'aime l'EPS, mais je n'aime pas la technologie.
– L'EPS, c'est quoi ça?
– Ah, c'est l'éducation physique et sportive. J'adore le sport.

4 – J'aime les sciences... mais je n'aime pas beaucoup la musique.

5 – Tu aimes quelles matières?
– J'aime le dessin et bien sûr, j'adore le français!

1 – Ta matière préférée, c'est quoi?
– Ma matière préférée, c'est la géographie. La géo, c'est super!

2 – Ma matière préférée, c'est les mathématiques. Les maths, c'est intéressant.

3 – Qu'est-ce que c'est ta matière préférée?
– Ma matière préférée, c'est l'EPS. C'est bien.

4 – Moi, ma matière préférée, c'est les sciences. J'adore ça.

AT 1.3 | **3 Regarde encore une fois. Note les opinions.**

- This revises likes and dislikes from Unit 2. Play the first half of the video again and pick out examples of the key phrases: *j'adore, j'aime (bien), je déteste, je n'aime pas (beaucoup).*
- Students listen again and draw a heart symbol beside each subject to represent the speaker's opinion (or they could note down the opinions in English).

Answers: 1 la géographie , l'histoire ;
2 les maths , l'anglais ; 3 l'EPS ,
la technologie ; 4 les sciences , la musique ;
5 le dessin , le français

AT 4.2 | **4 Donne ton opinion.**

- Students write down their own opinion of each subject on the key language list.

AT 2.2–3 | **5 A interviewe B. (B → A)**

- Students ask and answer questions to find out each other's opinions of school subjects.
- Tell them to put heart symbols beside each of their sentences from ex. 4 to show their partner's opinion of each subject, then compare each other's likes and dislikes.

AT 1.2 | **6 Note les matières préférées.**

- Play the second half of the video clip. Students note down each person's favourite subject.

Answers: 1 e (la géographie); 2 g (les maths);
3 c (l'EPS); 4 i (les sciences)

AT 2.3 | **7 Sondage.**

- Students carry out a survey in groups to find out the three most popular subjects, asking *Ta matière préférée, c'est quoi?* and answering *Ma matière préférée, c'est...*
- Provide dictionaries or a list of any extra subjects that students might need, e.g. *l'informatique* (ICT), *l'instruction religieuse* (RE), *l'art dramatique* (drama).
- Students feed back the results of their group survey to the class. Record the results for the whole class on the board or OHP. Collating the findings provides an opportunity to revise numbers.
- Students present the results graphically and compare them with the French results on page 49 (*Matières top en France*).

AT 3.2 |
AT 4.2 | **8 Mets les dominos dans le bon ordre.**

- When arranged end-to-end in the correct order, the dominoes form a continuous text about school and opinions of school subjects. Students solve the puzzle and write out the text.
- Less able students could copy out the dominoes onto sheets of paper, cut them out and physically arrange them into the correct order.
- Focus on the use of *et* and *mais* in the domino phrases: *J'aime bien les sciences <u>et</u> l'anglais <u>mais</u> ma matière préférée, c'est...* Point out the importance of using linking words to build more complex sentences.

Answers: Salut! Je m'appelle Nicolas. Mon collège, c'est le Collège Alain-Fournier. J'aime bien les sciences et l'anglais, mais ma matière préférée, c'est la musique. C'est super!

AT 4.2 | **9 À toi d'écrire ton paragraphe.**

- Students write their own paragraph about school, expressing their opinions of subjects. They use the ex. 8 text as a model.

W 34–35 | Pages 34–35 of the *En solo* Workbook provide further activities to practise school subjects and opinions of subjects.

3.2 Quelle heure est-il?

pages 50–51

Planner

> ### Objectives
> * Numbers up to 60 and how to tell the time

> ### Resources
> Students' Book, pages 50–51
> CD 2, tracks 3–4
> *En solo* Workbook, pages 36–37;
> *En solo* CD, track 25
> Copymasters 30, 32

> ### Key language
> Numbers up to 60
>
> *Quelle heure est-il?*
> *Il est (deux) heures. Il est (quatre) heures cinq.*
> *Il est (sept) heures dix. Il est (dix) heures quinze.*
> *Il est (trois) heures vingt. Il est (huit) heures vingt-cinq.*
> *Il est (neuf) heures trente. Il est (cinq) heures trente-cinq.*
> *Il est (quatre) heures quarante. Il est (six) heures quarante-cinq.*
> *Il est (une) heure cinquante. Il est (onze) heures cinquante-cinq.*
> *Il est midi. Il est minuit.*

> ### Framework reference
> R – 7C5

> ### Starters
> * Before introducing numbers up to 60, play "Number Shoot-out" to revise numbers up to 31. Two students stand up; call out a number in French and the pair compete to tell you the number required to add up to 31, e.g. if you call out *vingt*, the correct response would be *onze*. The first student to give you the correct number is the winner. The loser sits down and is replaced by another challenger.
> * Using a clock face with movable hands (either a real clock or a clock displayed on the OHP or interactive whiteboard), say some times and ask students to come out and move the hands to give the correct time. Alternatively, students take turns to move the clock hands themselves and ask *Quelle heure est-il?*

> ### Plenaries
> * For a variation on the starter activity using a clock face, ask a volunteer to come out and set the clock hands to a time that he/she keeps hidden from the class. Students take turns to try to guess the time. The person who guesses correctly comes out and takes over. Students inevitably have to use a wide range of time phrases before they guess the correct one, so this activity is particularly good for confirming what has been learned.
> * Display some digital clock faces with gap-fill times beside them, e.g. 10.45 –
> *Il est d _ x heures q _ _ r _ n t _ - c _ n q*
> Students fill in the missing letters. Vary the number of missing letters according to the ability of your students.
> Alternatively, students prepare similar clock faces and gap-fill sentences for a partner to complete.

 Preparation:
* Present and practise numbers up to 60 using OxBox *Interactif* CD-ROM.
* Play games to reinforce the numbers, e.g.
  – counting in pairs, with students saying alternate numbers
  – Mexican Wave around the class
  – Fizz/Buzz-style games, e.g. count around the class and replace multiples of a given number (e.g. three) with a French word/phrase (e.g. *Au revoir!* or *Salut!* or perhaps the name of a school subject).

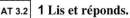 **1 Lis et réponds.**
* Students read the cartoon about Toto being late for school. They answer questions in English.

Answers: a Because Toto is late for the lesson. b He asks what time it is and what time lessons begin. c Toto is well aware that his teacher knows the answer to the question "What time do lessons begin?", but he asks him "Have you forgotten?" as if he really believes that the teacher needs a reminder. d He uses *vous*.

Follow-up: Look at the information panel on the use of *tu* and *vous*. Ask students which word they would use to address the person sitting next to them in class, their sister/brother, mother/father, the head teacher, a shopkeeper, their dog, the mother of their best friend.

 2a Écoute, répète et continue.
 * Students listen/repeat the numbers and fill in the next number in each sequence.

> 🎧 **CD 2, track 3**   page 50, activité 2a
>
> 1 – vingt... vingt et un...
>   – vingt-deux
> 2 – trente... trente et un...
>   – trente-deux
> 3 – quarante-quatre... quarante-cinq...
>   – quarante-six

4 – cinquante-cinq... cinquante-six...
– cinquante-sept
5 – trente-trois... trente-quatre...
– trente-cinq
6 – vingt-huit... vingt-neuf...
– trente
7 – trente... trente et un...
– trente-deux
8 – quarante-huit... quarante-neuf...
– cinquante
9 – cinquante-huit... cinquante-neuf...
– soixante
10 – quarante et un... quarante-deux...
– quarante-trois

AT 2.1 **2b À deux. (B ➤ A)**

- Students play their own version of the ex. 2a recording, giving two consecutive numbers and challenging their partner to add the next number in the sequence, e.g.
Student A: *Trente-huit, trente-neuf...*
Student B: *Quarante!... Cinquante-deux, cinquante-trois...*
Student A: *Cinquante-quatre!*

AT 3.1 **3a Un peu de maths.**

- Students work out the maths sums.

Answers: a soixante; b trente-trois; c cinquante-neuf; d cinquante-huit; e quarante-sept; f vingt et un; g vingt-neuf; h cinquante-six

AT 4.1 **3b À deux. (B ➤ A)**

- Pairs make up further maths sums to exchange with a partner.

AT 1.2 **4a Écoute 1–9. C'est quelle montre?**

- Students listen and choose a watch face to match each time

Answers: 1 d; 2 e; 3 a; 4 c; 5 i; 6 h; 7 b; 8 f; 9 g

 CD 2, track 4   page 51, activité 4a

1 – Quelle heure est-il?
– Il est quatre heures cinq.
2 – Quelle heure est-il?
– Il est une heure dix.
3 – Quelle heure est-il?
– Il est sept heures.
4 – Quelle heure est-il?
– Il est dix heures quinze.
5 – Quelle heure est-il?
– Il est deux heures cinquante-cinq.
6 – Quelle heure est-il?
– Il est dix heures trente-cinq.
7 – Quelle heure est-il?
– Il est deux heures trente.
8 – Quelle heure est-il?
– Il est six heures vingt.
9 – Quelle heure est-il?
– Il est huit heures quarante-cinq.

AT 2.1 **4b À deux. (B ➤ A)**

- Students play "Read my Lips": student A mouths a time (from ex. 4a) and student B points to the corresponding watch face.

AT 3.2 **4c Écris.**

AT 4.1

- Students separate out the words in the letter string to make a sentence.

Answers: Top secret. J'arrive au collège à quatre heures trente.

C30
C32 Ex. 1 (speaking) on Copymaster 30 and ex. 1 (writing) on Copymaster 32 are additional activities to practise clock times.

W 36–37 Pages 36–37 of the *En solo* Workbook provide further practice of clock times.

3.3 Mon emploi du temps

Planner

> ### Objectives
> - Talk about your school timetable

> ### Resources
> Students' Book, pages 52–53
> CD 2, track 5
> *En solo* Workbook, pages 38–39;
> *En solo* CD, track 26
> Copymasters 27, 28, 29, 32; CD 2, tracks 15–16

> ### Key language
> *Mon emploi du temps*
> *Le lundi, à onze heures, j'ai français.*
> *Le mardi, à neuf heures, on a EPS.*
> *C'est bien/nul.*
> *le déjeuner*
> *lundi, mardi, mercredi, jeudi, vendredi, samedi,*
> *dimanche*

> ### Grammar
> *on* + third person singular

> ### Framework reference
> **L** – 7S7; **R** – 7T2, 7C5

> ### Starters
> - If students have already been taught the days of
>   the week, write them up on the board or OHP
>   with all the vowels missing. Give students a time
>   limit to fill in the missing letters and arrange the
>   days in order.
> - Ask students to look at the French school
>   timetable on page 52 and to spot the three clear
>   differences between school routine in France and
>   the UK (no lessons on Wednesday, lessons on
>   Saturday morning, lunch lasts for two hours).
>   Talk about other features of French school
>   routine, e.g.

> - although this timetable shows no lessons at all
>   on Wednesday, some French schools have a
>   half day on Wednesdays, with lessons in the
>   morning only
> - lessons can start as early as 8 a.m. and may
>   not start at the same time each day.
> - To recap on school subjects, call out a
>   subject in English and ask students to either give
>   you the French word or to tell you whether they
>   like or dislike the subject, e.g. Science! – *Les
>   sciences / J'aime les sciences.*
> - Copymaster 27 *À tes marques!* ex. 1.

> ### Plenaries
> - Students play a memory game in groups of
>   three to practise the different parts of *avoir* and
>   school subjects. If necessary, display *j'ai, tu as*
>   and *il/elle/on a* prominently on the board or
>   OHP as support.
>   Student A begins by saying *j'ai* + one subject;
>   student B repeats this and adds to it using *tu as*;
>   student C adds on again, using *il/elle a*. Point
>   out that student A must concentrate carefully
>   on the subjects mentioned, because he/she has
>   to summarise what everyone has said using
>   *on a*. For example:
>   Student A: *J'ai histoire.*
>   Student B: *J'ai histoire et tu as anglais.*
>   Student C: *J'ai histoire, tu as anglais et il
>   a géo.*
>   Student A: *On a histoire, anglais et géo.*
>   It is then student B's turn to start the sequence
>   again with a different subject.
> - Students write sentences for a partner to fill in
>   about their own timetable, e.g.
>   *Le lundi, à onze heures, on a …*
>   *Le …, à … heures, on a maths.*
>   They check each other's sentences for accuracy,
>   not only in terms of spellings but also to make
>   sure they have correctly described their timetables.
> - Copymaster 28 *Bilan de leçon* ex. 2.

| AT 3.1 | **1 Lis et réponds.** |

- Students complete the sentences in English about
  the French school timetable.

Answers: a music; b English; c French

| AT 3.2 | **2 Qui est dans cette classe?** |

- Students read the four speech bubbles, in which
  teenagers give the days and times of specific
  subjects. They compare these with the timetable
  and work out whose timetable this is.

Answer: Manon et Thomas

| AT 3.2 | **3 Vrai ou faux?** |

This activity could replace task B in a Grade 2 Asset
Languages teacher assessment.

- Students refer to the timetable to work out whether
  statements a–f are true or false.
- If appropriate, students correct the false
  statements.
- Point out the information panel about *on*. Look at
  statements a–f and elicit from students that *on* is
  followed by the third person singular.

Answers: a vrai; b vrai; c faux (géographie); d faux
(EPS); e faux (on n'a pas cours); f faux (dessin)

4 À deux. (B ➝ A)

• Students take turns to tell each other true or false information about the days/times of subjects on the timetable, modelled on statements a–f in ex. 3. The partner refers to the timetable to work out whether the information is true or false.

 5 Écris. Explique. (B ➝ A)

• Students write ten sentences about their own timetable, saying which subjects they have on which days and at what times. Again, they use a–f in ex. 3 as a model.

• They read them out to their partner, trying to show by their tone of voice and facial expression whether they like these subjects or not.

• The partner works out their opinion, and responds with either *C'est bien* or *C'est nul*.

 6 Lis et écoute.

• Students read and listen to the conversation and work out whether Lola is happy. Ask them to explain why.

Answer: Lola isn't happy. (She has French at eleven o'clock with Mrs Martin, who is very strict, and Lola doesn't have her French book. She hates Mondays.)

🔊 **CD 2, track 5**   page 53, activité 6

– Il est dix heures cinquante-cinq. On a histoire à onze heures, non?
– Tu as histoire? Non! On a français!
– J'ai français? Oh non, je suis bête… je n'ai pas mon livre de français.
– Tu es sûre?
– Oui, et c'est Madame Martin…
– Oh là là… elle est super sévère, Madame Martin!
– Aaaaaaaah! Je déteste le lundi!

Follow-up: Ask comprehension questions about the conversation, in English or French.

 7 Lisez avec un(e) partenaire.

• Play the recording again and ask students to repeat it, imitating the pronunciation and intonation.

• Students practise reading the conversation aloud, in pairs, focusing on intonation.

---

8 Grammaire: trouve le français.

• Students search the conversation (ex. 6) for different parts of *être* and *avoir* (first, second and third person singular).

Answers: a je suis; b j'ai; c elle est; d on a; e tu as; f tu es

C29
C32
Ex. 2 on Copymaster 29 is a listening activity on school timetables. See also Copymaster 32, ex. 2 and 3, for additional reading/writing activities covering the language of this and the previous two spreads.

W 38–39
Pages 38–39 of the *En solo* Workbook provide further activities based on school timetables, practising times and days of the week.

3.4 Bien équipés!

Planner

> ### Objectives
> * School objects

> ### Resources
> Students' Book, pages 54–55
> CD 2, tracks 6–8
> *En solo* Workbook, pages 40–41;
> *En solo* CD, track 27
> Copymasters 27, 29, 30, 31; CD 2, tracks 15–16

> ### Key language
> *Les affaires d'école*
> *tu as...?*
> *j'ai..., il/elle/on a...*
> *on n'a pas de...*
> *nous avons..., vous avez...*
> *un bâton de colle, un cahier, une calculatrice, un cartable, un classeur, une clé USB, un crayon, une gomme, un livre, une règle, un stylo, une trousse*
>
> *Qu'est-ce qu'il y a dans ta classe?*
> *Il y a...*
> *une chaise, un ordinateur, un poster, une table, un tableau noir/blanc*

> ### Grammar
> Full present tense conjugation of *avoir* and *être*

> ### Framework reference
> **R** – 7W3, 7T3, 7L4, 7L5

> ### Starters
> * Before beginning work on this spread, students list in English the contents of their schoolbags and pencil cases. (To avoid long lists of irrelevant items, you could tell them to ignore anything that isn't directly related to school and schoolwork.) Students then open their books at page 54 and compare their own lists with the items in the grid. Which items do they have in common? Set them a time limit to look up any new vocabulary in a dictionary.

* Display a jumbled collection of vocabulary from the spread. Students compete to sort it into two groups: things you might have in your schoolbag, and classroom equipment/facilities.
* Before reading David's and Joseph's text on page 55, ask students to imagine what the schools in Burkina Faso might be like in terms of facilities and equipment. What do they imagine they would find in a typical classroom? Return to this discussion after working on the text: were students' assumptions correct?
* Copymaster 27 *À tes marques!* ex. 2.

> ### Plenaries
> * Working as a class or in groups, build up a Venn diagram showing which schoolbag items are specific to certain subjects (e.g. *maths: une calculatrice, une règle*) and which items are used in more than one subject.
> * Ask students to find the odd-one-out in sets of words/phrases from the whole of Unit 3, giving a reason for each choice, e.g.
>   – *samedi, lundi, midi, vendredi* (*midi* because it isn't a day of the week)
>   – *calculatrice, gomme, crayon, chaise* (*crayon* because it is masculine, or *chaise* because you wouldn't find it in your schoolbag)
>   – *on a, j'ai, nous sommes, vous avez* (*nous sommes* because it isn't part of *avoir*)
> * Students tell each other what they think are the most useful or interesting things they have learned in Unit 3, e.g. these could be details about school life in France and Burkina Faso, vocabulary or grammar points. Collect suggestions from the whole class.

---

  1 Qui parle?

* Students listen to three teenagers discussing the contents of their schoolbags.
* They track the items around the maze from one square to the next, as they are mentioned. When each speaker reaches the end of their list, students should find this corresponds with an arrow in the maze pointing to the name of the speaker.

Answers: 1 Joseph; 2 David; 3 Mathieu

 CD 2, track 6   page 54, activités 1 et 3

1 J'ai un cartable. J'ai une trousse. J'ai une règle.
  Tu as un crayon? Moi, j'ai un crayon.
  Tu as un stylo? Moi, j'ai un stylo.
  On a une gomme. On a un bâton de colle.
2 J'ai une clé USB! J'ai un crayon.
  Il a une règle. Il a une trousse.
  Elle a un livre. Elle a un classeur.
  Tu as une calculatrice?
3 J'ai un cartable. J'ai une trousse.
  Tu as une règle? On a un cahier.
  Il a un stylo. Elle a une gomme.

2 À deux: jeu de mémoire. (B ➤ A)

- In pairs, each student names six schoolbag items. Their partner tries to recall what they are, in the same sequence.

Follow-up:

- Say the number of an item from the maze. Students name the item. Do this first with books open, then ask students to try to memorise the layout of the maze and repeat the activity with books closed.
- Set up a memory chain around the class, e.g.
  Student A: *Un cahier.*
  Student B: *Un cahier et un livre.*
  Student C: *Un cahier, un livre et une règle.*
  Student D: *Un cahier, un livre, une règle et…*

3 Compte.

- Play the ex 1 recording again. Students count how many times they hear different parts of *avoir* (first, second and third person singular).

Answers: j'ai: 9; il a: 3; tu as: 4; elle a: 3; on a: 3

AT 1.2 **4a Note les objets.**

- Students listen and note down the schoolbag items (either the words or the numbers from the maze in ex. 1) that are being donated to schools in Burkina Faso. (Ex. 6 will return to this theme.)

Answers: 6, 8, 7, 3, 1, 2, 9 (see underlining in transcript)

 CD 2, track 7   page 54, activités 4a et 4b

- Nous avons des <u>crayons</u> pour le Burkina Faso.
- Nous avons des <u>gommes</u>. Ils ont des gommes au Burkina?
- Vous avez déjà des <u>stylos</u>? Nous, nous avons beaucoup de stylos.
- Vous avez des <u>règles</u>? Nous avons des règles pour votre association.
- Les élèves du Burkina Faso, ils ont des <u>cartables</u> et des <u>trousses</u>? Nous, dans notre l'école, nous avons plein de cartables et de trousses.
- Ils ont des <u>calculatrices</u> au Burkina? Nous avons des calculatrices à donner.

4b Compte.

- *Aim*: To introduce the first, second and third person plural forms of *avoir*.
- Play the recording again. Students count how many times they hear different parts of *avoir*.
- Draw attention to the grid for the dice game (ex. 5), which shows the full conjugation of *avoir*.

Answers: nous avons: 6; vous avez: 2; ils ont: 3

Follow-up:

- Point out the information panel on the use of *on* and the more formal *nous*. Ask students to recall another example of formal and informal subject pronouns (*tu* and *vous*, discussed on spread 3.2).

 5 Grammaire: fais des phrases avec le verbe *avoir*.

- Students play a dice game to practise the full present tense conjugation of *avoir*. The numbers on the die correspond to the different forms of *avoir*, as shown in the grid in the Students' Book.
- Students take turns to throw the die and make up a sentence using the corresponding part of *avoir*.
- If appropriate, encourage them to recycle previously learned language in addition to practising the school vocabulary, e.g. *j'ai douze ans, il a un chien, nous avons français à neuf heures, tu as une gomme?*

  6 Écoute et lis. C'est quoi en anglais?

- *Aim:* To promote intercultural awareness. This text compares classroom equipment in France and Burkina Faso.
- Students read and listen to the text. They locate French vocabulary items in the text and translate them into English. They should be able to work out most of them without a dictionary.

Answers: a a table; b a chair; c a blackboard; d an interactive whiteboard; e a computer; f a poster

 CD 2, track 8   page 55, activité 6

- Salut, Joseph! Qu'est-ce qu'il y a dans ta classe? Vous êtes bien équipés?
- Non, nous ne sommes pas bien équipés! Nous avons juste des tables, des chaises et un tableau noir. Et vous?
- Nous sommes bien équipés: nous avons des tables, des chaises, des ordinateurs, un TBI (tableau blanc interactif) et des posters.
- Les collèges en France sont super! Ils sont bien équipés. Vous avez de la chance!

Follow-up: The text in ex. 6 provides opportunities to focus on reading skills, thinking skills, etc.:

- Use the text to prompt a discussion on how students were able to work out the new vocabulary, e.g. cognates. Look at any similarities between French and English words (e.g. *chaise*, chair) that make them easier to remember.
- Discuss the wider issues raised in the text, e.g. aid to Africa. Ask students which schoolbag items (from the maze on page 54) would be inappropriate to donate to a village school in Burkina Faso (e.g. *une clé USB*).

- For further information: Edukafaso is an organisation set up to support education in Burkina Faso. Its website (http://www.edukafaso.org) gives details of the kinds of items and equipment needed by schools in Burkina Faso. These tend to be basic items such as chalk, slates, exercise books, pencils, etc.

 7a Grammaire: relis. Trouve.

- *Aim:* To introduce the first, second and third person plural forms of *être*.
- Students search the ex. 6 text for forms of *être*.
- Draw attention to the dice game grid, which gives the full conjugation of *être*.

Answers: a nous sommes; b vous êtes; c ils sont

7b Grammaire: complète.

- Students fill in the gaps with parts of *être*.

Answers: a sommes; b êtes; c sont; d sont

 Follow-up:

- Ask students to recall previous contexts in which they have used parts of *être*, e.g. nationalities (*je suis anglais, il est français*), birthdays (*mon anniversaire, c'est…*) and jobs (*il est acteur, elle est sportive*).
- Students use the dice game grid on page 55 to practise the present tense conjugation of *être*. The game is played in exactly the same way as the *avoir* dice game in ex. 5. Encourage them to recycle previously learned language.

 AT 4.2 **8 Réponds à la question de David.**

- Students give their own answer to David's questions: *Qu'est-ce qu'il y a dans ta classe? Vous êtes bien équipés?*

AT 4.2 **Défi!**

- Students copy out the letter string, separating out the words and adding punctuation.

Answers: Dans ma classe, il y a un cartable. Dans mon cartable, il y a une trousse. Dans ma trousse, il y a un crayon.

Follow-up: Encourage students to look for patterns in the conjugation of *avoir* and *être* to help them remember the different forms, e.g. there are similarities between *tu as* and *tu es*, and between *ils/elles ont* and *ils/elles sont*.

C29
C30
C31
Further activities to practise the language of Unit 3 are provided on Copymaster 29 ex. 1 (listening), Copymaster 30 ex. 2 (speaking) and Copymaster 31 (reading/writing).

W 40–41
Pages 40–41 of the *En solo* Workbook provide further activities based on schoolbag items.

Labo-langue

Planner

> **Objectives**
> • French verbs (2)
> • Learning vocabulary
> • The *é* sound

> **Resources**
> Students' Book, pages 56–57
> CD 2, tracks 9–10
> *En solo* Workbook, pages 42–43, 45;
> *En solo* CD, track 29
> Copymasters 33, 34, 35; CD 2, tracks 17–19

> **Framework reference**
> **R** – 7W5, 7W6, 7W7, 7W8 (via Workbook), 7L1,
> 7L6 (via Workbook)

Bien comprendre!

French verbs (2)

• These grammar notes introduce students to different categories of verbs (-*er*, -*ir* and -*re* verbs) and the notion of irregular verbs. They present the first, second and third person plural of regular -*er* verbs, and the full conjugation of *avoir* and *être*.

1 Separate these verbs into three groups.

Answers: -*er* verbs: détester, parler, jouer, arriver;
-*ir* verb: finir; -*re* verb: rendre

2 Copy the sentences, changing the infinitive in brackets to the right form.

Answers: a arrivons; b préférez; c adorent; d aimons;
e détestez; f parlent

3 Learn these special verbs by heart. Ask a partner to test you. Draw a large heart and write these verbs inside it.

• Students learn the present tense of *avoir* and *être*.
• In a subsequent lesson, discuss how students actually learned the verbs, e.g. by writing them out several times, chanting them aloud, etc.

4 Choose the right verb.

Answers: a suis; b avons; c sont; d es; e avez; f est;
g a

C33 | See Copymaster 33 for additional grammar practice focusing on verbs.

Pages 42–43 of the *En solo* Workbook provide further activities to practise these grammar points.

Bien apprendre!

Learning vocabulary

The activities in this section guide students through a checklist of things they can do to help them learn new words:
• find out what the word means
• find out how to pronounce it, then say it five times
• copy it out five times
• write it from memory, ask someone to check it, keep trying until you can write it accurately
• put the word into a sentence
Students follow the guidance and complete the activities.

C34 | Copymaster 34 focuses on vocabulary learning strategies and could be used at this point.

Bien parler!

The é sound

1 There are several ways to write the same sound. Look and listen. List the words that contain the same sound as *é*.

Answers: see underlining in transcript

CD 2, track 9   page 57, Bien parler! activité 1

– jou<u>é</u>
– d<u>é</u>teste
– <u>é</u>coutez
– parlent
– ador<u>er</u>
– la rentr<u>ée</u>
– activit<u>é</u>

2a Say these words aloud. Which word does not rhyme with the rest?

Answer: l'étude

2b Listen to check.

 CD 2, track 10   page 57, Bien parler! activité 2b
- une année
- aller
- j'ai téléphoné
- arriver
- l'étude
- vous venez

3 List any other words you know that include this sound.
- Students should find lots of examples in Units 1–3, e.g. *Sénégal, vélos, vidéo, école, Astérix, janvier, février, jouer, écouter, regarder, café, écossais, télé, cinéma, géo, préféré, avez.*

C35   Copymaster 35 provides further pronunciation practice of the *é* sound.

W45   Further language learning strategies are provided on page 45 of the *En solo* Workbook, which could be used at any appropriate point during Unit 3:
- *Speaking*: tips and activities to help students improve their pronunciation and intonation, focusing on the rhythm and sound of French
- *Reading*: cognates and false friends, including ways to help students remember which words are false friends

Blog-notes

Planner

> **Objectives**
  - To summarise the main points of the unit in context, in a format that is fun and familiar to students, i.e. a video blog
  - To provide a model enabling students to personalise the language of the unit
  - To provide opportunities for students to ask as well as answer questions

- To provide extended listening practice recycling the language of the whole unit

> **Resources**
Students' Book, page 58
Video clip 7
En solo Workbook, page 44;
En solo CD, track 30
Copymaster 26

> **Framework reference**
R – 7C3

AT 1.3 **1 Regarde le vidéo-blog. Choisis les bonnes réponses.**

- Students watch Yasmina's video diary and choose 1 or 2 to answer each question. Pause the video after each section to allow students time to answer.

Answers: a 2; b 1; c 2; d 1; e 1, 2, 4, 5; f 1; g 1; h 1

 Video clip 7   page 58, activité 1

Moteur! Action! Bienvenue sur mon vidéo-blog. Je m'appelle Yasmina, j'ai 13 ans. Je suis française et algérienne. J'adore le foot! Mon rêve c'est d'être une grande footballeuse.
a Bon... bref... Aujourd'hui, c'est samedi... Ah ahaha! Le samedi, c'est dur... J'ai des cours le samedi matin. Moi, j'adore le collège... le mercredi et le dimanche! Pas le lundi, pas le mardi, pas le jeudi, pas le vendredi... et pas le samedi matin...
b Mon collège, c'est le collège Jean-Moulin.
c Mon collège, il est nul, nous n'avons pas d'ordinateurs dans les classes! Pffff... nul.
d Bon. Quelle heure est-il? Oh là là... il est huit heures... Ahhhhhhh! Les cours commencent à huit heures trente!
e Vite, vite, mes affaires... mon cartable, ma trousse, mon emploi du temps...
f Alors le samedi, à huit heures trente, j'ai anglais! *I'm not very good at English... but I like it!* Moi, j'aime bien l'anglais. C'est intéressant. Mon livre d'anglais, et hop! Et toi, tu aimes quelles matières?
g Après, à neuf heures trente, j'ai maths... oh, maths... J'ai maths aussi le lundi à neuf heures trente. Je n'aime pas les maths, c'est nul! Mon classeur de maths... et ma calculatrice, hi hi hi!
h Après, à dix heures trente, on a deux heures d'EPS. Youpi! J'adore l'EPS! C'est super! C'est ma matière préférée! C'est quoi, ta matière préférée?
Voilà, je suis prête! Collège, j'arrive! Oh, pardon! Bonne journée!
Et à bientôt! Ciao!

AT 4.3 **2 À ton tour: réponds aux questions!**

- Students write their own answers to the questions.

Follow-up: These activities may be suitable for more able students only:

- Students interview each other using questions a–h.
- Students use their answers from ex. 2 to help them write their own blog. If the appropriate technology is available, allow students to record their own video blogs and play them to the class.

C26

W44

A checklist summarising the language of the unit is provided on Copymaster 26 and on page 44 of the *En solo* Workbook. It could be used in tandem with the *Blog-notes* page or at an appropriate point towards the end of the unit. It provides an opportunity for students to review what they have learned and reflect on areas for improvement.

Tu sais tout?

Planner

> **Objectives**
> • To enable students to recap on the language and structures of the unit
> • To provide an opportunity for quick testing of all four skills

The page is divided into four sections: listening, speaking, reading and writing. Each section can be marked out of 5 to give a total score out of 20.

> **Resources**
> Students' Book, page 59
> CD 2, track 12

| AT 1.2 | **1 Listen and note a or b.** |

• As extension, ask students to note down any extra details.

Answers: 1 b; 2 a (maths is on Thursday at three o'clock); 3 b (the subject they're discussing is science); 4 b; 5 a (the subject they're discussing is music)

 CD 2, track 12   page 59, activité 1

1 – Quelle heure est-il?
– Il est dix heures trente… Dépêche-toi!
2 – Le jeudi à quinze heures, on a maths… non?
– Oui! À quinze heures, on a maths.
3 – Tu aimes les sciences?
– Pff… c'est nul! Je n'aime pas les sciences.
4 – Tu as mon cahier?
– Ton cahier?
– Oui, je n'ai pas mon cahier.
5 – On a musique?
– Oui, on a musique à onze heures trente.
– Ah oui, c'est à onze heures trente.

| AT 2.2 | **2a Say these times…** |

Answers: a Il est neuf heures. b Il est onze heures trente. c Il est deux heures quinze.

| AT 2.2 | **2b Choose two different subjects, and explain the day and time you have them.** |

• If appropriate, ask students to add whether they like or dislike each subject.

| AT 3.2 | **3 Read Lola's message. List in English: a) three subjects she likes; b) two things she has in her schoolbag.** |

Answers: a English, geography, PE (she loves French); b pencils, textbooks

---

| AT 4.2 | **4 Copy out and complete these sentences to write about yourself.** |

This activity would be suitable as part of preparation for external assessment at Breakthrough stage.
• Students use the sentence beginnings as a framework to help them write a paragraph about subjects they like/don't like, the days/times when they have French, and items they have in their schoolbag.

En plus

Planner

➢ Objectives
- To provide extension material for more able students who are confident with the core language of the unit, and to introduce new language where appropriate
- To provide alternative class and homework material for students who finish other activities quickly

➢ Resources
Students' Book, page 60
CD 2, track 13

➢ Key language
Je n'ai pas terminé mes devoirs.
J'ai commencé mais je n'ai pas terminé.
J'ai cassé mon stylo.
J'ai oublié mon cahier.
On a volé ma règle.
Mon hamster a mangé mes devoirs.
Euh…

➢ Grammar
Introduction to the perfect tense of regular *-er* verbs with *avoir*

➢ Framework reference
L – 7S7; **R** – 7W3, 7W5, 7L4, 7L5

Problèmes et excuses

AT 3.2 **1 Relie.**

This activity would be suitable as part of preparation for external assessment at Breakthrough stage.
- Students match the pictures (representing different excuses) to the speech bubbles.

Answers: 1 c; 2 b; 3 e; 4 a; 5 d

AT 1.2 **2 Écoute.**
- Students listen and note down the numbers of the excuses given.

Answers: 3, 1, 4, 2

🔊 **CD 2, track 13**   page 60, activité 2

– Où sont tes devoirs?
– J'ai oublié mon cahier. Alors… je ne l'ai pas, madame.

– Où sont tes devoirs?
– Euh… excusez-moi, madame. J'ai eu un problème. J'ai cassé mon stylo.

– Où sont tes devoirs?
– J'ai… euh… j'ai commencé mais je n'ai pas terminé.

– Où sont tes devoirs?
– Mes devoirs? Euh… oui… Alors, ben… oui… c'est que… ah, oui… c'est mon hamster. Mon hamster a mangé mes devoirs!

Follow-up:
- Listen again. Ask students to consider who might be inventing their excuse. What makes them think this? (The final speaker is almost certainly making his excuse up, because he hesitates a lot instead of giving a direct answer and it is quite an unlikely

thing to happen!) Focus on the way the speakers hesitate: *euh…*
- Draw attention to the *é* sound at the end of the past participles. This sound is the pronunciation focus of *Bien parler!* on the Unit 3 *Labo-langue* spread.

AT 2.2 **3 Jeu de mémoire: à deux, en groupes ou avec toute la classe.**
- Students play a memory game:
  Student A: *On a volé ma trousse.*
  Student B: *On a volé ma trousse et j'ai cassé mon stylo.*
  Student C: *On a volé ma trousse, j'ai cassé mon stylo et j'ai oublié mon cahier.*
  Student D: *On a volé ma trousse, j'ai cassé mon stylo, j'ai oublié mon cahier et…*

 Follow-up:
- Students take turns to ask and answer the question *Où sont tes devoirs?* The person answering aims to sound as if they are making up an excuse, using the hesitation word *euh*.
- Students adapt the key phrases to make up different excuses, keeping the same verbs but altering the nouns. Provide dictionaries so that they can look up unknown nouns, and encourage them to come up with some outrageous excuses in addition to plausible ones, e.g. *On a volé mon cahier/mon cartable, Mon chien/lion/père a mangé mes devoirs, Mon hamster a mangé ma calculatrice.*
- Pairs/Groups report back their excuses to the class. Students list them, ranging from the most convincing down to the most unlikely.

4 N'oublie pas.

Student note down any new words or phrases they have learned on this page. They apply the learning strategies from *Bien apprendre!* (page 57) to help them learn them.

Clic.fr

Planner

➤ **Objectives**
- To raise awareness of France and French culture
- To promote intercultural understanding by providing opportunities to compare French culture with students' own culture

➤ **Resources**
Students' Book, page 61
Copymaster 36

➤ **Framework reference**
R – 7C2

Au college en France

AT 3.2 This page gives information in English about aspects of school life in France, including the school year, what class you're in at a certain age, and the foreign languages studied in different regions of France.

1 What class would you be in if you lived in France?

Answer: sixième

2 How is the school year in France different from yours?

Answer: It finishes at the end of June, i.e. a little earlier in France than in most parts of the UK.

3 Why do you think German and Spanish are taught in some parts of France?

Answer: German is taught in areas that are close to France's border with Germany, and Spanish is taught close to the border with Spain.

4 List in English the languages offered by French schools

Answers: English, German, Italian, Spanish, Portuguese, Greek, Danish, Arabic, Japanese, Chinese, Hebrew, Russian

5 Look back through pages 47–60. Make a note of anything else you have learned about school in France.

- You might like to add the following to anything already noted by students:
  - there is no daily assembly in French schools
  - there is no religious education in state schools
  - pupils' textbooks may have to be bought by their parents or are hired from the school and parents are invoiced
  - marks tend to be awarded out of 20 instead of being graded A, B, C, etc.

See also the teacher's notes for spread 3.3, second starter activity, on page 89 of this book.

C36 Copymaster 36 provides further activities focusing on school life in France.

Vocabulaire

Planner

> ### Objectives
> * *Vocabulaire:* to provide a theme-based summary of the key language of the unit, which students can use as a reference or as an aid to learning
> * To develop language learning strategies
> * *On chante!:* to reinforce the language of the unit in a fun way

> ### Resources
> Students' Book, pages 62–63
> CD 2, track 14
> *En solo* Workbook, pages 46–47;
> *En solo* CD, track 30
> Copymaster 25

> ### Framework reference
> **R** – 7W5, 7C4

C25
W 46–47

A list of key language from the unit, with associated activities, is also provided on Copymaster 25 and on pages 46–47 of the *En solo* Workbook.

Good value verbs

* *Aim*: To highlight the importance of knowing high-frequency verbs such as *avoir*.
* Students search pages 62–63 for different forms of *avoir*, then find three more verbs that they think they will use again.

Answers: A j'ai, tu as/vous avez, on a/nous avons; B aimer (j'aime), adorer (j'adore), détester (je déteste), être (c'est)

On chante!

 1 Écoute et lis. Trouve!

* Students listen and follow the words. They search the song lyrics for five days of the week and five school subjects.

Answers: a lundi, mardi, mercredi, jeudi, vendredi; b la géo, les mathématiques, le dessin, la musique, le français

CD 2, track 14   page 63, activité 1

Une semaine au collège

Aujourd'hui, c'est lundi
Le lundi, on a géo
J'aime, j'aime, j'aime
J'aime bien la géo
La géo, c'est rigolo.

Aujourd'hui, c'est mardi
Le mardi, on a mathématiques
J'aime, j'aime, j'aime
J'aime bien les mathématiques
Les mathématiques, c'est très pratique.

Aujourd'hui, c'est mercredi
Le mercredi, on a dessin
J'aime, j'aime, j'aime

J'aime bien le dessin
Le dessin, c'est super bien.

Aujourd'hui, c'est jeudi
Le jeudi, on a musique
J'aime, j'aime, j'aime
J'aime bien la musique
La musique, c'est fantastique.

Aujourd'hui, c'est vendredi
Le vendredi, on a français
J'aime, j'aime, j'aime
J'aime bien le français
En français, je suis parfait!

 2 Trouve.

* Students find in the song the French for five English adjectives.

Answers: a fantastique; b pratique; c bien; d parfait; e rigolo

AT 2.2 **3 Chante.**

* Students sing along with the recording.

Lecture

Planner

> ### Objectives
> - To encourage independent reading and develop reading strategies
> - To provide alternative class and homework material for students who finish other activities quickly

The texts and activities on *Lecture A* should be suitable for all; *Lecture B* is more challenging and may be suitable for more able students only.

> ### Resources
> Students' Book, pages 122–123

> ### Framework reference
> **R** – 7C4

Lecture A

Le collège, c'est cool?

This text focuses on positive and negative attitudes to school.

AT 3.2 **1 Read, find and give the French for...**

Answers: a *les maths* – maths, *les sciences* – science, *le dessin* – art, *l'anglais* – English, *l'EPS* – PE, *le français* – French; b j'aime bien..., ma matière préférée, c'est..., j'adore...; c je déteste..., c'est nul, je n'aime pas beaucoup..., ... n'est pas cool

AT 3.3 **2 Who likes school most? Who likes it least? Place the pupils in order, starting with the one you think is most positive.**

- Various answers are possible, but emphasise that students must be able to justify their responses with reference to the positive and negative comments made by each teenager.

Possible answers: 1 Caro (aime bien tous les cours); 2 Ali (collège est génial mais n'aime pas les maths); 3 Pierre (ça dépend, il adore les sciences mais il déteste le dessin, préfère la récréation/la cantine); 4 Malika (les classes ne sont pas cool); 5 Déborah (collège n'est pas cool, mais l'anglais est intéressant et le prof d'anglais est super)

 Défi!

- Students write a few lines expressing their own attitude to school, using the sentences on the page as a model.
- Less able students could copy out sentences from the page that apply to themselves.

Lecture B

Une décision difficile

This text uses language from Unit 3 in the context of a girl's first day at school.

AT 3.3 **1 Read and answer in English.**

Answers: a she's new at the school; b Séb; c because English is his favourite subject; d he's playing in a basketball match; e she has a geography lesson at ten o'clock on Saturday morning so she shouldn't really go to the basketball match

2 What would you do if you were Émilie? Turn the page round and read what she does.

- Émilie decides not to go to the match: what would students do if they were her?
- Discuss reasons for their choices, e.g. it's important to make friends when you start a new school, but it's also important not to get into bad habits of missing lessons.

Copymasters

Feuille 25 Vocabulaire

A list of key language from the unit is provided here as well as on pages 62–63 of the Students' Book and pages 46–47 of the *En solo* Workbook.

Feuille 26 Je sais…

Use this checklist with *Blog-notes* (Students' Book page 58) or towards the end of the unit. It provides an opportunity for students to review what they have learned and reflect on areas for improvement. This checklist is also provided on page 44 of the *En solo* Workbook.

Feuille 27 À vos marques!

These starter activities are intended for use with the following Students' Book pages:

• Use ex. 1 with pages 52–53.
• Use ex. 2 with pages 54–55.

1 C'est quel jour de la semaine? Utilise le code.

• Students solve the code to find the seven days of the week.

Answers: 1 jeudi; 2 dimanche; 3 lundi; 4 mercredi; 5 vendredi; 6 mardi; 7 samedi

2 Écris le mot correct pour l'image.

• Students label the pictures, choosing from the words and phrases provided.
• This activity includes language from the whole unit, including opinions, school subjects and classroom items.

Answers: a un stylo; b une gomme; c un livre; d la musique; e la technologie; f l'histoire; g j'aime; h je déteste; i je n'aime pas; j une chaise; k un tableau blanc; l un ordinateur

Feuille 28 Bilan de leçon

These plenary activities are intended for use with the following Students' Book pages:

• Use ex. 1 with pages 48–49.
• Use ex. 2 with pages 52–53.

1a Les codes secrets! Utilise les codes pour écrire les phrases.

• Students use the numbered words and phrases to build sentences expressing opinions of school subjects.

Answers: a J'adore le français parce que c'est super. b J'aime l'histoire parce que c'est intéressant. c Je déteste l'EPS parce que c'est difficile. d J'aime bien les sciences parce que c'est difficile. e Je n'aime pas l'anglais parce que c'est nul. f Je n'aime pas beaucoup la technologie parce que c'est difficile.

1b Traduis les phrases en anglais.

• Students translate the sentences from ex. 1a into English.

Answers: a I love French because it's great. b I like history because it's interesting. c I hate PE because it's hard. d I like science because it's hard. e I don't like English because it's rubbish. f I don't much like technology because it's difficult.

1c À deux. Fais des codes secrets pour ton/ta partenaire.

• Students write some coded sentences for their partner to solve, similar to those in ex. 1a.

2 Regarde les images et écris les phrases.

• Students write a sentence for each picture, giving a time and a school subject.

Answers: 1 À dix heures, j'ai histoire. 2 À une heure trente, j'ai français. 3 À neuf heures quinze, j'ai sciences. 4 À deux heures quarante-cinq, j'ai maths.

Follow-up: Challenge students to make up some picture sentences for their partner, similar to those in ex. 2.

Feuille 29 Écouter

• Use ex. 1 with Students' Book pages 54–55.
• Use ex. 2 with Students' Book pages 52–53.

 1 Écoute et coche la bonne image.

• Students listen and tick the items that are mentioned.
• This activity includes a range of language from Unit 3: school subjects, classroom equipment, clock times, problems, opinions.

Answers: 1 science; 2 pencil case; 3 ten past two; 4 blackboard; 5 frowning face; 6 broken pen

> 🔘 **CD 2, track 15**   Feuille 29, activité 1
>
> J'adore les sciences.
> Dans mon cartable, il y a une trousse.
> Il est deux heures dix.
> Regardez le tableau noir!
> Je n'aime pas beaucoup l'anglais. C'est nul.
> Je suis désolé, madame. J'ai cassé mon stylo.

 2 Écoute et remplis les blancs dans l'emploi du temps.

• Students listen to a description of a school timetable. They fill in seven blanks in the timetable provided.

Answers: <u>lundi</u>: français; <u>mardi matin</u>: EPS; <u>mardi après-midi</u>: anglais; <u>mercredi</u>: français; <u>jeudi matin</u>: maths; <u>jeudi après-midi</u>: musique; <u>vendredi</u>: technologie

 CD 2, track 16   Feuille 29, activité 2

1 Lundi matin, j'ai maths, soutien et français.
2 Mardi, nous avons informatique et sciences, puis la récréation et EPS. À deux heures, nous avons anglais.
3 Mercredi, j'ai français, sciences, informatique et maths.
4 Jeudi, on a histoire-géo et anglais, puis la récréation, maths et technologie. À deux heures, on a musique, puis à trois heures, informatique, et à quatre heures dix, français.
5 Vendredi, après la récréation, j'ai technologie et anglais.

Feuille 30   Parler

- Use ex. 1 with Students' Book pages 50–51.
- Use ex. 2 with Students' Book pages 54–55.

 1a Dessine l'heure (1–4) et réponds aux questions de ton/ta partenaire.

 1b Demande l'heure à ton/ta partenaire. Note ses réponses (5–8).

- Working in pairs, each student has eight blank clock faces. They each begin by drawing the time onto four of these faces.
- Students then take turns to ask and tell each the other the times they have drawn. They listen and fill in their partner's times on the four remaining blank clocks.

  2 Choisis six objets. Pose des questions à ton/ta partenaire.

- In pairs, each student secretly chooses six of the school items pictured on the copymaster.
- They take turns to ask each other questions to work out which items they have chosen.

Feuille 31   Lire et écrire 1

- Use with Students' Book pages 54–55.

AT 4.2 | **1 Tu travailles pour le site web www.cartable.fr. Écris une page pour le catalogue en ligne.**

- Students imagine they are compiling a price list for an online catalogue of school items, e.g. pens, pencils, pencil cases, etc.
- They complete a list of school items and invent a price for each.

AT 4.2 | **2 C'est quoi? Regarde les images et écris les phrases.**

- Students label the school items.

Answers: a C'est un stylo. b C'est une règle. c C'est une calculatrice. d C'est une trousse. e C'est une gomme. f C'est un bâton de colle.

AT 3.2 | **3 Mets les mots dans le bon ordre.**

- Students rearrange each set of words in the correct order to build four sentences relating to school.

Answers: a Je n'aime pas les sciences. b Ma matière préférée, c'est la musique. c Dans ma classe, il y a un ordinateur. d Dans ma trousse, il y a deux crayons et une gomme.

Feuille 32   Lire et écrire 2

- Use ex. 1 with Students' Book pages 50–51.
- Use ex. 2 and 3 with Students' Book pages 52–53.

AT 4.2 | **1 Quelle heure est-il?**

- Students write the time shown on each clock face.

Answers: a Il est cinq heures quinze. b Il est trois heures vingt-cinq. c Il est une heure vingt. d Il est six heures quarante-cinq. e Il est quatre heures cinquante. f Il est dix heures cinquante-cinq.

AT 3.2 | **2 Regarde l'emploi du temps. Lis les phrases 1–5: vrai ou faux?**

- Students look at the timetable and work out whether statements 1–5 are true or false.

Answers: 1 faux; 2 vrai; 3 faux; 4 vrai; 5 vrai

AT 3.3 | **3 You will need coloured pens or pencils for this activity. Read the email and underline the days in red, the times in blue, the subjects in green, the opinions in black and the reasons why in yellow.**

Answers:

<u>days</u>: mercredi, jeudi

<u>times</u>: il est neuf heures, à neuf heures trente, à dix heures quarante, à onze heures quarante, à deux heures, à trois heures

<u>subjects</u>: informatique, sciences, maths, géo, dessin, histoire

<u>opinions</u>: j'adore, je n'aime pas, beurk, ma matière préférée, je n'aime pas beaucoup, j'aime bien

<u>reasons why</u>: c'est génial, c'est difficile, c'est super-nul, c'est intéressant, ce n'est pas intéressant

Feuille 33   Labo-langue

- Use with Students' Book page 56.

1 Remplis le tableau.

- Students complete the table of subject pronouns and regular -er verb endings.
- The missing words and endings are provided for students to choose from.

Answers:

English pronouns	French pronouns	verb + ending
I	je	jou**e**
you	tu	jou**es**
he	il	jou**e**
she	elle	jou**e**
we	nous	jou**ons**
you	vous	jou**ez**
they (m)	ils	jou**ent**
they (f)	elles	jou**ent**

2 Mots-croisés.

- Students work out the regular -er verb endings and complete the crossword puzzle.

Answers:

Horizontalement: 1 regarde; 6 détestent; 9 laisse; 10 adorons; 12 oublie; 13 chantez; 14 jouent

Verticalement: 2 aimez; 3 casse; 4 casses; 5 terminent; 7 écoute; 8 termine; 11 volons

Feuille 34   Bien apprendre!

- Use with *Bien apprendre!* on Students' Book page 57.

Students are guided through a checklist of steps. They are asked to:

- choose five familiar words or phrases from a text about school, and write them down together with their English meanings
- practise saying each word or phrase aloud
- try writing them from memory
- use the words or phrases in sentences of their own.

Feuille 35   Bien parler!

- Use with *Bien parler!* on Students' Book page 57.

1a Encercle les mots avec le son é.

- Students circle all the words that contain an é sound.

Answers: see underlining in transcript for ex. 1b

1b Écoute et vérifie.

- Students listen to check their answers to ex. 1a.

 CD 2, track 17   Feuille 35, activité 1b

- je déteste – j'adore – j'aime – préférée
- la géographie – l'histoire – la matière – la récréation
- un cahier – une clé USB – un stylo – un ordinateur

1c Écoute et répète.

- Students listen and repeat.

 CD 2, track 18   Feuille 35, activité 1c

- je déteste – préférée
- la géographie – la récréation
- un cahier – une clé USB

2 Practise making the é sound by reading these picture captions out loud. Listen and copy the pronunciation you hear.

 CD 2, track 19   Feuille 35, activité 2

a – Aïe! On a volé mon vélo!
b – Désolé! J'ai oublié les cahiers!
c – Léa a cassé la télé au musée!
d – Félix et son bébé jouent à la pétanque au café.

Feuille 36   Culture

- Use with Students' Book page 61.

1 Which foreign languages are likely to be taught in the three shaded areas on the map? Write the languages into the boxes: choose from Dutch, German, Italian, Portuguese, Spanish.

Answers: south-west: Spanish; north-east: German; south-east: Italian

2 What do you know about the school system in France? Use the *Clic! 1* Students' Book to help you, and circle the correct answer.

Answers: 1 no; 2 yes; 3 no; 4 yes; 5 yes; 6 sometimes; 7 sometimes; 8 no; 9 sometimes; 10 *students' own answers*

En solo Workbook

Pages 34–35 3.1 Les matières: top ou flop?

- Use with Students' Book pages 48–49.

AT 3.1
AT 4.1
1 Find ten school subjects in the wordsnake, then use them to label the symbols.

Answers: a les maths; b la musique; c les sciences; d l'anglais; e l'EPS; f l'histoire; g le dessin; h le français; i la technologie; j la géographie

AT 1.2
2 Do you have more in common with Morgane, Bastien or Amina? Listen and circle the subjects they like.

- As extension, ask students to listen out for a third subject mentioned by Amina and what she says about it (she doesn't like maths).

Answers: <u>Morgane</u>: music and geography; <u>Bastien</u>: English and art; <u>Amina</u>: likes technology and history

 En solo CD, track 24   page 35, activité 2

- Salut! Je m'appelle Morgane. J'aime la musique… et j'aime beaucoup la géographie.
- Salut! Je m'appelle Bastien. J'aime l'anglais et j'adore le dessin.
- Salut! Je m'appelle Amina. Au collège, j'aime bien la technologie… mais… je n'aime pas les maths. Et euh… j'aime beaucoup l'histoire. L'histoire, c'est intéressant.

AT 3.2
3 Read the speech bubbles. Which is the right one for Simon? Tick A or B.

Answer: B

Follow-up: Students write similar speech bubbles based on their answers for ex. 2.

AT 4.2
4 Which subjects do you like? Which don't you like?

- Students use ex. 3 as a model to express their own likes and dislikes.

Pages 36–37 3.2 Quelle heure est-il?

- Use with Students' Book pages 50–51.

AT 3.2
1 Look at the clocks. Tick the correct time: is it a or b?

Answers: 1 b; 2 a; 3 b; 4 b

AT 3.2
2 Fill in the correct time on the watches.

Answers: a 8.15; b 9.00; c 11.30; d 3.10; e 5.25; f 13.15

AT 4.2
3 Write the correct time.

Answers: a Il est six heures cinq. b Il est deux heures. c Il est quatre heures quinze. d Il est six heures trente. e Il est dix heures dix. f Il est quinze heures quarante-cinq.

AT 1.2
4 How many people will arrive at the holiday camp in time for lunch at 12.30? Listen and circle each person's time of arrival.

Answers: Mathilde: 11 h; Pierre: 12 h; Julie: 13 h 20; Dylan: 10 h 30; Pauline: 12 h 05; Mohammed: 13 h 15 (Mathilde, Pierre, Dylan and Pauline are in time for lunch)

En solo CD, track 25   page 37, activité 4

- Mathilde, tu arrives quand?
- J'arrive à onze heures.

- Pierre, tu arrives quand?
- J'arrive à midi.

- Julie, tu arrives quand?
- J'arrive à treize heures vingt.

- Dylan, tu arrives quand?
- J'arrive à dix heures trente.

- Pauline, tu arrives quand?
- J'arrive à midi cinq.

- Mohammed, tu arrives quand?
- J'arrive à treize heures quinze.

Pages 38–39 3.3 Mon *emploi du temps*

- Use with Students' Book pages 52–53.

AT 3.2
1 Are statements 1–5 about the timetable true or false?

Answers: 1 vrai; 2 faux; 3 faux; 4 vrai; 5 vrai

AT 3.2
2 Read sentences a–e and underline all the times.

Answers: a à huit heures; b à neuf heures; c à dix heures vingt; d à onze heures vingt; e à quinze heures quarante-cinq

AT 3.2

AT 4.1

3 Read sentences a–e again and write the missing subjects into the timetable.

Answers:

	lundi	mardi	mercredi
8 h	dessin	dessin	technologie
9 h	histoire	anglais	français
R É C R É A T I O N			
10 h 20	sciences	français	EPS
11 h 20	français	géo	EPS
D É J E U N E R			
13 h 45	anglais	sciences	–
14 h 45	géo	musique	–
15 h 45	maths	histoire	–

AT 4.2

4a Fill the gaps to complete what Toto is saying.

Answers: see transcript for ex. 4b

AT 1.2

4b Listen to check your answers.

En solo CD, track 26   page 39, activité 4b

1 Le mardi, à quatorze heures, on a histoire.
2 Le mercredi, à neuf heures, on a français.
3 Le lundi, à onze heures, on a anglais.
4 Le samedi, à dix heures trente, on a musique.
5 Le jeudi, à treize heures, on a EPS.
6 Le vendredi, à quatorze heures dix, on a sciences.

AT 4.2 **Défi!**

* Students write six sentences about their own school timetable, giving the day and the time of each subject they mention.

Pages 40–41   3.4 Bien équipés!

* Use with Students' Book pages 54–55.

AT 3.1

AT 4.1

1 Can you complete the captions? Find the missing endings in the box and write them in.

Answers: a un bâton de colle; b un cahier; c une calculatrice; d un livre; e une règle; f un stylo; g une trousse; h un cartable; i un classeur; j une clé USB; k un crayon; l une gomme

AT 1.2

AT 3.1

2 Léa thinks she has more things in her schoolbag than Marc has in his. Listen and mark the items on their lists. Is Léa right?

Answers: <u>Léa</u>: un bâton de colle, un cahier, un classeur, des livres, une règle, un stylo, une trousse; <u>Marc</u>: un bâton de colle, un classeur, des livres, un stylo (Léa is right – she has most items)

En solo CD, track 27   page 41, activité 2

[*Léa:*] Dans mon cartable, j'ai un bâton de colle… j'ai un cahier… je n'ai pas de calculatrice… j'ai un classeur… j'ai des crayons… je n'ai pas de gomme… j'ai des livres… j'ai une règle…. j'ai un stylo… et j'ai une trousse. C'est bien!
[*Marc:*] Dans mon cartable, j'ai un bâton de colle… je n'ai pas de cahier… je n'ai pas de calculatrice… j'ai un classeur… je n'ai pas de crayons… je n'ai pas de gomme… j'ai des livres… je n'ai pas de règle…. j'ai un stylo… mais je n'ai pas de trousse. Hmmm!

AT 3.2

3 Read Toto's speech bubble. Does the picture show his bag? Give a reason.

Answer: no, because the picture shows a book and Toto says he doesn't have any books

AT 3.1 **Défi!**

AT 4.2

* Students tick the items listed in ex. 2 to show the contents of their own schoolbag, then write sentences explaining what they do and don't have.

Pages 42–43   Labo-langue

* Use with Students' Book pages 56–57.

1 Do the quiz on verbs. Circle a, b or c. Explain your choices.

Answers: 1 b (it isn't a regular -er verb); 2 b (because the *tu* ending is -es); 3 b (*il* and *on* are third person singular, *ils* is third person plural); 4 b (it's the correct form of the verb to go with *elle*, and it makes a logical sentence – *elle est maths* doesn't make sense); 5 c (*mes parents* needs to be followed by the third person plural form of the verb); 6 c (it's part of the verb *être*); 7 a (it is likely to be more common than the other two)

2 Underline the right form of the verb. (They're all -er verbs.)

Answers: a aimons; b aimes; c adorent; d parlez; e parlons; f arrivent

3 Write in the right form of *avoir* or *être*.

Answers: a sont; b ai; c est; d as; e ont; f sont; g sommes, sont

4 Translate the sentences in activities 2 and 3 into English.

Answers:

Ex. 2: a We like maths. b Do you like French? c They love it/that. d Do you speak English? e We speak a little French. f The teachers arrive at seven thirty.

Ex. 3: a The maths teachers are great. b I have chemistry at nine o'clock. c The teacher is cool. d Do you have a glue stick, please? e Max and Léo don't have an exercise book. f Chemistry homework is difficult. g We are clever but they are stupid.

5 Choose words from each column to write five different sentences.

• A range of answers are possible.

Follow-up: Ask students to write as many sentences as they can in 30 seconds, similar to the ones they wrote in ex. 5. Encourage them to use previously learned language in addition to language from Unit 3.

Page 44   Checklist

• Use with *Blog-notes* (Students' Book page 58) or towards the end of the unit.

The checklist, recording and follow-up activities provide opportunities for students to review what they have learned, test themselves orally on key language and reflect on areas for improvement.

 En solo CD, track 28   page 44, activité 2

1 technology [*beep*] la technologie
2 I like French. [*beep*] J'aime bien le français.
3 I don't like history. [*beep*] Je n'aime pas l'histoire.
4 My favourite subject is art. [*beep*] Ma matière préférée, c'est le dessin.
5 It's eleven fifteen. [*beep*] Il est onze heures quinze.
6 Monday, Tuesday [*beep*] lundi, mardi
7 On Thursdays, at ten o'clock, I have PE. [*beep*] Le jeudi, à dix heures, j'ai EPS.
8 a pencil case [*beep*] une trousse
9 Have you got a calculator? [*beep*] Tu as une calculatrice?
10 I haven't got a glue stick. [*beep*] Je n'ai pas de bâton de colle.
11 There is a poster. [*beep*] Il y a un poster.
12 There isn't a blackboard. [*beep*] Il n'y a pas de tableau noir.
13 I like, you like, he likes, she likes [*beep*] j'aime, tu aimes, il aime, elle aime
14 I have, you have, he has, she has [*beep*] j'ai, tu as, il a, elle a
15 I am, you are, he is, she is [*beep*] je suis, tu es, il est, elle est

Follow-up: Encourage students to draw up their own individual action plan of steps they could take to help them improve. Provide a checklist of suggestions for them to choose from, e.g. try harder to learn vocabulary, read the grammar notes again and make sure they understand them/ask for help if they don't understand, check written work carefully for mistakes, etc.

Page 45   Top tips and strategies

Speaking

This section provides tips and activities to help students improve their pronunciation and intonation, focusing on the rhythm and sound of French. It can be used at any appropriate point during Unit 3.

1 Read sentences a–d to yourself. Which of the tips above will help you say them more like a French person? Prepare each sentence, then listen and repeat. (Each one is said twice in the recording.)

 En solo CD, track 29   page 45, activité 1

a J'aime les jeux. [*pause*] J'aime les jeux.
b C'est ma fête préférée. [*pause*] C'est ma fête préférée.
c Tu aimes la musique. [*pause*] Tu aimes la musique.
d Luc a un lapin, mais Lulu préfère les chiens. [*pause*] Luc a un lapin, mais Lulu préfère les chiens.

Reading

This section focuses on cognates and false friends. It can be used at any appropriate point during Unit 3.

2 Are these useful cognates or false friends? Use the *Vocabulaire* pages in *Clic! 1* Students' Book to help you. Circle the false friends.

Answers: all cognates apart from d (it's a pencil, not a crayon) and f (it's a coach, not a car)

 3 How can you make sure you remember which are cognates and which are false friends? Discuss with a partner.

• Ideas might include: draw a warning sign (e.g. red warning triangle, red exclamation mark) beside them; keep them in a separate list; mark them with a highlighter pen; draw a wiggly line underneath them in a bright colour.

Pages 46–47   Vocabulaire

• Use with the Students' Book page 62–63.

A list of key language from the unit is provided here as well as in the Students' Book and on Copymaster 25.

1 Listen and tick the phrases you hear.

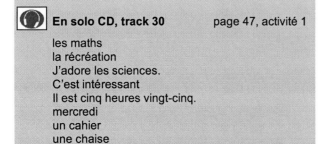

En solo CD, track 30   page 47, activité 1

les maths
la récréation
J'adore les sciences.
C'est intéressant
Il est cinq heures vingt-cinq.
mercredi
un cahier
une chaise

2 Underline in coloured pencil...

* Students search the list for key language items.

3 Note: a) your favourite word/phrase in this unit; b) 3 key words/phrases to remember.

* Challenge students to make up some sentences using their favourite word/phrase.

Unité 4: Mon coin du monde   Overview grid

Page reference	Contexts and objectives	Grammar	Language strategies and pronunciation	Key language	Framework	AT Level
66–67 **4.1 Ma région**	• Your area and the weather			*le nord, l'ouest, le sud, l'est, le centre, le nord-ouest, le sud-ouest, le nord-est, le sud-est* *Ma région, c'est… C'est dans le nord de la France.* *Quel temps fait-il? Il fait beau. Il ne fait pas beau. Il fait chaud. Il fait froid. Il y a du vent. Il y a du soleil. Il y a de l'orage. Il y a du brouillard. Il y a des nuages. Il pleut. Il neige.*	**R** – 7C1	1.1–2, 2.2, 3.1, 4.2
68–69 **4.2 Tu habites où?**	• Where you live	• Agreement of adjectives (masculine and feminine)		*Tu habites où? J'habite… dans une grande/petite ville, dans un village à la campagne, à la montagne, au bord de la mer* *dans une maison, dans un appartement* *C'est comment?* *grand(e), petit(e), moderne, beau (belle), ancien(enne)*	**R** – 7S9, 7T5	1.2–3, 2.2–3, 3.1–2, 4.2–3
70–71 **4.3 C'est comment, chez toi?**	• Flats and houses	• Agreement of adjectives (masculine, feminine, plural)		*Chez moi, il y a… une pièce, une chambre, une cuisine, une salle à manger, une salle de bains, une douche, une piscine, un salon, un bureau, un garage, un jardin, un balcon, des toilettes* *au rez-de-chaussée, au premier étage* *vieux (vieille)*	**R** – 7W1, 7T5	1.1–3, 2.2, 3.3, 4.2–3
72–73 **4.4 Dans ma chambre**	• Things in your bedroom	• Position of adjectives		*un lit, un bureau, un tableau, un miroir, un tapis, une chaise, une armoire, une table, une table de chevet, une lampe, une moquette, des rideaux, le mur, le plancher, la porte, la fenêtre* *simple, confortable* *assez, très, trop*	**R** – 7W1, 7S6, 7T5	1.2, 2.2–3, 3.1–2, 4.2–3
74–75 **Labo-langue**	• Grammar • Skills • Pronunciation	Adjectives: • Agreement • Position	• How to listen well • Pronunciation of adjective endings **Workbook:** • Why literal translations don't always work • Out-of-school learning		**R** – 7W4, 7S1, 7S2, 7L2	
76–79 **Blog-notes / Tu sais tout? / En plus / Clic.fr**	• End-of-unit summary and assessment • Extension • **Cultural focus:** geography of France			**En plus:** *devant, derrière, entre, sur, sous, dans*	**R** – 7W2, 7T3, 7T6, 7C1, 7C2, 7C3, 7C4	1.2–3, 2.2, 3.2–3, 4.2–3

CLIC! 1 STAR UNIT 4 MEDIUM TERM PLAN

About Unit 4, *Mon coin du monde*: In this unit, students learn to exchange information and opinions about weather and climate, different living environments (town, countryside, seaside, etc.), types of home, rooms in a house, and bedroom furniture. The grammar focus of the unit is adjectives, including agreement and position, and pronunciation of adjective endings. Students are also given tips on improving listening skills, and prepositions are introduced on the *En plus* page for the benefit of able students. There are opportunities to compare house styles in France and the UK, and students find out about features of different areas of France and Burkina Faso.

Framework objectives (reinforce)	Teaching and learning	Week-by-week overview (assuming 6 weeks' work or approximately 10–12.5 hours)
7W1: Everyday words	Build stock of vocabulary relating to own home, including rooms, adjectives, bedroom furniture.	**Week 1 – Opening spread/4.1 Ma région** Opening spread: introduction to unit themes and objectives, focusing on facts and figures relating to French housing and different styles of houses in France and the UK Spread 4.1: areas of France; home area; weather and climate
7W2: High-frequency words	Importance of knowing high-frequency words that can be used in a range of contexts, e.g. *assez, très, trop* (p. 81).	
7W4: Gender and plural	Adjective agreement (masculine, feminine, plural) (p. 74).	
7S1: Typical word order	Position of adjectives (pp. 73–74).	
7S2: Sentence gist	Why word-for-word translations don't always work (Workbook p. 59); expressions that are different in French and English, e.g. *il y a du soleil* translates as "it is sunny" although the literal translation is "there is some sun".	**Week 2 – 4.2 Tu habites où?** Different living environments, e.g. town, countryside, seaside; adjectives
7S6: Compound sentences	Focus on the word *mais* in Van Gogh's speech bubble on p. 72 and use it as an opportunity to highlight the importance of linking words in building more complex sentences. Encourage students to use *et* and *mais* in their own descriptions (p. 73 ex. 7), e.g. *Dans ma chambre, il y a … et… mais il n'y a pas de…*	
7S9: Using simple sentences	Exchange basic information about own home and home area, e.g. *J'habite dans un village à la campagne*.	**Week 3 – 4.3 C'est comment, chez toi?** Houses and flats; rooms in a house; adjectives
7T3: Checking before reading	Students work through a series of activities to help them access a text about the Camargue (p. 124), e.g. predict content by looking at the photos, find key points by matching simple questions to paragraphs of the text, find captions for the photos.	
7T5: Assembling text	Build short texts about own region and own home/ideal home using key words and phrases and by adapting model texts.	**Week 4 – 4.4 Dans ma chambre** Bedroom furniture; more about adjectives
7T6: Texts as prompts for writing	Use multiple-choice questions about the video blog (p. 76) as a stimulus for writing own answers to questions about home and region. If appropriate, encourage students to build a continuous text from their answers.	
7L2: Following speech	Tips and strategies to help with listening (p. 75).	**Week 5 – Labo-langue** Adjectives (agreement and position); listening skills; pronunciation of adjective endings
7C1: Geographical facts	Regions and climate of France (pp. 66–67, p. 79, p. 124).	
7C2: Everyday culture	House styles in France and the UK (p. 65, pp. 68–69); a village in Burkina Faso (p. 125).	
7C3: Contact with native speakers	Video clip of native speakers talking about where they live (p. 68); video blog (p. 76).	**Week 6 – Blog-notes, Tu sais tout?, En plus, Clic.fr, On chante!, Lecture** Reinforcement and extension of the language of the unit; review of progress via the Checklist in the Workbook/on Copymaster; revision and assessment
7C4: Stories and songs	Song on the theme of home (p. 81).	

4 Mon coin du monde

Unit objectives

Contexts: Homes and regions
Grammar: Adjectives
Language learning: Listening skills
Pronunciation: Adjective endings
Cultural focus: Regions of France

Assessment opportunities

Reading: Students' Book, page 71, activity 4b
Writing: Students' Book, page 73, activity 7

See also **Clic! 1** OxBox Assessment CD-ROM

 1 Regarde. C'est en France ou en Grande-Bretagne?

- *Aim*: To develop cultural awareness and visual observation skills.
- Students look at the photos and try to work out whether each house is in France or the UK.

Answers: 1 France; 2 France; 3 UK; 4 UK

Follow-up:

- Discuss styles of houses in France and the UK (reinforcing Framework Objective 7C2). If possible, bring in (or find on the Internet) some photos showing the variety of French regional architecture, e.g. thatched cottages in Normandy, chalets in the Alps, Provençal mas (traditional farmhouses or country houses), and typical Breton houses with their grey-slated roofs, whitewashed walls and shutters to keep out the wind and rain. Point out that terraced houses are rare in France.
- Discuss the statistics about housing in France, population centres (town versus countryside) and trends in ownership of holiday homes. How do students think these statistics compare with the situation in the UK?

 2 Complète.

- Students complete the sentences to say which houses they like/don't like.
- Encourage them to add to the sentences using *parce que…,* e.g. *J'aime bien la maison numéro… parce que…*

4.1 Ma région

Planner

> ### Objectives
> * Your area and the weather

> ### Resources
> Students' Book, pages 66–67
> CD 2, tracks 20–22
> *En solo* Workbook, pages 48–49;
> *En solo* CD, track 31
> Copymasters 40, 41; CD 2, tracks 38–40

> ### Key language
> <u>Ma région</u>
> *le nord, l'ouest, le sud, l'est, le centre*
> *le nord-ouest, le sud-ouest, le nord-est, le sud-est*
> *Ma région, c'est...*
> *C'est dans le nord de la France.*
>
> <u>Le temps</u>
> *Quel temps fait-il?*
> *Il fait beau. Il ne fait pas beau.*
> *Il fait chaud. Il fait froid.*
> *Il y a du vent. Il y a du soleil.*
> *Il y a de l'orage. Il y a du brouillard.*
> *Il y a des nuages.*
> *Il pleut. Il neige.*

> ### Framework reference
> **R** – 7C1

> ### Starters
> * Ask whether any students have visited the areas labelled on the map of France. What was the weather like?
> * Write a list of counties/areas of the UK on the board, and divide the class into two teams. A student from team A stands up, chooses a county and says where it is, e.g. *Ma région, c'est le Devon. C'est dans le sud-ouest de*

l'Angleterre. If both sentences are correct, cross this region off the list and award two points to team A (one point for each correct sentence). A student from team B then stands up and repeats this for a different area on the list. Continue until all the areas have been crossed off. The winning team is the one with the most points.
> * Play "Weather Bingo". Students copy down three or four weather symbols from page 67. Call out random weather phrases and students cross out the corresponding symbols as you mention them. The winner is the first person to cross out all their symbols. A confident student could take over as the Bingo caller.

> ### Plenaries
> * In pairs, students invent and draw out a new set of weather symbols, different from the ones in the Students' Book, e.g. they could use a melting ice-cream cone for *il fait chaud*, sunglasses for *il y a du soleil*, an umbrella blown inside-out for *il y a du vent*, etc. They exchange their symbols with another pair, who label each one with a corresponding weather phrase. Pairs give each other feedback on the accuracy of the French and the clarity/effectiveness of the symbols.
> * List on the board a few areas of the UK. Give brief details in English about the location of each place and two weather conditions. For example: <u>Sutherland</u>: N Scotland; windy, snow.
> Students choose a couple of areas and describe them to their partner. Provide a model on the board if necessary, e.g. *Ma région, c'est le Sutherland. C'est dans le nord de l'Écosse. Il y a du vent et il neige.*
> The partner provides feedback.
> * Copymaster 40 *Bilan de leçon* ex. 3.

 AT 1.2

1 Écoute. Qui parle?

* Students look at the photos of five teenagers linked to different areas of a map of France. Draw attention to the compass points (*nord, sud, est, ouest, centre*, etc.).
* Ask them to predict what each person might say about where they live. Give them a model to adapt, e.g. *Ma région, c'est <u>le Poitou-Charentes</u>. C'est dans <u>l'ouest</u> de la France.*
* Students listen to the recording to check their predictions, and work out the name of each speaker.

Answers: 1 Léo; 2 Anya; 3 Éric; 4 Suzie; 5 Simon

 CD 2, track 20   page 66, activité 1

1 Ma région, c'est le Poitou-Charentes. C'est dans l'ouest de la France.
2 Ma région, c'est la Provence. C'est dans le sud de la France.
3 Ma région, c'est l'Alsace. C'est dans l'est de la France.
4 Ma région, c'est la Picardie. C'est dans le nord de la France.
5 Ma région, c'est l'Auvergne. C'est dans le centre de la France.

AT 4.2 **2 Écris et lis.**

- Students write a speech bubble for each of the five teenagers, similar to their predictions in ex. 1, e.g. *Je m'appelle Léo. Ma région, c'est le Poitou-Charentes. C'est dans l'ouest de la France.*
- They read out their bubbles.

Follow-up: Égide is a French organisation providing information, advice and assistance for foreign students wishing to study or find work experience in France. Their website is a useful source of information about the regions of France (http://www.egide.asso.fr/fr/guide/connaitre/regions). Students could visit the site (an English version is available), choose a region and find out a few facts about it, which they then present to the class in a subsequent lesson.

AT 2.2 **3 Parle.**

- Students adapt the speech bubble from ex. 2 to say where they themselves live, e.g. *Je m'appelle… Ma région, c'est le Devon. C'est dans le sud-ouest de l'Angleterre.*
- They do the same for their favourite celebrities, e.g. *Je m'appelle Sean Bean. Ma région, c'est le Yorkshire. C'est dans le nord-est de l'Angleterre.*
- Point out the information panel on *de l'Angleterre*, *de l'Écosse*, *de l'Irlande du Nord* and *du pays de Galles*. (Use of *du, de la, de l'* and *des* will be explained in Unit 6.)

AT 1.1 **AT 3.1** **4 Relie. Écoute et vérifie.**

- Students match the weather pictures to the phrases, then listen to the recording to check their answers.

Answers: 1 j (il pleut); 2 k (il neige); 3 f (il y a du soleil); 4 g (il y a du brouillard); 5 d (il fait froid); 6 c (il fait chaud); 7 h (il y a de l'orage); 8 i (il y a des nuages); 9 e (il y a du vent)

CD 2, track 2 page 67, activité 4

1 – Quel temps fait-il?
  – Il pleut.
2 – Quel temps fait-il?
  – Il neige.
3 – Quel temps fait-il?
  – Il y a du soleil.
4 – Quel temps fait-il?
  – Il y a du brouillard.
5 – Quel temps fait-il?
  – Il fait froid.
6 – Quel temps fait-il?
  – Il fait chaud.
7 – Quel temps fait-il?
  – Il y a de l'orage.
8 – Quel temps fait-il?
  – Il y a des nuages.
9 – Quel temps fait-il?
  – Il y a du vent.

Follow-up: Play Noughts and Crosses using the grid of weather pictures. In order to win a square, students say the weather phrase represented by the picture.

AT 1.2 **AT 4.2** **5 Écris et vérifie.**

This activity would be suitable as part of preparation for external assessment at Breakthrough stage.
- Students look at the weather map of France, and refer back to the map on page 66 to remind themselves of where the five teenagers live.
- They write a speech bubble for each teenager, describing the weather today in their region, then listen to the recording to check their answers.

Answers: Léo: Dans ma région, il y a du vent et il pleut. Anya: Dans ma région, il fait chaud et il y a du soleil. Éric: Dans ma région, il fait froid et il neige. Suzie: Dans ma région, il y a des nuages et il y a du brouillard. Simon: Dans ma région, il y a de l'orage

CD 2, track 22 page 67, activité 5

– Quel temps fait-il dans ta région aujourd'hui, Léo?
– Aujourd'hui, dans ma région, il ne fait pas beau. Il y a du vent et il pleut.
– Quel temps fait-il dans ta région aujourd'hui, Anya?
– Aujourd'hui, dans ma région, il fait beau. Il fait chaud et il y a du soleil.
– Quel temps fait-il dans ta région aujourd'hui, Éric?
– Aujourd'hui, dans ma région, il ne fait pas beau. Il fait froid et il neige.
– Quel temps fait-il dans ta région aujourd'hui, Suzie?
– Aujourd'hui, dans ma région, il ne fait pas beau. Il y a des nuages et il y a du brouillard.
– Quel temps fait-il dans ta région aujourd'hui, Simon?
– Aujourd'hui, dans ma région, il ne fait pas beau. Il y a de l'orage.

AT 4.2 **6 À toi.**

- Students describe today's weather in your own region.

C41 Ex. 3 on Copymaster 41 is a listening activity on the weather.

W 48–49 Pages 48–49 of the *En solo* Workbook provide further activities to practise the weather phrases and compass points.

4.2 Tu habites où?

Planner

> ### Objectives
> • Where you live

> ### Resources
> Students' Book, pages 68–69
> CD 2, tracks 24–25
> Video clip 8
> *En solo* Workbook, pages 50–51;
> *En solo* CD, tracks 32–34
> Copymasters 39, 41; CD 2, tracks 38–40

> ### Key language
> *Tu habites où?*
> *J'habite...*
> *dans une grande/petite ville*
> *dans un village*
> *à la campagne, à la montagne, au bord de la mer*
> *dans une maison, dans un appartement*
>
> *C'est comment?*
> *grand(e), petit(e), moderne, beau (belle),*
> *ancien(enne)*

> ### Grammar
> Agreement of adjectives (masculine/feminine)

> ### Framework reference
> **R** – 7S9, 7T5

> ### Starters
> • Call out numbers between one and six (corresponding to the six pictures in ex. 1 on page 68). Students respond with the place and an opinion, e.g.
> Teacher: *Le numéro cinq!*
> Student: *À la montagne! J'adore, c'est génial!*
> • Students answer the register using sentences or phrases from the spread, e.g. *une grande ville, J'adore ma maison*, etc.
> • *C'est en France ou en Grande-Bretagne?* Students work out whether the houses and flats shown (page 69) are in France or the UK. (Numbers 1, 2, 4 and 5 are in France.) Ask them what clues they notice in the photos, e.g. shutters.
> • Copymaster 39 *À tes marques!* ex. 1.

> ### Plenaries
> • Say a word from the lesson; students say a sentence containing the word, e.g.
> Teacher: *Petite!*
> Student: *J'habite dans une petite maison.*
> • In pairs or groups, students play Word Tennis to build sentences based on the language of the spread. The aim is to keep the "rally" going for as long as they can, e.g.
> Student A: *J'habite...*
> Student B: *... dans un appartement...*
> Student A: *... à la montagne.*
> Student B: *Il est...*
> Student A: *... grand et...*
> Student B: *... moderne.*
> Provide key words/phrases on the board as support.

The phrases *une maison mitoyenne* (a terraced house) and *une maison jumelle* (a semi-detached house) do not appear as key language in the Students' Book because they are rarely used in France. However, students may need these expressions in order to refer to their own houses, so you may wish to introduce them.

 1 Regarde. Note dans l'ordre.

• Students watch the video clip, in which people give brief details about where they live. They note down the order in which places a–f (*dans une petite ville, dans une grande ville*, etc.) are mentioned.
• They also note whether each speaker likes where they live.

Answers: 1 b; 2 c, d; 3 a, f; 4 c, e; 5 c, f
Speakers 1, 3, 4 and 5 like where they live.

 Video clip 8   page 68, activité 1

> – Bonjour! Aujourd'hui... on parle de là où tu habites... Tu habites où? En ville? À la campagne? Dans un village?
> 1 – Tu habites où?
>   – J'habite dans une grande ville. C'est super!
> 2 – Tu habites où?
>   – J'habite dans un village, à la campagne. C'est nul!
> 3 – J'habite dans une petite ville, au bord de la mer. J'aime bien.
> 4 – Tu habites où?
>   – J'habite dans un village, à la montagne. C'est génial!
> 5 – J'habite dans un petit village au bord de la mer. Moi, j'adore!

Follow-up: Ask students to rate the places mentioned on the video on a scale of 1–6. Which would be their favourite place to live? And their least favourite?

2 À deux. (B ➤ A)

- Students take turns to throw a die and say a sentence corresponding to photos 1–6 and the number they have thrown, e.g. (student throws a 3) *J'habite dans un village.*
- The first student to throw all six numbers and say all six sentences correctly is the winner.
- Point out the note about pronunciation and emphasise that students must say the sentences correctly in order to win.

 3 Relie et vérifie.

- Students read the four sentences about where the teenagers live. They match each sentence to a photo, then listen to the recording to check their answers.

Answers: Suzie: C (Amiens); Léo: A (Tusson); Anya: D (Sanary); Éric: B (Bellefontaine)

CD 2, track 24   page 68, activité 3

– Salut! Je suis Suzie. J'habite à Amiens. Amiens, c'est une grande ville. Amiens, c'est super!

– Bonjour, moi, je suis Léo. J'habite à Tusson. Tusson, c'est un village à la campagne. Tusson, c'est nul!

– Salut. Je m'appelle Anya. J'habite à Sanary. C'est une petite ville au bord de la mer. Sanary, moi, j'adore!

– Bonjour! Moi, je m'appelle Éric. J'habite à Blllefontaine. C'est un village à la montagne. C'est génial!

Follow-up: Play the recording again and ask students to note the opinions.

4 Et toi?

- Students write about where they live, including their opinion.

 5 Décris.

This activity could replace task B in a Grade 2 Asset Languages teacher assessment.
- Students select adjectives to go with each photo. (Accept any appropriate answers for *beau*.)

Answers: 1 grand, moderne, beau; 2 ancien; 3 grand, ancien, beau; 4 moderne, beau; 5 ancien; 6 petit, moderne

6 Relie. Vérifie.

- Students read six teenagers' descriptions of where they live.
- They match each description to a photo in ex. 5, then listen to the recording to check their answers.

Answers: 1 Simon; 2 Éric; 3 Jez; 4 Anya; 5 Suzie; 6 Alex

 CD 2, track 25   page 69, activité 6

– Éric, tu habites dans une maison ou un appartement?
– J'habite dans une maison.
– C'est comment?
– Ma maison est belle et ancienne. C'est la maison numéro 2.

– Suzie, tu habites dans une maison ou un appartement?
– J'habite dans un appartement.
– C'est comment?
– Mon appartement est petit et assez ancien. C'est l'appartement numéro 5.

– Alex, tu habites dans une maison ou un appartement?
– J'habite dans une maison.
– C'est comment?
– Ma maison est petite et moderne. C'est la maison numéro 6.

– Jez, tu habites dans une maison ou un appartement?
– J'habite dans une maison.
– C'est comment?
– Ma maison est grande et ancienne. C'est la maison numéro 3.

– Anya, tu habites dans une maison ou un appartement?
– J'habite dans un appartement.
– C'est comment?
– Mon appartement est beau, grand et moderne. C'est l'appartement numéro 4.

– Simon, tu habites dans une maison ou un appartement?
– J'habite dans une maison.
– C'est comment?
– Ma maison est belle, assez grande et moderne. C'est la maison numéro 1.

---

 7 À deux. (B ➤ A)

This activity would be suitable as part of preparation for external assessment at Breakthrough stage.

- Students ask and answer basic questions about where they live, following the model question-and-answer sequence provided.

Follow-up: Students make up similar mini-conversations based on the photos on this spread.

8 Grammaire: choisis des adjectifs.

- Students choose the correct forms of the adjectives to describe each noun in the list, supported by the grammar notes on adjective endings.
- Accept any appropriate adjectives for each noun, as long as they correspond with the gender of the noun.

AT 4.2 **Follow-up**: Students refer back to the adjectives they selected to describe the photos in ex. 5. They describe each house or flat using the correct masculine or feminine forms of the adjectives. (Accept any appropriate suggestions for *beau/belle*.)

Model answers:
Numéro 1: J'habite dans une maison. Elle est grande, moderne et belle.
Numéro 2: J'habite dans une maison. Elle est ancienne.
Numéro 3: J'habite dans une maison. Elle est grande, ancienne et belle.
Numéro 4: J'habite dans un appartement. Il est moderne et beau.
Numéro 5: J'habite dans un appartement. Il est ancien.
Numéro 6: J'habite dans une maison. Elle est petite et moderne.

AT 4.2–3 **Défi!**

- Students write four sentences about where they live, following the model provided.

C41 Ex. 1 and 2 on Copymaster 41 are listening activities on home and home area.

W 50–51 Pages 50–51 of the *En solo* Workbook provide further activities to practise the language of this spread.

4.3   C'est comment, chez toi?

Planner

➢ **Objectives**
- Flats and houses

➢ **Resources**
Students' Book, pages 70–71
CD 2, tracks 26–28
En solo Workbook, pages 52–53;
En solo CD, track 34
Copymasters 39, 40, 44

➢ **Key language**
Chez moi, il y a...
une pièce, une chambre, une cuisine, une salle à manger, une salle de bains, une douche, une piscine un salon, un bureau, un garage, un jardin, un balcon des toilettes

la maison de mes rêves
au rez-de-chaussée, au premier étage

vieux (vieille)

➢ **Grammar**
Agreement of adjectives (masculine/feminine/plural)

➢ **Framework reference**
R – 7W1, 7T5

➢ **Starters**
- Students play a memory game in groups or as a class:
  Student A: *Chez moi, il y a un salon.*
  Student B: *Chez moi, il y a un salon et une salle de bains.*
  Student C: *Chez moi, il y a un salon, une salle de bains et...,* etc.
- For this activity, you will need to prepare a set of small blue and red (or pink) cards. Each student in the class will need one blue card and one red card.
  Before working on plural forms of adjectives (page 71), brainstorm adjectives students have learned so far that could be used to describe where you live, e.g. *moderne, ancien, grand, petit, beau*. Call out each one in its masculine or feminine form. Students stand up. They hold up a blue card when they hear a masculine adjective, a red card when they hear a feminine adjective, and both cards together when

the adjective could be either masculine or feminine.
- Copymaster 39 *À tes marques!* ex. 2.

➢ **Plenaries**
- Divide the class into two teams. Write *Chez moi* on the board in large letters, and a set of six boxes containing the following elements:
  – *il y a*
  – names of rooms, e.g. *un salon, une salle à manger*, etc.
  – *au rez-de-chaussée, au premier étage*
  – adjectives, e.g. *grand/grande, moderne, petit/petite*, etc.
  – *assez, très*
  – *et, mais*
  Challenge the teams to build a long sentence by taking turns to choose extra words/phrases. For example:
  Team A: *Chez moi, il y a...*
  Team B: *Chez moi, il y a un salon.*
  Team A: *Chez moi, au rez-de-chaussée, il y a un salon.*
  Team B: *Chez moi, au rez-de-chaussée, il y a un grand salon.*
  Team A: *Chez moi, au rez-de-chaussée, il y a un très grand salon.*
  Team B: *Chez moi, au rez-de-chaussée, il y a un très grand salon et...*
  This activity is ideal for use with an interactive whiteboard, especially if a drag-and-drop function is available, since it allows students to physically move the words around on-screen.
- Students choose the odd-one-out from several groups of words taken from Unit 4, e.g.
  – *grands, modernes, petite, vieux* (*vieux* because you can't tell whether it's masculine singular or masculine plural, *petite* because it's the only feminine singular, *modernes* because you can't tell whether it is masculine or feminine)
  – *salle de bains, chambre, cuisine, jardin* (*jardin* because it's masculine, or because it isn't a room)
  – *maison, appartement, salle de bains* (*appartement* because it's masculine, *salle de bains* because it isn't a type of residence)
  – *piscine, balcon, toilettes* (*balcon* because it's the only masculine noun, *toilettes* because it's the only plural or because it's the only essential feature of a house – the others are luxuries)
- Copymaster 40 *Bilan de leçon* ex. 1.

This page is based on the idea of The Sims computer games. A budget of 24,000 euros is available to spend on features for an ideal home. Ask students to suggest other features they might want to buy in addition to those mentioned here, e.g. *une salle de gym, une salle de jeux, un bar, un sauna, un Jacuzzi, un héliport pour le hélicoptère.*

AT 1.1

1 Note les prix.
- Students list items 1–12 from the key language panel.
- Play the recording. Beside each item in their list, students note down the price.

Answers: see transcript

CD 2, track 26   page 70, activité 1

1 une chambre… 2000 euros
2 une cuisine… 3000 euros
3 un salon… 3000 euros
4 une salle à manger… 2000 euros
5 une salle de bains… 2000 euros
6 une douche… 1000 euros
7 des toilettes… 1000 euros
8 un bureau… 2000 euros
9 un garage… 1000 euros
10 un jardin… 3000 euros
11 un balcon… 1000 euros
12 une piscine… 4000 euros

AT 1.2 **2a Écoute. Note les pièces.**

- Luc, Sophie and Lola each describe their ideal home. Students listen and note down the numbers (from the house plan on page 70 of the Students' Book) of the rooms and features they mention.

Answers: <u>Luc</u>: 10, 12, 9, 1, 3, 11, 2, 5, 7; <u>Sophie</u>: 10, 12, 9, 8, 1, 3, 11, 2, 4, 5, 6, 7; <u>Lola</u>: 5 (x 3), 6, 7, 1 (x 3), 2, 3, 11, 4, 11, 8, 11

 CD 2, track 27   page 70, activité 2a

– Luc, elle est comment, la maison de tes rêves?
– Au rez-de-chaussée, il y a un jardin avec une piscine et un garage. Au premier étage, il y a trois pièces: une chambre, un salon avec un balcon et une cuisine. Il y a aussi une salle de bains et des toilettes.

– Sophie, elle est comment, la maison de tes rêves?
– Dans ma maison, au rez-de-chaussée, il y a un jardin avec une piscine, un garage et un bureau. Au premier étage, il y a quatre pièces: une chambre avec un balcon, un salon, une cuisine et une salle à manger. Il y a aussi une salle de bains, une douche et des toilettes.

– Lola, elle est comment, la maison de tes rêves?
– Moi, je préfère un appartement. Dans mon appartement, il y a sept pièces, trois salles de bains, une douche et des toilettes. Il y a trois chambres, une cuisine, un salon avec un balcon, une salle à manger avec un balcon et un bureau avec un balcon. J'adore les balcons!

Follow-up: Students use their answers from ex. 1 and 2a to calculate the cost of each teenager's ideal home. Tell them that only one home will be within budget (bearing in mind that the budget is 24,000 euros): which one is it?

Answers:
<u>Luc</u>: 3000 + 4000 + 1000 + 2000 + 3000 + 1000 + 3000 + 2000 + 1000 = 20 000 euros

<u>Sophie</u>: 3000 + 4000 + 1000 + 2000 + 2000 + 3000 + 1000 + 3000 + 2000 + 2000 + 1000 + 1000 = 25 000 euros
<u>Lola</u>: 2000 (x 3) + 1000 + 1000 + 2000 (x 3) + 3000 + 3000 + 1000 + 2000 + 1000 + 2000 + 1000 = 27 000 euros (Lola and Sophie's houses are over budget)

2b Qui choisit la maison?

- Students use their answers from ex. 2a to work out which teenager would choose the house pictured on page 70.

Answer: Sophie

AT 2.2 **3 À deux! (B → A)**

- Each student sketches a rough plan of their ideal home (or their actual house/flat) within a budget of 24,000 euros.
- They read out the rooms and features to their partner, saying what is on the ground floor and what is on the first floor. Model sentences are provided.
- Their partner listens carefully and sketches out a plan of the building. Students then check each other's sketches to see how accurate they are.

AT 1.3
AT 3.3

4a Où habite Lucie? Et Jean? (1–4)

- Students read and listen to the two texts. They work out which picture (1–4) shows Lucie's home and which shows Jean's home.

Answers: 1 Lucie; 3 Jean

 CD 2, track 28   page 71, activité 4a

– J'habite dans un lotissement au bord de la mer. J'aime beaucoup habiter ici: les maisons sont <u>modernes</u>. Ma maison est très très <u>belle</u>. Les pièces sont <u>grandes</u>. Au rez-de-chaussée, il y a une <u>grande</u> cuisine, deux <u>petits</u> salons et une <u>grande</u> salle à manger. Au premier étage, il y a quatre <u>grandes</u> chambres et deux <u>petites</u> salles de bains.

– J'habite dans un appartement en ville. Je n'aime pas beaucoup chez moi. L'immeuble est très <u>vieux</u>! Les appartements sont <u>vieux</u>, ils sont <u>petits</u> et ils ne sont pas <u>beaux</u>! Il n'y a pas de balcon! Les chambres sont trop <u>petites</u>! La cuisine et la salle de bains sont <u>vieilles</u> et elles ne sont pas <u>belles</u>! La douche est très <u>vieille</u>! Je rêve d'habiter dans une maison super <u>moderne</u> avec un jardin et une piscine!

AT 3.3 **4b Décris en anglais.**

- Students describe in English what Lucie and Jean say about their homes.

Answers:
<u>Lucie</u>: She lives on a residential estate by the sea. She likes it: the houses are very modern. Her own house is beautiful. The rooms are big. On the ground floor, there's a large kitchen, two small living rooms and a large dining room. On the first floor, there are

four large bedrooms and two small bathrooms.

Jean: He lives in a flat in town. He doesn't like it. The block of flats is very old. The flats are old, small and not very nice. There's no balcony. The bedrooms are too small; the kitchen and bathroom are old and aren't very nice; the shower is very old. He dreams of living in a very modern house with a garden and a swimming pool.

Follow-up: More able students could describe the other two pictures, 2 and 4. They will need to invent details such as rooms and features.

5a Grammaire: compte!

* Students find 18 adjectives in Lucie's and Jean's texts. They translate them into English and explain why their endings are different.
* Point out the grammar notes on adjective endings.

Answers: see underlining in the transcript for ex. 4a.

 ### 5b Fais des paires.

* Students make matching pairs with the adjectives from ex. 5a.
* They may pair them in any way they wish, as long as they provide a logical explanation. For example, they could match opposites (*grandes/petites*), or they could match masculine singular adjectives to their corresponding feminine singular (*vieux/ vieille*), or they could match singular and plural forms of the same adjective (*moderne/modernes*).

Défi!

* Students describe their own home or ideal home using at least six adjectives (two masculine, two feminine and two plural).

 Follow-up: For further practice with plural forms of adjectives, display the following "adjective maths" puzzle:

Exemple: une grande chambre 3 2 = deux grandes chambres
un petit salon 3 2 = ?
un beau jardin 3 2 = ?
une vieille douche 3 2 = ?
un vieux garage 3 2 = ?
Students rewrite the sentences with the nouns and adjectives in their plural forms.

Answers: deux grandes chambres; deux petits salons; deux beaux jardins; deux vieilles douches; deux vieux garages

 Additional reading/writing activities on the theme of property descriptions are provided on Copymaster 44.

Pages 52–53 of the *En solo* Workbook provide further activities to practise rooms/features of a house.

4.4 Dans ma chambre

Planner

➤ **Objectives**
- Things in your bedroom

➤ **Resources**
Students' Book, pages 72–73
CD 2, tracks 29–30
En solo Workbook, pages 54–55;
En solo CD, track 35
Copymasters 39, 40, 42, 43

➤ **Key language**
un lit, un bureau, un tableau, un miroir, un tapis
une chaise, une armoire, une table, une table de
chevet, une lampe, une moquette
des rideaux
le mur, le plancher, la porte, la fenêtre

simple, confortable
assez, très, trop

➤ **Grammar**
Position of adjectives

➤ **Framework reference**
R – 7W1, 7S6, 7T5

➤ **Starters**
- Students name the colours they see in the Van Gogh painting.
- Play Hangman to practise furniture items.

- Speed duel. Two students stand up. Call out a colour in English. The pair compete to say a phrase containing the colour, e.g. Yellow! – *Un lit jaune!*
The first student to say a correct phrase is the winner. The other student sits down and another challenger stands up to take his/her place.
To increase the difficulty, call out two adjectives and/or ask students to form a complete sentence instead of a short phrase, e.g. Small, modern! – *J'aime ma petite chambre moderne!*
- Copymaster 39 *À tes marques!* ex. 3.

➤ **Plenaries**
- Divide the class into small groups. Call out an adjective. Members of each group collaborate to make up a sentence showing whether the adjective goes before or after the noun and what the endings are, e.g.
Teacher: *Bleu!*
Students: *Il y a une armoire bleue, un miroir bleu, des rideaux bleus et deux chaises bleues.*
Continue with a few more adjectives. The group with the greatest number of correct sentences is the winner.
- In pairs or groups, students draw out a mind map on the theme of *Chez moi*, summarising everything they have learned in Unit 4. Key topics: *Ma région. Le temps. Ma ville/Mon village. Ma maison/Mon appartement. Ma chambre. Opinions.* Allow time for feedback with the whole class.
- Copymaster 40 *Bilan de leçon* ex. 2.

 1a Qu'est-ce qu'il y a dans la chambre de Van Gogh?

This activity could replace task B in a Grade 1 Asset Languages teacher assessment.
- Begin by revising colours: ask students to name all the colours they see in the Van Gogh painting.
- Students then list the key language items that appear in Van Gogh's room.

Answers: 1 a (un lit); 2 b (une table); 3 d (une chaise); 4 h (un miroir); 5 i (un tableau)

 1b Écoute et vérifie.
- Students listen to the recording to check their answers to 1a.

 CD 2, track 29   page 72, activité 1b

Ah… bonjour! Ça va? Je m'appelle Vincent, Vincent Van Gogh. Je suis peintre. Je suis hollandais mais j'habite à Arles, une petite ville en Provence, dans le sud de la France.

J'habite dans une maison ancienne, en ville. Voici ma chambre! Alors, qu'est-ce qu'il y a dans ma chambre?

Dans ma chambre, il y a un lit (c'est le numéro 1), une table (numéro 2), deux chaises (numéro 3), un miroir (numéro 4) et des tableaux (numéro 5). Et voilà!

Mais dans ma chambre, il n'y a pas tout! Voici ce qu'il n'y a pas: alors, une armoire, une table de chevet, une lampe, un bureau, des rideaux, une moquette et un tapis…

Mais j'aime bien ma chambre: elle est simple et assez confortable… et elle est très belle, non? J'adore les couleurs de ma chambre!

Follow-up:
- Ask students some *vrai/faux* questions about the recording and the painting, e.g. *Van Gogh a une armoire* (faux); *Il n'a pas de tapis* (vrai); *Le lit est jaune* (vrai); *Il y a trois chaises* (faux); *Il n'aime pas sa chambre* (faux).

- Focus on the word *mais* in Van Gogh's speech bubble and use it as an opportunity to highlight the importance of linking words in building more complex sentences. Encourage students to use *et* and *mais* in their own descriptions in ex. 7, e.g. *Dans ma chambre, il y a... et... mais il n'y a pas de...*

2 Donne ton opinion.

- Students use the model sentences and adjectives provided to help them express their opinion of Van Gogh's room.
- Encourage students to use the words *assez, très* and *trop*, as in the examples.
- Students could work on this in pairs, then compare their opinions with those of another pair. They decide whose sentences are the best in terms of accuracy, interest, variety, etc. This type of activity exemplifies Assessment for Learning (AfL) (see page 14 of the Introduction).

3 Écoute et choisis.

- Students listen to another description of Van Gogh's room, this time with adjectives added. They complete the gap-fill text using the adjectives provided.
- Alternatively, students try to fill in the gaps before listening to the recording. They should be able to do this using their knowledge of adjective agreement. Once students have filled in the gaps, play the recording so that they can check their answers.
- All the adjectives needed are provided as support, but make sure students realise they have to choose the correct form of the adjective in each case.

Answers: 1 bleus; 2 bleues; 3 vieux; 4 marron; 5 grande; 6 verte; 7 petit; 8 jaune; 9 petite; 10 confortable

---

CD 2, track 30   page 73, activité 3

– Vincent, qu'est-ce qu'il y a dans ta chambre?
– Alors, dans ma chambre, il y a des murs bleus et deux portes bleues. Il y a un vieux plancher marron. Il y a une grande fenêtre verte. Il y a un petit lit jaune. J'aime bien ma chambre. C'est une petite chambre confortable.

---

4 Grammaire: écris.

- Students rewrite phrases a–d with the words in the correct order.

Answers: a une petite chambre confortable; b une grande table bleue; c une vieille armoire jaune; d un beau tableau vert et rouge

5 "Vincent, qu'est-ce qu'il y a dans ta chambre maintenant?" Décris.

This activity could replace task A or B in a Grade 2 Asset Languages teacher assessment.

- Students write a description of the modern-day version of Van Gogh's room.
- Encourage them to use a variety of adjectives, together with *assez, très* and *trop*, and some opinions, to add interest and variety to their writing.

6 À deux: discutez.

- Students work in pairs to invent their own modern-day version of Van Gogh's bedroom. First, they need to agree on the furniture and colours: a model dicussion is provided in the Students' Book. They then draw/colour the room and write sentences to describe it.

7 Dessine et décris ta chambre.

- Students draw and describe their own room or their ideal room.

Copymaster 42 provides speaking activities on the language of the whole unit, including information and opinions about home area, house/flat and own room. Additional reading/writing activities based on bedroom descriptions are provided on Copymaster 43.

Pages 54–55 of the *En solo* Workbook provide further activities to practise bedroom furniture and colours.

Labo-langue

Planner

> **Objectives**
> * Adjectives
> * How to listen well
> * Adjective endings

> **Resources**
> Students' Book, pages 74–75
> CD 2, tracks 31–33
> *En solo* Workbook, pages 56–57, 59
> Copymasters 45, 46, 47; CD 2, tracks 41–43

> **Framework reference**
> R – 7W4, 7S1, 7S2 (via Workbook), 7L2

Bien comprendre!

Adjectives

 These grammar notes focus on the position of adjectives and adjective endings. After working through the grammar explanations, students complete the activities.

1 Copy the sentences, adding the adjectives in the right place.

Answers: a C'est une petite prof blonde. b Il y a des belles maisons roses. c J'ai tros gros chiens noirs.

2 Copy the sentences, adding the adjectives in the right form and right place.

Answers: a Il y a trois grandes chambres. b J'ai deux bonnes copines. c Il y a des vieux rideaux bleus.

C45 Copymaster 45 could be used at this point. It focuses on masculine and feminine singular and plural forms of adjectives.

W 56–57 Pages 56–57 of the *En solo* Workbook provide further activities to practise adjectives.

Bien apprendre!

How to listen well

This section helps students to identify good practice in listening and develop listening strategies.

1 Decide what you feel (grade 5–1) about what Toto says on the right.

* Students reflect on listening activities in French. How easy do they find them? How well are they able to concentrate? What do they find helps? Have they developed any strategies to help them cope in listening activities?

 2 Discuss with a partner. Then recap with the teacher in class. What can you do to improve your listening skills?

* Talk about the strategies listed in the Students' Book and try to give some examples of how they might help. For example, point out that it is often possible to predict the sort of language that will come up in a listening activity by reading the question carefully: if the question mentions where someone lives, you know you might hear language related to home area, houses/flats, rooms, and maybe some furniture.

C46 Copymaster 46 provides additional activities to practise these listening strategies.

W59 Further language learning strategies are provided on page 59 of the *En solo* Workbook, which could be used at any appropriate point during Unit 4:

* *Vocabulary*: expressions that are different in English and French; why word-for-word translations don't always work
* *Autonomous learning*: tips on how to practise French outside class

Bien parler!

Adjective endings

1 Listen. Who is Toto's penpal, A or B?

* *Aim*: To raise awareness of how knowledge of grammar and pronunciation can help to work out meaning.
* Make sure students realise that the key to this activity lies in focusing on the adjective endings in the spoken description. The adjectives are masculine, so Toto's penpal must be male.

Answer: A

 CD 2, track 31   page 75, Bien parler! activité 1

– Toto, voici la photo de Micka. Micka est petit et blond.
– Petit et blond? Oh non…! Moi, je préfère petite et blonde!

2 Listen (1–20). Is it masculine (M) or feminine (F)?

Answers: 1 M; 2 F; 3 M; 4 M; 5 M; 6 F; 7 F; 8 M; 9 F; 10 F; 11 F; 12 M; 13 F; 14 M; 15 F; 16 M; 17 F; 18 M; 19 M; 20 M

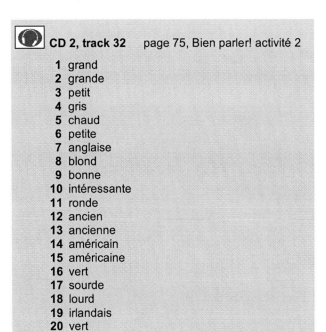

CD 2, track 32   page 75, Bien parler! activité 2

1 grand
2 grande
3 petit
4 gris
5 chaud
6 petite
7 anglaise
8 blond
9 bonne
10 intéressante
11 ronde
12 ancien
13 ancienne
14 américain
15 américaine
16 vert
17 sourde
18 lourd
19 irlandais
20 vert

3 Listen to these adjectives. What do you notice?

- Students listen while looking at three sets of adjectives, which are shown in their masculine and feminine singular and plural forms.
- They focus on the sound of the words compared to their spelling: all the words sound the same even though they have different endings.

CD 2, track 33   page 75, Bien parler! activité 3

1 bleu – bleue – bleus – bleues
2 clair – claire – clairs – claires
3 équipé – équipée – équipés – équipées

Follow-up:

- Ask students to think of other adjectives they have met so far that could be added to the lists in ex. 3, e.g. *préféré, nul*.
- Point out that some adjectives are invariable (e.g. *super, cool, marron*), and others have only a singular and a plural form but don't change in the feminine (e.g. *confortable, moderne, simple, rouge*), so these will always sound the same too.

 C47 Copymaster 47 provides further pronunciation practice focusing on adjective endings.

Blog-notes

Planner

▷ Objectives

- To summarise the main points of the unit in context, in a format that is fun and familiar to students, i.e. a video blog
- To provide a model enabling students to personalise the language of the unit
- To provide opportunities for students to ask as well as answer questions
- To provide extended listening practice recycling the language of the whole unit

▷ Resources

Students' Book, page 76
Video clip 9
En solo Workbook, page 58;
En solo CD, track 36
Copymaster 38

▷ Framework reference

R – 7T6, 7C3

AT 1.3

1 Regarde le vidéo-blog. Choisis 1 ou 2.

- Students watch Manon's video diary and choose 1 or 2 in answer to questions about her home. Pause the video after each section to allow pupils time to answer.

Answers: a 2; b 2; c 1; d 1; e 1; f 1; g 2, 1; h 1

▶ Video clip 9   page 76, activité 1

– Salut! Bienvenue sur mon vidéo-blog! Et bienvenue chez moi!
Je m'appelle Manon! J'ai 12 ans et je suis française.
a Mon pays, c'est la France. Ma région s'appelle les Pays de la Loire. Ici.
b Et les Pays de la Loire, c'est ici... dans l'ouest de la France. Et toi? Comment s'appelle ta région? C'est où?
c Bon, aujourd'hui, il fait très beau! Il n'y a pas de nuages, et il fait chaud. Quel temps fait-il chez toi?
d Moi, j'habite en ville, à Pornichet. Pornichet, c'est une petite ville, au bord de la mer. Et toi, tu habites en ville ou à la campagne?
e J'aime beaucoup habiter ici! C'est super! À côté de Pornichet, il y a une assez grande ville: c'est Nantes. J'adore Nantes! Oui, moi, j'aime beaucoup habiter ici. Et toi, tu aimes là où tu habites?
f J'habite dans une maison au bord de la mer. Elle est assez grande et assez moderne. Au rez-de-chaussée, il y a une cuisine... des toilettes... un salon-salle à manger... Au premier étage, il y a deux grandes chambres... et deux petites chambres et une salle de bains. Il y a aussi un garage et un jardin, mais le jardin est assez petit. Et chez toi, c'est comment?
g Comment est la maison de tes rêves? Moi, la maison de mes rêves, c'est une grande maison moderne, au bord de la mer. Il y a un grand jardin, et une piscine, bien sûr! Les chambres sont grandes, très grandes, et très confortables!

---

h Regarde ma chambre! Elle est assez petite.
i Qu'est-ce qu'il y a dans ma chambre? Et bien, il y a un lit bien sûr, un bureau, une chaise, des étagères. Qu'est-ce qu'il y a dans ta chambre, à toi?
– Manon, tu es prête? Tu as rangé ta chambre? On t'attend!
Oh là là! C'est maman! Bon, j'y vais... Je range ma chambre!! Salut!

AT 4.3 **2 À toi de répondre!**

- Students write their own answers to questions a–h.

Follow-up:

These activities may be suitable for more able students only:

- Students interview each other using questions a–h.
- Students use their answers from ex. 2 to help them write their own blog. If the appropriate technology is available, allow students to record their own video blogs and play them to the class.

C38
W58

A checklist summarising the language of the unit is provided on Copymaster 38 and on page 58 of the *En solo* Workbook. It could be used in tandem with the *Blog-notes* page or at an appropriate point towards the end of the unit. It provides an opportunity for students to review what they have learned and reflect on areas for improvement.

Tu sais tout?

Planner

The page is divided into four sections: listening, speaking, reading and writing. Each section can be marked out of 5 to give a total score out of 20.

> **Objectives**
> • To enable students to recap on the language and structures of the unit
> • To provide an opportunity for quick testing of all four skills

> **Resources**
> Students' Book, page 77
> CD 2, track 35

| AT 1.2 | **1 Listen and match. Who lives…?**

This activity would be suitable as part of preparation for external assessment at Breakthrough stage.

Answers: 1 f; 2 d; 3 b; 4 e; 5 a; 6 c

 CD 2, track 35　　　　page 77, activité 1

– Tu habites où?
1　J'habite dans un petit appartement, à Lyon. Lyon, c'est une grande ville.
2　Moi, j'habite dans un petit appartement dans un village.
3　J'habite dans un appartement moderne dans une petite ville.
4　J'habite dans une grande maison à la campagne.
5　J'habite dans une petite maison à Carnac, au bord de la mer.
6　J'habite dans une vieille maison à l'Alpe d'Huez, à la montagne.

| AT 3.2 | **2 Read the description and look at the picture. Spot six differences.**

Answers: In the picture: 1 the carpet is brown, not blue; 2 there are no curtains; 3 there is no bedside table; 4 there is no chair; 5 the lamp is small, not large; 6 there is no mirror on the wardrobe door

---

| AT 4.2 | **3 Write the weather report.**

Answers: Dans le centre, il fait froid. Dans le nord, il neige. Dans l'est, il y a du brouillard. Dans le sud, il pleut. Dans l'ouest, il y a des nuages.

| AT 2.2 | **4 Complete these sentences to speak about yourself.**

• Students use the sentence beginnings as prompts to help them talk about their own home and region.

En plus

Planner

> **Objectives**
> * To provide extension material for more able students who are confident with the core language of the unit, and to introduce new language where appropriate
> * To provide alternative class and homework material for students who finish other activities quickly

> **Resources**
> Students' Book, page 78
> CD 2, track 36

> **Key language**
> *devant, derrière, entre, sur, sous, dans*

C'est où?

This page introduces six additional prepositions of place and reinforces furniture vocabulary.

| AT 1.3 | **1 Écoute.** |

* Students listen to the recording: a mobile phone is ringing and a boy and girl are trying to find it. Students choose a picture to represent each place where they look.

Answers: 1 c; 2 d; 3 b; 4 f; 5 a; 6 e

CD 2, track 36   page 78, activité 1

1 – Où est mon portable?
  – Il est sur le bureau!
  – Non, il n'est pas là.
2 – Ah, où est mon portable?
  – Ben… il est sous le lit!
  – Non, il n'est pas là.
3 – Ah, où est mon portable?
  – Pfff… il est devant l'ordinateur!
  – Non, il n'est pas là.
4 – Ah là là, où est mon portable?
  – Il est derrière les rideaux!
  – Non, il n'est pas là.
5 – Grrrrrr, où est mon portable?
  – Oh là là, il est entre le bureau et l'armoire!
  – Non, non, non, il n'est pas là.
6 – Mais où est mon portable?!
  – Je sais! Il est dans l'armoire!
  – Oui! Il est dans l'armoire! Allô! Allô! Allô! Oh non!

---

2 Réécoute.

* Students listen again and list the prepositions in the order they hear them.

Answers: 1 b; 2 c; 3 e; 4 d; 5 f; 6 a

| AT 3.3 | **3 Complète.** |

* Referring to the bedroom picture, students fill the gap in each sentence with a suitable preposition to describe the layout of the room.

Answers: 1 sous; 2 sur; 3 devant; 4 derrière; 5 dans; 6 entre

| AT 4.3 | **4 Décris ta chambre.** |

* Students write six sentences describing the layout of their own (or an imaginary) bedroom. They receive a point for each correct sentence, and a bonus point for each preposition used.

Clic.fr

Planner

> **Objectives**
> • To raise awareness of France and French culture
> • To promote intercultural understanding by providing opportunities to compare French culture with students' own culture

> **Resources**
> Students' Book, page 49
> Copymaster 48

> **Framework reference**
> **R** – 7C1

Les régions de la France

This page provides key geographical facts in English about areas of France, e.g. climate, altitude, population, etc

| AT 3.2 | **1 Which places are these?** |

Answers: a Toulon; b Bourg-Saint-Maurice; c l'Alsace; d le Luberon; e Biarritz; f le Jura; g Midi-Pyrénées; h Ajaccio

Follow-up:

• Students take turns to tell each other facts about places on the map. Their partner works out which place they are referring to. Encourage them to give the location of each place as well as its name, e.g.
Student A: *Ici, il pleut!*
Student B: *C'est Biarritz, dans le sud-ouest de la France!... Ici, il fait froid!*
Student A: *C'est le Jura...*

• Students make a similar map of their own country, with captions giving key information about selected places. This could be used in a classroom display, or sent to a partner school.

| C48 | Additional activities on the geography and features of France are provided on Copymaster 48. |

Vocabulaire

Planner

> ### Objectives
>   • *Vocabulaire*: to provide a theme-based summary of the key language of the unit, which students can use as a reference or as an aid to learning
>   • To develop language learning strategies
>   • *On chante!*: to reinforce the language of the unit in a fun way

> ### Resources
> Students' Book, pages 80–81
> CD 2, track 37
> *En solo* Workbook, pages 60–61;
> *En solo* CD, track 37
> Copymaster 37

> ### Framework reference
> **R** – 7W2, 7C4

A list of key language from the unit, with associated activities, is also provided on Copymaster 37 and on pages 60–61 of the *En solo* Workbook.

A few words can go a long way!

• *Aim*: To highlight the importance of knowing high-frequency words that can be reapplied in different contexts.

• Students search pages 80–81 for six words/phrases that can be used only to speak about the weather, then for three words that can be used in any context.

Answers: A any six weather phrases; B assez, très, trop

On chante!

AT 2.2 **1 Chante avec le CD!**

AT 1.2 • Students listen to the song while reading the lyrics. Encourage them to join in.

AT 3.2

 CD 2, track 37   page 81, activité 1

Viens chez moi!

Sur la Terre, il y a un pays
C'est la France, où j'habite!
C'est la France, où j'habite!
Viens chez moi, je t'invite!

Dans mon pays, il y a une ville
C'est Paris, où j'habite!
C'est Paris, où j'habite!
Viens chez moi, je t'invite!

Dans ma ville, il y a une rue
C'est Belleville, où j'habite!
C'est Belleville, où j'habite!
Viens chez moi, je t'invite!

Dans ma rue, il y a une maison
C'est la maison, où j'habite!
C'est la maison, où j'habite!
Viens chez moi, je t'invite!

Dans ma maison, il y a une chambre
C'est la chambre, où je suis!
C'est la chambre, où je suis!
Viens chez moi, je t'attends!

AT 3.2 **2 Adapte pour toi!**

• Students adapt the song to give details of where they themselves live.

Follow-up: Students replace the repeated line in each verse (*C'est… où j'habite!*) with an opinion, e.g.

Dans mon pays, il y a une ville
C'est Paris, où j'habite!
J'aime Paris, c'est joli!
Viens chez moi, je t'invite!

Lecture

Planner

> **Objectives**
> * To encourage independent reading and develop reading strategies
> * To provide alternative class and homework material for students who finish other activities quickly

The texts and activities on *Lecture A* should be suitable for all; *Lecture B* is more challenging and may be suitable for more able students only.

> **Resources**
> Students' Book, pages 124–125

> **Framework reference**
> **R** – 7T3, 7C1, 7C2

The reading texts on these pages provide cultural information about life in two different French-speaking areas: the Camargue, in the south-west of France, and Burkina Faso in West Africa.

Lecture A

La Camargue

Before students begin these activities, ask them to look first at the photos: what do the photos tell them about life in the Camargue? What can they work out about this region of France from looking at the photos before they even begin reading the text?

AT 3.3 **1 Read the text. Match each question on the notepad (1–5) with a paragraph (a–e).**

Answers: 1 a; 2 b; 3 e; 4 c; 5 d

AT 3.3 **2 Write a short caption for each photo.**

Answers: A Mon rêve, c'est d'être gardian. B Il y a les gardians, les cowboys de Camargue. C J'habite dans un mas, une maison traditionnelle de Camargue. D Il y a beaucoup d'oiseaux.

3 Find three words specific to the Camargue region.

Answers: *le mistral* (a strong wind that blows through southern France/Provence); *un mas* (a traditional country house or farmhouse); *une manade* (a farm where bulls or horses are raised); *un gardian* (a Camargue cowboy, who works at a *manade*)

 4 Do you think Sylvain will stay in his region? Why?
* Encourage students to think about wider issues that might lead Sylvain to move away from the Camargue, e.g. lack of work and study opportunities in the area, rise of tourism and holiday-home ownership leading to a shortage of housing for local people.

Lecture B

Un village au Burkina Faso

AT 3.3 **1 Read the text. Look at the plan of Nora's home: what are the places numbered 1–8?**

Answers: 1 her father's hut; 2 her father's first wife's hut; 3 her mother's hut (Nora's mother is her father's second wife); 4 her grandmother's hut; 5 the visitors' hut; 6 the hut for boys who are over ten years old; 7 an area for the animals; 8 toilets and showers

AT 3.3 **2 True, false or we don't know?**

Answers: a vrai; b vrai; c on ne sait pas; d faux

3 What do you think are the good and bad things about Nora's village?
* Encourage students to focus on cultural aspects as well as on details such as buildings, facilities, weather, etc.

Copymasters

Feuille 37 Vocabulaire

A list of key language from the unit is provided here as well as on pages 80–81 of the Students' Book and pages 60–61 of the *En solo* Workbook.

Feuille 38 Je sais...

Use this checklist with *Blog-notes* (Students' Book page 76) or towards the end of the unit. It provides an opportunity for students to review what they have learned and reflect on areas for improvement. This checklist is also provided on page 58 of the *En solo* Workbook.

Feuille 39 À vos marques!

These starter activities are intended for use with the following Students' Book pages:

- Use ex. 1 with pages 68–69.
- Use ex. 2 with pages 70–71.
- Use ex. 3 with pages 72–73.

1 Relie les adjectifs aux traductions.

- Students match the French adjectives to the English.
- If this activity is used as a starter with Students' Book pages 68–69, the adjective *confortable* won't yet have been introduced (it is introduced on Students' Book pages 72–73). However, students should be able to cope with it here by a process of elimination and because of its similarity to English.

Answers: 1 c; 2 f; 3 d; 4 e; 5 a; 6 b

2 Trouve les six pièces dans la spirale.

- Students find the names of six rooms in the spiral.

Answers: une cuisine, un salon, des toilettes, un bureau, une chambre, une salle de bains

3a Relie les images aux descriptions.

- Students match the furniture vocabulary to the pictures.

Answers: 1 b; 2 f; 3 c; 4 e; 5 d; 6 a

3b Colorie les objets.

- Students colour in the furniture items to match the descriptions in ex. 3a.

Answers: 1 grey; 2 black; 3 red; 4 pink; 5 green; 6 blue and white

Feuille 40 Bilan de leçon

These plenary activities are intended for use with the following Students' Book pages:

- Use ex. 1 with pages 70–71.
- Use ex. 2 with pages 72–73.
- Use ex. 3 with pages 66–67.

1 Quelle image pour quel mot? Note les lettres (a–h).

- Students match the words to the pictures of features of a house.

Answers: 1 d; 2 f; 3 b; 4 e; 5 g; 6 c; 7 h; 8 a

2 Relie les parties de phrase.

- Students match sentence halves to build a description of a bedroom.

Answers: 1 d; 2 a; 3 c/f; 4 b; 5 e; 6 c/f

3a Regarde la carte A. Quel temps fait-il? Coche les phrases correctes.

- Students look at the weather map of France (A). They compare this with statements 1–8 and tick the statements that are correct.

Answers: the correct statements are: 2, 4, 5

3b Décris le temps pour la carte B.

- Students describe the weather for map B.

Answers: Dans l'ouest, il y a du soleil. Dans le nord, il y a du vent. Dans l'est, il fait chaud. Dans le sud-ouest, il neige.

Feuille 41 Écouter

- Use ex. 1 and 2 with Students' Book pages 68–69.
- Use ex. 3 with Students' Book pages 66–67.

AT 1.2 **1 Écoute. Quelle personne pour quelle image?**

- Students listen to five people saying where they live. They match each speaker to a picture.

Answers: 1 b; 2 a; 3 e; 4 c; 5 d

 CD 2, track 38   Feuille 41, activité 1

1 Moi, j'habite dans une petite maison.
2 J'habite dans un appartement moderne en ville.
3 J'habite dans une grande maison. Elle est très belle.
4 Alors moi, j'habite dans un ancien appartement. J'aime bien.
5 Moi, j'habite dans une belle maison à la campagne.

2 Écoute et coche la bonne réponse.

- Students listen and choose a picture to represent where they lives.

Answers: a big city; b village; c mountains; d seaside; e small town; f countryside

 CD 2, track 39   Feuille 41, activité 2

a Moi, j'habite à Rouen, une grande ville dans le nord-ouest de la France.
b J'habite dans un village, près de Castres dans le sud de la France.
c Salut! J'habite à la montagne dans les Pyrénées. C'est une très belle région.
d J'habite au bord de la mer dans l'ouest de la France.
e J'habite à Aurillac. C'est une petite ville dans le Massif central.
f J'habite à la campagne, en Provence.

 3 Écoute la météo. Coche les cinq images correctes.

- Students listen to the weather forecast and tick the five corresponding weather symbols.

Answers: cold, rain, windy, snow, fog

 CD 2, track 40   Feuille 41, activité 3

Voici la météo. Aujourd'hui, il fait très froid. Il pleut et il y a un peu de vent. À la montagne, il neige et il y a du brouillard…

Feuille 42 Parler

- Use with Students' Book pages 72–73.

 1 Pose à ton/ta partenaire les questions suivantes. Note ses réponses.

 2 Choisis tes réponses et réponds aux questions.

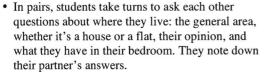
- In pairs, students take turns to ask each other questions about where they live: the general area, whether it's a house or a flat, their opinion, and what they have in their bedroom. They note down their partner's answers.
- Instead of giving real details, the person answering the questions invents the information, using the picture prompts provided.

Feuille 43 Lire et écrire 1

- Use with Students' Book pages 72–73.

 1 Remplis.

- Students label the picture of a bedroom using the vocabulary provided.

Answers: 1 une fenêtre; 2 un ordinateur; 3 un bureau; 4 un poster; 5 une table de chevet; 6 un lit; 7 un tapis; 8 une chaise; 9 un miroir

 2a Lis la description de la chambre d'Aurélie. Lis les phrases a–h: vrai, faux ou pas mentionné?

- Students compare Aurélie's description of her room with statements a–h. They work out whether each statement is true, false or not mentioned in the text.

Answers: a faux; b vrai; c pas mentionné; d faux; e faux; f pas mentionné; g pas mentionné; h faux

2b Corrige les phrases fausses.

- Students correct the false statements from ex. 2a.

Answers: a La chambre est assez grande. d Il y a deux fenêtres. e Le tapis est grand. h Aurélie aime bien sa chambre.

Feuille 44 Lire et écrire 2

- Use with Students' Book pages 70–71.

1 Lis les quatre bulles. Trouve une maison ou un appartement pour chaque personne.

- Students read the details of the type of property each person is looking for. They compare these with the property advertisements and choose a suitable house or flat for each person.

Answers: 1 b; 2 a; 3 d; 4 c

2 Écris ta propre bulle.

- Students imagine they are house-hunting. They write a description of the sort of property they are looking for, similar to the speech bubbles in ex. 1.

Feuille 45 Labo-langue

- Use with Students' Book page 74.

1 Encercle la bonne forme de l'adjectif.

- Students circle the correct form (masculine or feminine) of each adjective.

Answers: a grande; b préférée; c petit; d blanc; e bonne; f belle

2a Mets les adjectifs dans la bonne colonne.

- Students complete the table of masculine and feminine singular and plural adjectives.
- Point out that one of the adjectives can be placed in more than one column.

Answers:

masculine	feminine	plural
bon	belle	beaux (m)
bleu	ronde	petites (f)
moderne	moderne	jolies (f)
		grands (m)

2b Décide si les adjectifs pluriels sont masculins ou féminins.

- Students label the plural adjectives in ex. 2a as masculine or feminine.

Answers: see grid in ex. 2a

2c Tu connais d'autres adjectifs?

- Students add extra adjectives to the grid, taking care to put them in the correct columns.

Feuille 46   Bien apprendre!

- Use with *Bien apprendre!* on Students' Book page 75.

1a Look at the pictures in activity 1b. Then read the list of words and circle the ones you might expect to hear.

- This encourages students to prepare for listening by trying to predict any language they are likely to hear.

Answers: students should circle the words *chien, ville, femme, France, neuf heures, bus*

1b Now listen. What are these people talking about? Tick the right box.

- Students listen and check their predictions from ex. 1a.

Answers: a dog; b France; c nine o'clock

 CD 2, track 41   Feuille 46, activité 1b

a – Tu as un animal?
   – Oui, j'adore les animaux. Moi, j'ai un chien adorable. Il est noir et blanc. J'adore jouer avec mon chien!
b – La Provence, c'est une région de la France dans le sud du pays.
c – Le lundi, à neuf heures, on a maths. Génial! J'aime bien les maths.

2a Look at activity 2b and note down some words that you are likely to hear.

- Students use statements a–f in ex. 2b as clues to help them work out the sort of language they might hear.

2b Listen to Alice. Are statements a–f true or false?

Answers: a vrai; b faux; c vrai; d faux; e faux; f vrai

 CD 2, track 42   Feuille 46, activité 2b

Bonjour! Je vous présente ma région. Ma région, c'est la Normandie. C'est dans le nord-ouest de la France. En été, il fait beau, mais en automne, il pleut. Il y a de belles villes. C'est super!

Feuille 47   Bien parler!

- Use with *Bien parler!* on Students' Book page 75.

1 Listen to Yann describing his bedroom. Circle the adjectives you hear.

Answers: a petite; b gris; c verte; d belle; e grande; f blanche

 CD 2, track 43   Feuille 47, activité 1

a Ma chambre est petite.
b Il y a un bureau gris.
c Il y a aussi une table verte…
d … et une belle chaise.
e À côté du lit, j'ai une grande armoire.
f Et en face de la porte, j'ai une chaise blanche.

 2 In pairs, practise saying each pair of adjectives from activity 1.

3a Now write sentences for six of the adjectives in activity 1. Remember to put the adjective in the right position.

 3b Read your sentences out to your partner who will give you marks out of 5 for your pronunciation!

Feuille 48   Culture

- Use with Students' Book page 79.

1 Complète.

- Students label the map of France using the words and phrases provided.

Answers: 1 les montagnes; 2 au bord de la mer; 3 la capitale; 4 une grande ville; 5 la campagne; 6 une banlieue; 7 l'Angleterre; 8 une petite ville; 9 un village

2 Relie les parties de phrase.

- Students match sentence halves to build statements about the map of France.

Answers: 1 c; 2 a; 3 d; 4 e; 5 b

3 Dessine une carte pour la Grande-Bretagne.

- Students copy a simple outline map of Britain and label it with the captions from ex. 1.

En solo Workbook

Pages 48–49 4.1 Ma région

- Use with Students' Book pages 66–67.

 AT 3.1 **1 Draw lines to match up the symbols and the weather phrases.**

Answers: 1 il fait chaud; 2 il fait froid; 3 il y a des nuages; 4 il y a du vent; 5 il y a du soleil; 6 il y a du brouillard; 7 il y a de l'orage; 8 il neige; 9 il pleut

AT 1.2 **2 Listen to the weather forecast. How should Toto dress? Tick A or B.**

Answer: B

En solo CD, track 31   page 48, activité 2

Bonjour! Aujourd'hui, il fait vraiment beau: il y a un peu de vent mais il n'y a pas de nuages et il ne pleut pas. Il y a du soleil et il fait chaud. Bonne journée!

AT 3.2 **3 Read the weather report. Which is the right map?**

Answer: B

AT 4.2 **4 Complete the weather report for the other map.**

Answers: Dans le nord, il fait froid et il y a du brouillard. Dans l'est, il neige. Dans le sud, il fait chaud et il y a du soleil. Dans l'ouest, il pleut et il y a du vent. Dans le centre, il y a de l'orage.

AT 4.2 **5 Answer the question:** *Quel temps fait-il aujourd'hui dans ta région?* **To help you, first underline useful phrases in the report in activity 3.**

- Students describe the weather today in your own area.

Pages 50–51 4.2 Tu habites où?

- Use with Students' Book pages 68–69.

AT 3.2 **1 Read the speech bubbles (1–6) and match them to the pictures (A–F).**

Answers: 1 F; 2 A; 3 E; 4 C; 5 B; 6 D

AT 4.1 **2 Fill in a speech bubble for this picture.**

Answer: J'habite dans un appartement au bord de la mer.

AT 3.2 **3a Circle the correct words in sentences 1–6 below.**

Answers: see underlining in transcript for 3b

AT 1.2 **3b Listen to check.**

En solo CD, track 32   page 51, activité 3b

1 J'habite dans une maison. Elle est <u>ancienne</u> mais j'aime bien.
2 J'habite dans <u>un appartement</u> en ville. Il est nul parce qu'il est petit.
3 J'habite dans une maison à la campagne. J'aime bien parce qu'elle est <u>belle</u>.
4 J'habite dans un appartement. Je n'aime pas beaucoup parce qu'<u>il</u> est <u>petit</u>.
5 J'habite dans une maison. J'adore ma maison parce qu'elle est très <u>moderne</u>.
6 J'habite dans <u>un appartement</u> dans un village. J'adore parce qu'<u>il</u> est très grand.

AT 1.2 **AT 4.2** **4 Listen and fill in the gaps.**

Answers: see underlining in transcript

En solo CD, track 33   page 51, activité 4

Bonjour! Je <u>m'appelle</u> Julie. J'habite dans un <u>village</u> à la <u>montagne</u>. C'est dans le <u>sud</u> de la France. Il fait <u>beau</u> ici. J'habite dans une <u>maison</u> ancienne. Elle est très <u>belle</u>.

Pages 52–53 4.3 C'est comment, chez toi?

- Use with Students' Book pages 70–71.

AT 1.1 **1 Listen to Toto and tick the parts of his house as you hear him mention them.**

Answers: he mentions all the rooms/features 1–12

En solo CD, track 34   page 52, activité 1

Bienvenue chez moi! Voici le jardin… les chambres… la salle de bains… les toilettes… la salle à manger… la douche… le balcon… la cuisine… le garage… la piscine… le salon… et le bureau! Ouf…

AT 4.1 **2 Look at the picture of Toto's house on page 52. Write the names of the parts of the house here. Then use the letters in the grey squares and discover where Toto is hiding!**

Answers: 1 le jardin; 2 les chambres; 3 la salle de bains; 4 les toilettes; 5 la salle à manger; 6 la douche; 7 le balcon; 8 la cuisine; 9 le garage; 10 la piscine; 11 le salon; 12 le bureau (Toto est dans le bureau)

AT 3.2 **3 Circle the correct adjectives in Toto's description of his house.**

Answers: 1 grand; 2 belle; 3 petites; 4 confortable; 5 vieille

AT 4.1 **4 Draw and label the ideal house for your favourite celebrity.**

• Encourage students to add a few simple sentences using adjectives to describe the rooms, like the sentences in ex. 3 (e.g. *Le salon est confortable*).

Pages 54–55 4.4 Dans ma chambre

• Use with Students' Book pages 72–73.

AT 4.1 **1 Beat the clock. How quickly can you complete the labels?**

Answers: un mur, une porte, une fenêtre, un lit, une table de chevet, une armoire, un bureau, une chaise, une table, un tableau, des rideaux, une moquette

AT 3.2 **2 Read the description and colour in the picture on page 54.**

Answers: white walls, blue door, yellow window, red bed, red bedside table, blue desk, blue chair, white wardrobe, blue/yellow curtains

AT 4.2 **3 Choose colours for the other things in the bedroom and write the description.**

• The remaining items are the table, painting and carpet.

AT 3.2 **4 Read and add to the picture the things that are mentioned.**

Answers: blue/white mirror, small red lamp, small blue/white/red rug

AT 1.2 **5 Listen to Yohann. Is the bedroom on page 54 his?**

Answer: yes

 E solo CD, track 35 page 55, activité 5

Dans ma chambre, il y a des murs blancs et une porte bleue. Il y a une fenêtre jaune. J'ai un lit rouge, une table de chevet rouge, un bureau bleu, une chaise bleue et une armoire blanche. Les rideaux sont bleus et jaunes.
Il y a aussi un miroir bleu et blanc. J'ai une petite lampe rouge et il y a un petit tapis bleu blanc rouge!

AT 4.2–3 **6 Choose a person and imagine their bedroom. Write a short description.**

• Students make up a bedroom description for one of the characters shown, using the texts on this page as a model.

Pages 56–57 Labo-langue

• Use with Students' Book pages 74–75.

1 Do the quiz on adjectives. Circle a, b or c. Explain your choices.

Answers: 1 a (it isn't an adjective); 2 b (*bon* is the masculine form); 3 b (it has a feminine ending); 4 c (it's the feminine form of *blanc*); 5 c (it isn't plural); 6 c (it's masculine and plural); 7 a, c (both can be used with a feminine singular noun); 8 c (because it's masculine and goes before the noun)

2 Find the pairs (masculine/feminine).

Answers: petit, petite; vieux, vieille; grand, grande; blanc, blanche; beau, belle; préféré, préférée; bon, bonne; ancien, ancienne

3 With a red pen, add letters to the adjectives in activity 2 to make them all plural.

Answers: petits, petites; vieux, vieilles; grands, grandes; blancs, blanches; beaux, belles; préférés, préférées; bons, bonnes; anciens, anciennes

4 Use the correct adjective from the box in each sentence.

Answers: 1 belle; 2 bon; 3 blanc; 4 bonne; 5 blanches; 6 beaux

5 Rewrite each sentence in the correct order.

Answers: 1 J'ai un beau chien blanc et noir. 2 J'ai une très bonne copine française. 3 J'habite dans un grand appartement moderne.

Page 58 Checklist

• Use with *Blog-notes* (Students' Book page 76) or towards the end of the unit.

The checklist, recording and follow-up activities provide opportunities for students to review what they have learned, test themselves orally on key language and reflect on areas for improvement.

 En solo CD, track 36 page 58, activité 2

1 My region is Normandy. [*beep*] Ma région, c'est la Normandie.
2 It's in the north. [*beep*] C'est dans le nord.
3 The weather's fine. [*beep*] Il fait beau.
4 It's hot. [*beep*] Il fait chaud.
5 It's windy. [*beep*] Il y a du vent.
6 It's snowing. [*beep*] Il neige.
7 Where do you live? [*beep*] Tu habites où?
8 I live in a village by the sea. [*beep*] J'habite dans un village au bord de la mer.
9 My flat is beautiful. [*beep*] Mon appartement est beau.
10 I live in a big house. [*beep*] J'habite dans une grande maison.
11 There is a dining room and a sitting room. [*beep*] Il y a une salle à manger et un salon.

12 There is a bed and a wardrobe. [*beep*] Il y a un lit et une armoire.

13 The curtains are green. [*beep*] Les rideaux sont verts.

14 I live in a village and it's great, I love it! [*beep*] J'habite dans un village et c'est génial, j'adore!

15 I don't like my house – there's no garden. [*beep*] Je n'aime pas ma maison – il n'y a pas de jardin.

Follow-up: Encourage students to draw up their own individual action plan of steps they could take to help them improve. Provide a checklist of suggestions for them to choose from, e.g. try harder to learn vocabulary, read the grammar notes again and make sure they understand them/ask for help if they don't understand, check written work carefully for mistakes, etc.

Page 59 Top tips and strategies

Vocabulary

This section focuses on expressions that are different in English and French, and shows why word-for-word translations don't always work. It could be used at any appropriate point during Unit 4.

1 Give the literal translation and also the way we say it in English.

Answers: a She has 15 years. (She's 15 years old.) b It is what, your nationality? (What nationality are you?) c The Monday, one has maths. (On Mondays, we have maths.)

Follow-up: Ask students to think of other expressions they've met that can't be translated literally, e.g. some of the weather phrases from the beginning of Unit 4.

 2 Here's one way of highlighting an expression that is different in French and English. Can you think of any other ways?

- In pairs, students discuss ways to remember any expressions that are different in English and French, e.g. by marking them with an asterisk, a warning triangle or an exclamation mark.
- Pairs report back their ideas to the class.
- Remind them of any strategies they came up with in Unit 3 when working on page 45 of the *En solo* Workbook (ex. 3, how to remember cognates and false friends): see page 107 of this book.

Autonomous learning

This section gives suggestions on ways to learn and practise French outside class. It could be used at any appropriate point during Unit 4.

3 Grade each of the suggestions above.

- Students rate the tips according to how effective they think they'd find them. Point out that what works very well for one person might not work so well for someone else.

4 Try the suggestions and keep a note of which you found useful.

- Remember to set aside some time in a subsequent lesson for feedback on this.

Pages 60–61 Vocabulaire

- Use with Students' Book pages 80–81.

A list of key language from the unit is provided here as well as in the Students' Book and on Copymaster 37.

1 Listen and tick the phrases you hear.

 En solo CD, track 37 page 61, activité 1

le nord-ouest
Quel temps fait-il?
Il fait froid.
Il pleut.
Il ne fait pas beau.
Tu habites où?
J'habite dans une petite ville.
à la montagne
dans une maison
C'est comment?
assez... moderne
très... confortable
une cuisine
au rez-de-chaussée
dans ma chambre
un tapis

2 Underline in coloured pencil...

- Students search the list for key language items.

3 Note: a) your favourite word/phrase in this unit; b) 3 key words/phrases to remember.

- Challenge students to make up some sentences using these words/phrases.

Unité 5: Ma famille — Overview grid

Page reference	Contexts and objectives	Grammar	Language strategies and pronunciation	Key language	Framework	AT Level
84–85 **5.1 Voici ma famille**	• Family			*les grands-parents, le grand-père, la grand-mère, les parents, le père, la mère, le beau-père, la belle-mère, l'oncle, la tante, les enfants, le fils, la fille, le frère, la sœur, le cousin, la cousine* *Tu as des frères et des sœurs? Oui, j'ai un frère et deux sœurs. Non, je n'ai pas de frères et sœurs. Je suis fils/fille unique.* *Tu habites avec qui? J'habite avec ma mère. Mes parents sont divorcés.*	**R** – 7S2, 7S9, 7L3	1.3, 2.2–3, 3.1–3, 4.3
86–87 **5.2 Le matin, chez moi**	• Morning routines	• Reflexive verbs		*je me réveille, je me lève, je prends mon petit déjeuner, je me douche, je me brosse les dents, je m'habille, je quitte la maison, j'arrive au collège* *À quelle heure (tu te réveilles)? Je me réveille à sept heures quinze.* *tous les jours, ça dépend, jamais moi aussi, pas moi*	**R** – 7S5, 7S8	1.1–2, 2.3, 3.1–2, 4.3
88–89 **5.3 Il est comment?**	• Describe someone's appearance	• Adjective agreement		*Tu es comment? Il/Elle est comment?* *Je suis/Il est/Elle est grand(e), petit(e), gros(se), mince, de taille moyenne.* *De quelle couleur sont tes cheveux?* *Je suis/Il est/Elle est brun(e), blond(e), roux (rousse). J'ai/Il a/Elle a les cheveux longs/courts/frisés/raides. De quelle couleur sont tes yeux? J'ai/Il a/Elle a les yeux marron/bleus/verts/gris. J'ai/Il a/Elle a un long/petit nez. Tu portes/Il porte/Elle porte des lunettes? Je/Il/Elle porte des lunettes.*	**R** – 7W4	1.2, 2.3, 3.2, 4.3
90–91 **5.4 Qui es-tu?**	• Describing personality	• Adjective agreement		*bavard(e), drôle, égoïste, gentil(le), généreux(euse), intelligent(e), optimiste, paresseux(euse), sportif(ive), têtu(e), timide, travailleur(euse)* *un peu, assez, très*	**R** – 7W4, 7T4	1.1–2, 2.2–3, 3.1, 3.3, 4.1, 4.3
92–93 **Labo-langue**	• Grammar • Skills • Pronunciation	French verbs (3): • Present tense of common irregular verbs • Reflexive verbs (incl. negatives)	• Using connectives • The *e/ais* sound **Workbook:** • Speaking strategies • Reading strategies		**R** – 7W5, 7W7, 7S1, 7S5, 7S6, 7S8, 7T1, 7T7, 7L1, 7L5	
94–97 **Blog-notes / Tu sais tout? / En plus / Clic.fr**	• End-of-unit summary and assessment • Extension • **Cultural focus:** French surnames			**En plus:** *s'entendre avec*	**R** – 7S3, 7T3, 7T5, 7C2, 7C3, 7C4	1.3–4, 2.3, 3.2–4, 4.3

CLIC! 1 STAR UNIT 5 MEDIUM TERM PLAN

About Unit 5, *Ma famille*: In this unit, students work in the context of families, including their own family and famous/imaginary families from popular TV series, and they find out about aspects of family life in France. They re-apply their knowledge of adjective agreement to describe themselves and others in terms of personality and physical appearance, and describe morning routines (recycling clock times from Unit 3). On the *En plus* page, able students learn to talk about relationships between family members. Work on verbs continues: students learn how to form the present tense of reflexive verbs, and they get to grips with some common irregular verbs. They also consider the importance of using connectives, and practise the pronunciation of è/ai.

Framework objectives (reinforce)	Teaching and learning
7W4: Gender and plural	Masculine/Feminine/Plural agreement of adjectives (pp. 88–91).
7W5: Verbs present (+ past)	Irregular verbs (p. 92); reflexive verbs (pp. 86–87, p. 92).
7W7: Learning about words	Using verb tables in the *Grammaire* section to check the endings of irregular verbs (p. 92).
7S1: Typical word order	Reflexive verbs: subject + reflexive pronoun + verb; negatives with reflexive verbs, e.g. *je + ne + me + lève + pas* (p. 92).
7S2: Sentence gist	Use of apostrophe in English possessives compared with use of *de/d'* in French, e.g. *l'oncle de Théo* – Théo's uncle (p. 85).
7S3: Adapting sentences	Importance of being able to re-use and adapt language to communicate personal information (p. 99).
7S5: Basic negatives	How to form negatives with reflexive verbs, e.g. *Je ne me lève pas* (p. 92); *jamais* (p. 87).
7S6: Compound sentences	Use of connectives: *mais, et, ou* (p. 93).
7S8: Punctuation	Reflexive pronouns *me, te* and *se* become *m', t'* and *s'* before a vowel or silent *h*, e.g. *tu t'habilles* (p. 86, p. 92).
7S9: Using simple sentences	Exchange basic information about families, e.g. *Tu as des frères et des sœurs? J'ai deux sœurs. Je n'ai pas de frères.*
7T1: Reading using cues	Use visual and context clues to help with reading (Workbook p. 73).
7T3: Checking before reading	Find family members and adjectives in an extended text as a preliminary to summarising the text in English (p. 127).
7T4: Using resources	Use the glossary to find the meanings of personality adjectives (p. 90 ex. 1).
7T5: Assembling text	Adapt the answers to questions about Yasmina's video blog (p. 94) to compile own personal answers to the same questions. If appropriate, encourage students to build a continuous text from their answers and create their own video blog.
7T7: Improving written work	Use of connectives to make work more interesting (p. 93).
7L1: Sound patterns	Pronunciation: è/ai (p. 93).
7L3: Gist and detail	Watch video and identify mistakes in a list of family members, then watch again and note down extra details (p. 84).
7L5: Spontaneous talk	How to cope when you want to say something but don't know the word for it, e.g. rephrase it or use mime/gestures (Workbook p. 73).
7C2: Everyday culture	Common French surnames (p. 97).
7C3: Contact with native speakers	Video clips of students talking about families (p. 84, p. 94).
7C4: Stories and songs	Song on the theme of morning routine (p. 99).

Week-by-week overview (assuming 6 weeks' work or approximately 10–12.5 hours)

Week 1 – Opening spread/5.1 Voici ma famille
Opening spread: introduction to unit themes and objectives, including common French surnames and aspects of family life in France
Spread 5.1: family vocabulary

Week 2 – 5.2 Le matin, chez moi
Morning routines; reflexive verbs

Week 3 – 5.3 Il est comment?
Describing someone's appearance

Week 4 – 5.4 Qui es-tu?
Describing personality

Week 5 – Labo-langue
French verbs (irregular verbs, reflexive verbs); using connectives; pronunciation of è/ai

Week 6 – Blog-notes, Tu sais tout?, En plus, Clic.fr, On chante!, Lecture
Reinforcement and extension of the language of the unit; review of progress via the Checklist in the Workbook/on Copymaster; revision and assessment

5 Ma famille

Unit objectives

Contexts: Family and other people
Grammar: Verbs (3)
Language learning: Using connectives
Pronunciation: The *è/ais* sound
Cultural focus: Family life in France and French-speaking countries

Assessment opportunities

Reading: Students' Book, page 91, activity 9
Writing: Students' Book, page 89, ex. 7 (if done individually as a written exercise before any oral work in pairs)

See also **Clic! 1** OxBox Assessment CD-ROM

1 Regarde les photos.

- *Aim*: To introduce the themes of the unit and promote cultural awareness.
- Do students recognise any of the French TV programmes shown in the photos? Ask them what the common theme of the photos is (families).
- Brainstorm other TV programmes based on families. List these for students to describe towards the end of Unit 5.

 AT 3.2 ### 2 Vrai ou faux?

- Students say whether the statements about the TV families are true or false. Encourage them to use the glossary to look up unknown words.
- Ask students to correct the false statements.
- This provides an opportunity for students who have learned French in primary school to recycle family-related vocabulary. However, if your students don't yet know enough language to do this activity, hold a brief discussion about the photos in English and return to this towards the end of Unit 5.

Answers: a faux (il y a sept personnes); b vrai; c vrai; d vrai; e faux (à 20 h 10)

Follow-up:

- Use the clips from TV magazines as an opportunity to revise times, e.g. *"Les Simpson" est à quelle heure?*

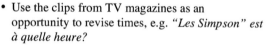

- Discuss the information panels. What do students think are the most common surnames in the UK? (There is more about French surnames on the Unit 5 *Clic.fr* page.) Talk about *la médaille de la famille* and *livert de famille*? Do students think we should have these in the UK?

5.1 Voici ma famille

Planner

> **Objectives**
> • Family

> **Resources**
> Students' Book, pages 84–85
> CD 3, track 2
> Video clip 10
> *En solo* Workbook, pages 62–63;
> *En solo* CD, track 38
> Copymasters 51, 53, 55; CD 3, tracks 14–16

> **Key language**
> *ma famille*
> *les grands-parents: le grand-père, la grand-mère*
> *les parents: le père, la mère, le beau-père, la*
> *belle-mère*
> *l'oncle, la tante*
> *les enfants: le fils, la fille, le frère, la sœur, le cousin,*
> *la cousine*
>
> *Tu as...? J'ai... Je n'ai pas de...*
> *Tu as des frères et des sœurs? Oui, j'ai un frère et*
> *deux sœurs.*
> *Non, je n'ai pas de frères et sœurs.*
> *Je suis fils/fille unique.*
>
> *Tu habites avec qui?*
> *J'habite avec ma mère.*
> *Mes parents sont divorcés.*

> **Framework reference**
> R – 7S2, 7S9, 7L3

> **Starters**
> • In pairs or groups, students try to predict any
>   previously learned language that they might find
>   useful when working on Unit 5, given that the
>   themes are family and other people. For example,
>   they might suggest adjectives to describe
>   appearance and personality (position and

agreement of adjectives), colours, *il/elle* forms
of verbs, numbers (to talk about ages and
birthdays), opinions, likes and dislikes. Collect
ideas and use this as an opportunity to show that
language learned in one context can often be
transferred to different contexts.
• Play a memory game with the family vocabulary.
  Write out the family members on an OHT, cut
  out the words and display them on the OHP.
  Give students a minute to look at it, then switch
  off the OHP and remove one of the words.
  Switch the OHP back on; students work out
  what is missing. Alternatively, give students a
  minute to study the words on the OHP, then
  switch if off and ask students to recall what
  was there.
• Copymaster 51 *À tes marques!* ex. 1 and 2.

> **Plenaries**
> • Write some family puzzles on the board or
>   OHP, e.g.
>   *C'est qui?*
>   – *C'est la mère de ma mère. (ma grand-mère)*
>   – *C'est le frère de mon père. (mon oncle)*
>   – *C'est la fille de la sœur de ma mère. (ma*
>   *cousine)*
>   – *C'est le frère de la fille du frère de ma mère.*
>   *(mon cousin)*
> • Display some jumbled sentences on the board,
>   OHP or interactive whiteboard. Set a time limit
>   for students to put the words into the correct
>   order, e.g.
>   *Je / pas / n' / frères / de / ai / sœurs / et*
>   *(Je n'ai pas de frères et sœurs)*
>   *Ma / s' / Helen / mère / appelle*
>   *(Ma mère s'appelle Helen)*
> • Play Word Tennis with the class divided into
>   two teams. A student from team A calls out a
>   word from the spread (e.g. *Cousin!*); a student
>   from team B puts the word into a sentence (*J'ai*
>   *un cousin*). Team B then calls out a word for
>   team A, and so on.

 AT 3.1 **1 C'est qui?**

• Students translate the list of family vocabulary into
English.

Answers: les grands-parents: grandparents; *le grand-
père*: grandfather; *la grand-mère*: grandmother; *les
parents*: parents; *le père*: father; *la mère*: mother; *le
beau-père*: stepfather; *la belle-mère*: stepmother;
l'oncle: uncle; *la tante*: aunt; *les enfants*: children; *le
fils*: son; *la fille*: daughter; *le frère*: brother; *la sœur*:
sister; *le/la cousin(e)*: cousin

 AT 1.3 **2 Regarde et écoute.**

• Play the video clip: three teenagers describe their
families. Students watch the whole clip for gist,
without writing anything down.
• Play Yasmina's interview (the first part of the
video clip) again. Students spot two mistakes in
the list of Yasmina's family members in the
Students' Book.

Answers: the mistakes are: Yasmina doesn't have a
grandfather, she has lots of cousins

Video clip 10   page 84, activité 2

– Aujourd'hui, on parle de la famille… Tu habites avec qui? Tu as des frères et sœurs?

– Salut Yasmina! Aujourd'hui on parle de la famille. Tu habites avec qui?
– J'habite avec mes parents… mon père et ma mère.
– Tu as des frères et sœurs?
– Oui, j'ai un frère et deux sœurs. Voilà une photo…
– Est-ce que tu as des grands-parents?
– Je n'ai pas de grand-père mais j'ai une grand-mère.
– Est-ce que tu as des oncles et des tantes… ou des cousins et des cousines?
– J'ai beaucoup d'oncles et beaucoup de tantes. Et j'ai beaucoup beaucoup beaucoup de cousins et cousines!
– Ah bon? C'est vrai? OK, merci, Yasmina.

– Salut, Manon!
– Salut!
– Tu habites avec qui?
– J'habite avec ma mère et ma grand-mère.
– Et ton père?
– Mes parents sont divorcés, je vois mon père le week-end.
– Tu as des frères et sœurs?
– Non, je n'ai pas de frères et sœurs. Je suis fille unique.
– Tu as donc ta grand-mère… tu n'as pas de grand-père?
– Non, je n'ai pas de grand-père.
– Tu as des oncles et des tantes?
– Oui, j'ai trois oncles et une tante.
– Trois oncles et une tante… Et des cousins et des cousines?
– Oui, j'ai un cousin et une petite cousine.

– Et toi, Thomas… tu habites avec qui?
– J'habite avec ma mère et mon beau-père.
– Tu as des frères et sœurs?
– Oui, j'ai deux frères – un grand et un petit – et aussi, j'ai une sœur.
– Une grande sœur?
– Euh, non… une petite sœur.
– Tu as des grands-parents aussi?
– Oui, j'ai des grands-parents… deux grands-mères et deux grands-pères. Ils habitent à Nantes aussi… Mon grand-père est très cool.
– Génial! Et… euh… Tu as des oncles et des tantes?
– Oui, j'ai cinq tantes et cinq oncles. Et beaucoup de cousins… j'ai sept cousins et quatre cousines. C'est sympa!
– Ben oui. Merci, Thomas.

AT 1.3 **3 Regarde encore une fois.**

• Play the clip again: first Manon's interview, then Thomas's interview. Students make notes on each person's family members. Allow them to watch several times if they need to.

• To make students' note-taking easier, agree on abbreviations for the family members, e.g. M = *mère*, 2 x Fr = *deux frères*. Alternatively, ask students to list the family members before listening, so that they can tick them as they are mentioned, or you could prepare and photocopy a grid/answer sheet for them to tick.

AT 2.2 **4 À deux: jouez. (B ➔ A)**

• Students play a game based on their notes from ex. 3, taking turns to tell each other facts about Manon's and Thomas's families.
• Their partner works out, from memory, which teenager they are referring to, e.g.
Student A: *Je n'ai pas de frères et sœurs.*
Student B: *Tu es Manon!*
• If unable to do this from memory, less able students refer to their ex. 3 answers.
• Point out the information box on *J'ai un/une…* and *Je n'ai pas de.*

AT 4.3 **5 Écris.**
• Using their notes from the video, students write a few sentences on behalf of Manon and Thomas, giving details of each teenager's family.
• Work through an example paragraph first for Yasmina with the whole class.

AT 4.3 **6 Et toi?**

This activity would be suitable as part of preparation for external assessment at Breakthrough stage.
• Students write a few sentences about their own family.
• If this might be a sensitive issue with some of your students, suggest that they choose a famous or cartoon family instead, e.g. *Je m'appelle Bart Simpson. J'habite avec ma mère, Marge, mon père, Homer, et mes deux sœurs, Lisa et Maggie.*

AT 3.2 **7 Oui ou non?**

• Students answer straightforward *Oui/Non* questions about Théo's family tree.
• Ask them to correct the false statements.
• Compare different ways of indicating possession in French and English: French uses *de* or *d'* (e.g. *l'oncle de Théo*) whereas English uses *'s* (Théo's uncle).
• If appropriate, focus on the format of the family tree, and make sure students understand the way in which the relationships are presented.

Answers: a oui; b non (l'oncle de Théo s'appelle Michel); c non (Lucien est le grand-père de Kévin); d non (Elsa est la fille de Maryline)

AT 3.3 **8a Regarde et lis.**

• Students read the conversation with Théo about his family. They fill in the missing family members by referring to his family tree.
• If appropriate, do this orally as a whole class before students tackle it individually in writing. Ask additional questions about Théo's family, e.g. *Il a une cousine? La tante s'appelle…?*

Answers: see underlining in transcript

8b Écoute et vérifie.

- Students listen to the recording to check their answers to ex. 8a.

🔊 **CD 3, track 2**   page 85, activité 8b

- Yo, Théo! C'est moi, Shamu12! Ça va? Une question… tu habites avec qui?
- Salut, Shamu12! Ça va bien. J'habite avec mes <u>parents</u>. Ma mère s'appelle Magali et mon <u>père</u> s'appelle Arnaud.
- Tu as des frères et sœurs?
- Oui, j'ai un petit <u>frère</u>. Il s'appelle Kévin. Mais je n'ai pas de <u>sœurs</u>.
- Tu as des grands-parents?
- Oui, j'ai un <u>grand-père</u> et une grand-mère.
- Tu as des oncles et des tantes et des cousins?
- Oui, un oncle et une <u>tante</u>… et j'ai un cousin et une <u>cousine</u>.

 8c À deux: lisez le dialogue à haute voix.

- Students read aloud the conversation in pairs.

 9 À deux: interviewe ton/ta partenaire.

- Students interview each other about their families, using the questions from the ex. 8 dialogue.

Défi!

- Students use the ex. 8 dialogue as a model for writing an interview with Dracula about his family.
- This could be done in writing and/or as oral work in pairs.
- Point out that there is no right or wrong version of this, so students can be as imaginative as they like, inventing details of names, ages, etc. If possible, allow students to perform their dialogues for the class or record them.

C53   Additional activities on the theme of family are provided on Copymaster 53 ex. 2 (listening) and C55   Copymaster 55 (reading/writing).

W 62–63   Pages 62–63 of the *En solo* Workbook provide further activities focusing on brothers, sisters and family members.

5.2 Le matin, chez moi

pages 86–87

Planner

> ### Objectives
> - Morning routines

> ### Resources
> Students' Book, pages 86–87
> CD 3, tracks 3–4
> *En solo* Workbook, pages 64–65;
> *En solo* CD, track 39
> Copymasters 52, 53, 56; CD 3, tracks 14–16

> ### Key language
> *Le matin*
> *je me réveille, je me lève, je prends mon petit
> déjeuner, je me douche, je me brosse les dents, je
> m'habille, je quitte la maison, j'arrive au collège
> À quelle heure (tu te réveilles)? Je me réveille à sept
> heures quinze.
> tous les jours, ça depend
> non, jamais
> moi aussi, pas moi*

> ### Grammar
> Reflexive verbs

> ### Framework reference
> **R** – 7S5, 7S8

> ### Starters
> To recap on times from Unit 3, display on the
> board/OHP some digital clock faces together with
> the corresponding times written in words, in
> jumbled order. Number the clock faces 1, 2, 3,

etc. and label the written times a, b, c, etc. Give
students 30 seconds to match them up. If
appropriate, give them extra time to copy the
times out in sequence, starting with the earliest.
- In groups, students play a version of Charades,
taking turns to mime the daily routine phrases for
each other to guess.
- Write out the daily routine phrases on an OHT
and cut them up into individual words. If
appropriate, include a question using *Tu...?* and
examples in the first and third person singular.
Jumble the pieces on the OHP screen and invite
students out to build sentences.
(Instead of using the OHP, an interactive
whiteboard with drag-and-drop function can be
used for this type of activity.)

> ### Plenaries
> - In groups, students brainstorm strategies for
> learning and remembering the daily routine
> phrases. Collect ideas and discuss as a whole
> class, then challenge students to try out their
> preferred ideas for homework. Some students
> might like to try writing a rap or setting the
> words to a well-known tune.
> - Students work in pairs. Give them a sentence
> starter: *Je me réveille...* Students then take turns
> to add to the sentence, trying to make it as long
> as possible. If necessary, provide some ideas or
> prompts on the board (e.g. *à sept heures, dans la
> cuisine, et*). Allow time for feedback on students'
> sentences. Which pair have built the longest
> correct sentence?
> - Copymaster 52 *Bilan de leçon* ex. 3.

| AT 1.1 | **1 Écoute et lis.** |

| AT 3.1 |

- Students listen and work out which daily routine
phrase is missing from the recording.

  Answer: j'arrive au collège

 CD 3, track 3   page 86, activité 1

Je me réveille.
Je me lève.
Je me douche.
Je me brosse les dents.
Je m'habille.
Je prends mon petit déjeuner.
Je quitte la maison.

| AT 3.2 | **2 Relie.** |

This activity would be suitable as part of preparation
for external assessment at Breakthrough stage.
- Students match each daily routine phrase to a
picture.

Answers: a je me brosse les dents; b je me douche;
c je me réveille; d je me lève; e j'arrive au collège;
f je quitte la maison; g je prends mon petit déjeuner;
h je m'habille.

Preparation: Revise telling the time, if appropriate,
before beginning ex. 3.

| AT 1.2 | **3 Mets les actions dans le bon ordre. Écoute et
vérifie.** |

- Students note down the letters of the daily routine
pictures in the correct order, then listen to the
recording to check their answers.

Answers: c, d, b, h, g, a, f, e

 CD 3, track 4   page 86, activité 3

– Le matin, chez moi, c'est comme ça...
  Je me réveille à sept heures.
  À sept heures cinq, je me lève.
  À sept heures dix, je me douche... et à sept
  heures vingt, je m'habille.

> Je prends mon petit déjeuner dans la cuisine avec ma mère et mon frère.
> Après le petit déjeuner, je me brosse les dents…
> Je quitte la maison à huit heures.
> Et j'arrive à l'école à huit heures quinze.
> – Hé, Théo! Salut!…

4 Grammaire.

- Students copy out the morning routine phrases and underline the reflexive verbs.
- Ask them to think about why these verbs are reflexive. (They are reflexive because the subject of the verb is "doing" the action of the verb to itself, e.g. I wash myself, I dress myself, I wake myself.)

Follow-up: Students work out the present tense *tu* and *il/elle* forms for all the reflexive verbs used in the morning routine phrases, either orally or in writing. Draw their attention to the grammar notes, and point out that the verbs shown here follow the same pattern as all regular -*er* verbs, i.e. with final -*s* in the *tu* form.

5 Enregistre des "bruits mystère".

- *Aim*: To provide opportunities to practise the *tu* form of reflexive verbs and ask questions.
- Students prepare a "mystery sounds" recording of their morning routine, e.g. alarm clock ringing, running water, etc.
- Play the recordings to the class and ask them to guess what each sound represents, e.g. *Tu te douches? Tu te brosses les dents?*
- Listen to the recordings before you play them to the class, in case some of them need to be censored!

 AT 3.2 **AT 4.3** ### 6 Sondage: lis et réponds.

- Students write their answers to the survey questions about morning routine.
- Decide in advance whether to insist on full sentences for students' answers. A few clock times and other phrases (*jamais, ça dépend, tous les jours*) are provided as support.
- The first question (*Tu aimes le matin?*) is not included in the key language for this spread, but students should by now be able to recognise and use *aimer* (introduced in Unit 2).

 AT 2.3 ### 7 A interviewe B. (B ➤ A)

- Students complete the survey in pairs and compare each other's responses.

AT 2.3 **AT 4.3** ### 8 Décris.

- Students describe Dracula's routine using the third person singular, either orally or in writing.
- Alternatively, less able students could use the first person singular, speaking or writing as if they are Dracula.

Answers: Dracula se réveille à minuit. Il se lève à minuit dix. Il se brosse les dents à minuit quinze. Il se douche à minuit vingt. Il s'habille à minuit trente.

C53 **C56** Ex. 3 on Copymaster 53 is a listening activity on morning routine. An additional reading/writing activity is provided on Copymaster 56, ex. 2.

W 64–65 Pages 64–65 of the *En solo* Workbook provide further activities to practise morning routine phrases and reflexive verbs.

5.3 Il est comment?

Planner

> ### Objectives
> - Describing someone's appearance

> ### Resources
> Students' Book, pages 88–89
> CD 3, tracks 5–6
> *En solo* Workbook, pages 66–67`
> Copymasters 53, 54; CD 3, tracks 14–16

> ### Key language
> *Tu es comment? Il/Elle est comment?*
> *Je suis/Il est/Elle est grand(e), petit(e), gros(se), mince.*
> *Je suis/Il est/Elle est de taille moyenne.*
> *De quelle couleur sont tes cheveux?*
> *Je suis/Il est/Elle est brun(e), blond(e), roux (rousse).*
> *J'ai/Il a/Elle a les cheveux longs/courts/frisés/raides.*
> *De quelle couleur sont tes yeux?*
> *J'ai/Il a/Elle a les yeux marron/bleus/verts/gris.*
> *J'ai/Il a/Elle a un long/petit nez.*
> *Tu portes/Il porte/Elle porte des lunettes?*
> *Je/Il/Elle porte des lunettes.*

> ### Grammar
> Adjective agreement

> ### Framework reference
> **R** – 7W4

> ### Starters
> - Display some magazine photos of celebrities and start describing one of them (using either the first person or the third person singular). Students compete to be the first to recognise who you are talking about. Continue with the other photos, or allow confident students to take over your role. Alternatively, students could do this activity in pairs.
> - Display some jumbled sentence halves and give students a time limit to match them up, e.g.
>   *Il est / brun.*
>   *J'ai les yeux / verts.*
>   *Elle a les cheveux / frisés.*
>   *Elle est / petite.*
>   *Je porte / des lunettes.*
>   *Il a / un petit nez.*

> ### Plenaries
> - Students will need access to coloured pencils for this activity. Working in pairs, each student prepares a description of appearance, which they then read out to their partner. The partner draws a rough sketch. Afterwards, they compare the written description and the drawing: they should be roughly the same!
> - In pairs/groups, students compare the structure of English and French phrases from this spread, e.g. *Elle a les cheveux raides* (She has the hairs straight), *De quelle couleur sont tes yeux?* (Of what colour are your eyes?), *Il est comment?* (He is how?). Ask them to think of other phrases they've learned that can't be translated literally between French and English. Allow time for a whole-class discussion.
> - Students work in pairs to recap on everything they know about French adjectives. Challenge them to write down some phrases that show examples of: adjectives that go before the noun; adjectives that go after the noun; adjective agreement. Allow time for feedback.

AT 3.2

1 Lis et choisis.
- Students choose a or b to complete each statement and build up a description of Harry Potter.
- Alternatively, begin by putting similar questions orally to the whole class. Students could then do the activity in writing using the key vocabulary list as support.
- Students may challenge the statement *Il est brun* (referring to Harry Potter), because it literally means "He has brown hair", whereas Harry actually has black hair. Explain that *brun(e)* also means "dark-haired". Introduce *Il a les cheveux noirs* for students who wish to be more precise!

Answers: 1 b; 2 b; 3 a; 4 b; 5 a; 6 b

AT 1.2

2 Écoute.
- Students listen and work out which of the three descriptions refers to Harry Potter.

Answer: C

  CD 3, track 5   page 88, activité 2

Il a les cheveux courts, il a les yeux verts… et il est roux. Il a un long nez. Il ne porte pas de lunettes.
Il est brun. Il a les cheveux longs et frisés. Il a les yeux bleus. Il porte des lunettes.
Il est brun. Il a les cheveux courts et il a les yeux raides. Il a les yeux marron. Il porte des lunettes. Il a un petit nez.

Follow-up:

- Ask questions about Harry's appearance (e.g. *Il est grand ou petit? Il est gros ou mince?*), using *assez* and *très* if appropriate.
- To revise language from spread 5.1, ask: *Il habite avec qui?*
- If students are familiar with the Harry Potter films, question them about the appearance of Harry's relatives or other characters.

 3 Vrai ou faux?

- Students listen and note down whether each statement about Ron Weasley is true or false.

Answers: 1 vrai; 2 faux; 3 vrai; 4 vrai; 5 faux; 6 faux

 CD 3, track 6   page 89, activité 3

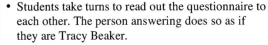

– Tu connais Ron Weasley? Il est comment?
   Il est roux.
   Ron Weasley?... Il a les yeux bleus.
   Il ne porte pas de lunettes.
   Euh... il a un très long nez.
   Il a les cheveux frisés.
   Il a les cheveux longs.

 Follow-up: Students make up additional true/false statements about the appearance of other characters from the Harry Potter films. They exchange these with a partner. Alternatively, pairs work together to compile a true/false quiz to exchange with other pairs.

4 Lis.

- Students read Tracy Beaker's speech bubble and note down in English four things she says about herself.
- Draw attention to the feminine adjectives in Tracy's speech bubble. Compare these with the masculine forms used in the Harry Potter section.

Answers: any four details from: small, quite thin, long dark curly hair, brown eyes, pointed nose

5 À deux: questionnaire. (B → A)

- Students take turns to read out the questionnaire to each other. The person answering does so as if they are Tracy Beaker.
- Alternatively, students could do this as a written exercise.

Answers: 1 Je m'appelle Tracy Beaker. 2 Je suis petite. 3 Oui, je suis (assez) mince. 4 J'ai les yeux marron. 5 Je suis brune. 6 J'ai les cheveux longs et frisés. 7 Non, je ne porte pas de lunettes.

---

 6 À deux. (A → B)

 • Students repeat ex. 5 for Harry Potter.

Answers: 1 Je m'appelle Harry Potter. 2 Je suis assez grand. 3 Oui, je suis mince. 4 J'ai les yeux marron. 5 Je suis brun. 6 J'ai les cheveux courts et raides. 7 Oui, je porte des lunettes.

 7 Et toi?

- Students give their own answers to the questionnaire.
- After doing this orally in pairs, students write out their answers to the questions.

Follow-up: Students describe the appearance of family members and friends.

C53
C54 Ex. 1 on Copymaster 53 is a listening activity focusing on descriptions of appearance. An additional speaking activity is provided on Copymaster 54, ex. 1.

W 66–67 Pages 66–67 of the *En solo* Workbook provide further activities to practise descriptions of appearance.

5.4 Qui es-tu?

Planner

> **Objectives**
> • Describing personality

> **Resources**
> Students' Book, pages 90–91
> CD 3, tracks 7–8
> *En solo* Workbook, pages 68–69;
> *En solo* CD, tracks 40–41
> Copymasters 51, 52, 54, 56

> **Key language**
> *Je suis...*
> *bavard(e), drôle, égoïste, gentil(le), généreux(euse),*
> *intelligent(e), optimiste, paresseux(euse),*
> *sportif(ive), têtu(e), timide, travailleur(euse)*
> *un peu, assez, très*

> **Grammar**
> Adjective agreement

> **Framework reference**
> **R** – 7W4, 7T4

> **Starters**
> • Students choose the odd-one-out in groups of
>   words, e.g.
>   – *drôle, vert, intelligent* (*vert* because it's a
>   colour and not a personality adjective, or *drôle*
>   because it's both masculine and feminine)
>   – *sportive, travailleur, paresseuse* (*paresseuse*
>   because the other two imply being busy and
>   active, or *travailleur* because it's masculine)

> – *égoïste, gentil, généreuse* (*égoïste* because the
>   other two are good qualities, or because it
>   could be masculine or feminine, or *généreuse*
>   because it's the only one that is definitely
>   feminine)
> • Display the personality adjectives in English and
>   French, in jumbled order, on the board or OHP.
>   Students race against the clock to match up the
>   English to the French.
> • Copymaster 51 *À tes marques!* ex. 3.

> **Plenaries**
> • Draw a Noughts and Crosses grid on the board
>   with a number (in figures, not words) written in
>   each square. In advance, prepare a question or
>   instruction corresponding to each number, e.g.
>   *Tes cheveux sont comment? De quelle couleur*
>   *sont tes yeux/cheveux? Décris tes qualités/ta*
>   *personnalité. Tu habites avec qui? Daniel*
>   *Radcliffe* (or other celebrity) *est comment?*
>   Divide the class into two teams. Team A choose
>   a number and nominate a spokesperson. Read
>   out the corresponding question. If the student
>   answers correctly, erase the number from the
>   grid and write "A" in the square. Team B then
>   call out a number, and so on. The aim is to win
>   a line of three squares.
> • Write a mixture of old and new vocabulary on
>   the board and ask students to sort it into groups.
>   Students themselves decide on the groupings.
>   Allow time for feedback. Ask students to assess
>   which types of grouping would make it easier to
>   remember/learn the vocabulary.
> • Copymaster 52 *Bilan de leçon* ex. 1 and 2.

 Preparation:

• Students brainstorm any personality adjectives
  they already know (e.g. *cool, patient*).

• Recap on what they already know about adjective
  agreement.

 AT 3.1 **1 Traduis.**
• Students find the English meanings of the
  adjectives in the key language list.
• Discuss how to do this without using the glossary
  or a dictionary, e.g. by focusing on cognates/near-
  cognates and words that are based on French
  words they already know. Go through the list
  orally as a whole class.

AT 4.1 **2 Écris une liste d'adjectifs.**
• Students list the personality adjectives in order of
  importance, to reflect the qualities they would like
  to have.

 • They compare their lists with a partner. They
  might hold different views on some of the
  adjectives, e.g. some students might consider being
  talkative to be a good quality, whereas others
  might not.

AT 1.1–2 **3 Joue au Loto.**
• *Aim*: To familiarise students with the
  pronunciation of masculine and feminine forms of
  the adjectives.
• There are two games of Adjective Bingo on the
  recording. The words in game 1 are masculine
  only; game 2 has a mixture of masculine and
  feminine forms used in short sentences.
• For each game, students choose four adjectives from
  the key language list. They listen and tick them off as
  they hear them. The winner is the first person to tick
  all the adjectives off their list.
• In game 2, make sure students realise that in order
  to tick an item off their list it must not only be the
  correct adjective but also the correct form
  (masculine or feminine) of the adjective, e.g. if

they have *bavard* (masculine) on their list, they cannot tick it off when the bingo caller says *Elle est bavarde*.

Similarly, if they have *gentille* on their list, they cannot tick it off when they hear *Il est gentil*, even though *gentil* and *gentille* sound the same – because the word *il* tells them that the adjective will be in its masculine form.

 CD 3, track 7   page 90, activité 3

On joue au Loto?

Jeu numéro un. Écoutez bien…
drôle… drôle
sportif… sportif
têtu… têtu
paresseux… paresseux
travailleur… travailleur
timide… timide
égoïste… égoïste
gentil… gentil
bavard… bavard
généreux… généreux
intelligent… intelligent
optimiste… optimiste

Jeu numéro deux. Écoutez bien…
Je suis timide… Je suis timide.
Il est gentil… Il est gentil.
Elle est bavarde… Elle est bavarde.
Je suis généreux… Je suis généreux.
Elle est intelligente… Elle est intelligente.
Il est optimiste… Il est optimiste.
Tu es drôle… Tu es drôle.
Je suis sportive… Je suis sportive.
Il est têtu… Il est têtu.
Tu es paresseuse… Tu es paresseuse.
Elle est travailleuse… Elle est travailleuse.
Il est égoïste… Il est égoïste.

 4 Jeu de mime.

- Students take turns to mime adjectives for the class to guess. They could do this in small groups instead of as a whole class.

 AT 1.2   **5 Écoute et note trois adjectifs pour Alex, et trois pour Yasmina.**

- Students listen and note down three adjectives used by Alex to describe himself, and three used by Yasmina.

Answers: Alex: travailleur, généreux, têtu; Yasmina: paresseuse (pas travailleuse), intelligente, sportive

 CD 3, track 8   page 90, activité 5

– Je suis travailleur. Oui… je suis très travailleur… Je suis assez généreux. Et mes défauts? Euh… je suis un peu têtu.

– Moi, je ne suis pas travailleuse. Je suis assez paresseuse. Je n'aime pas beaucoup le travail! Mais je suis intelligente… et euh… j'aime beaucoup le sport… je suis sportive.

Follow-up: Play the recording again and ask students to spot *un peu, très* and *assez*. Point out the information box about them and encourage students to use these words in their own speaking and writing.

 AT 2.2   **6 À deux.**

 - Each student secretly writes down three adjectives from the list to describe the sort of person they are. Their partner asks questions to work out their choice of adjectives.

Follow-up*:* Students write a few sentences describing their own personality. Encourage them to use *assez, très* and *un peu*.

AT 2.3   **7 À deux. Donne ton opinion.**

AT 4.3

- Students look at the photos and imagine what sort of people these are. They work with a partner to build up a character description of each one. (A range of answers are acceptable.)
- Students put their descriptions in writing.

8 Grammaire.

- Students complete the grammar rules about adjective endings. Refer them to the grammar section at the back of the Students' Book if they need help with this.
- With less able groups, provide the missing elements on the board or OHP for students to match to rules a–d.

Answers: a the feminine form doesn't change; b the feminine form adds *e*; c the feminine form is -*euse*; d the feminine form is -*ive*

AT 3.3   **9 Lis et réponds.**

- *Aim*: To provide an opportunity for students to meet the key vocabulary and some irregular verbs in a slightly longer text.
- Students read three problem page letters and answer questions in English.

Answers: a problem page letters; b he has no friends, is rather shy and not very sociable; c he is intelligent, hard-working and gets good marks at school, whereas she isn't intelligent, is quite lazy and doesn't do her homework; d his (female) cousin; e because she is selfish and not very generous; f *aller (ma sœur va), faire (je ne fais pas mes devoirs), venir (ses copines viennent), voir (je vois ma cousine)*

| C54 | Additional practice of the language of the unit is provided on Copymaster 54 ex. 2 (speaking) and |
| C56 | Copymaster 56 ex. 1 (reading/writing). |

| W 68–69 | Pages 68–69 of the *En solo* Workbook provide further activities to practise descriptions of personality. |

5.5 Labo-langue

Planner

> **Objectives**
> • French verbs (3)
> • Using connectives
> • The *è/ai* sound

> **Resources**
> Students' Book, pages 92–93
> CD 3, tracks 9–10
> *En solo* Workbook, pages 70–71, 73
> Copymasters 57, 58, 59; CD 3, tracks 17–18

> **Framework reference**
> R – 7W5, 7W7, 7S1, 7S5, 7S6, 7S8, 7T1 (via Workbook), 7T7, 7L1, 7L5 (via Workbook)

Bien comprendre!

French verbs (3)

These grammar notes focus on the present tense of some common irregular verbs, reflexive verbs (*je*, *tu*, *il/elle/on*) and reflexive verbs with negatives.

1 Complete these verbs.

• Refer students to the verb tables on Students' Book pages 137–138 to help them complete the conjugation of the verbs listed. If appropriate, with less able groups, focus on the first, second and third person singular forms only and omit *nous*, *vous* and *ils/elles*.
• Point out that the tip on *tu* endings (*tu* forms always end in *-s* or *-x*) is very handy to know when checking written work.
• Draw attention to the "Three for the price of one!" tip (i.e. *il*, *elle* and *on* endings are always the same): it is important to lighten the workload psychologically for less able students!

2 Copy the sentences, using the right form of the verbs.

Answers: a prends; b vois; c va, veut

3 How would you say these in French, using reflexive verbs?

Answers: a Je me lève à six heures. b Tu te réveilles à sept heures trente. c Il se douche. d Elle s'habille dans sa chambre. e Je ne me brosse pas les dents. f Elle ne se douche pas.

 See Copymaster 57 for further grammar practice of *-ir* and *-re* verbs, and reflexive verbs.

 Pages 70–71 of the *En solo* Workbook provide further activities to practise these grammar points.

Bien apprendre!

Using connectives

1 Match these words with the French connectives in the cartoon.

Answers: or: *ou*; and: *et*; but: *mais*

 2 Can you think of reasons why it is useful to use connectives when you speak or write? Discuss with a partner.

• Students discuss the importance of using connectives (e.g. to avoid short choppy sentences, to build longer, more impressive/more complex utterances, to add interest and variety).
• Collect ideas and discuss as a class.

3 Link each pair of sentences with a different connective.

Answers: a Je suis sportif <u>mais</u> je n'aime pas le tennis. b Laura quitte la maison <u>et</u> elle va au collège. c On va au cinéma <u>ou</u> on fait du shopping?

Défi!

• Students use some of the phrases in the box, plus *et, ou* and *mais*, to imagine and describe Toto's Saturday morning routine.

 Copymaster 58 provides additional activities to practise connectives.

 Further language learning strategies are provided on page 73 of the *En solo* Workbook, which could be used at any appropriate point during Unit 5:

• *Speaking:* ways to cope when you don't know the word for something
• *Reading:* tips on using visual and context clues to help with reading

Bien parler!

The *è/ai* sound

1 Count the *è* sounds in Toto's bubble.

- Once students have spotted the *è* sounds, practise reading the sentence aloud in pairs and as a whole class.
- Words like *les* and *mes* are pronounced slightly differently in different parts of France, but strictly speaking they should be pronounced as an *é* sound, not as *è*. Note also that the *e* in *paresseux* is an *é* sound (unlike in *paresse*, where it is an *è* sound).

Answers: Je suis paresseux et très t<u>ê</u>tu... m<u>ai</u>s mes parents m'<u>ai</u>ment!

2 Listen. Do you hear the *è/ai* sound or not?

Answers: 1 ✓; 2 ✗; 3 ✓; 4 ✗; 5 ✓; 6 ✓; 7 ✓; 8 ✗; 9 ✓; 10 ✗; 11 ✗; 12 ✗; 13 ✓; 14 ✓; 15 ✓

 CD 3, track 9   page 93, Bien parler! activité 2

1 père
2 grand
3 frère
4 petit
5 grand-mère
6 je me lève
7 au collège
8 tu te douches
9 à sept heures
10 à huit heures
11 mes parents
12 ma sœur
13 tu portes des lunettes?
14 non, jamais!
15 il est très têtu

3 Listen to this sentence. Can you say it with a really French accent?

- The sentence is repeated several times on the recording as a tongue-twister.

 CD 3, track 10   page 93, Bien parler! activité 3

Je mets mes lunettes et je vais au collège.

C59 Copymaster 59 provides further pronunciation practice of the *è/ai* sound.

Blog-notes

Planner

> ### Objectives
> * To summarise the main points of the unit in context, in a format that is fun and familiar to students, i.e. a video blog
> * To provide a model enabling students to personalise the language of the unit
> * To provide opportunities for students to ask as well as answer questions
> * To provide extended listening practice recycling the language of the whole unit

> ### Resources
> Students' Book, page 94
> Video clip 11
> *En solo* Workbook, page 72;
> *En solo* CD, track 42
> Copymaster 50

> ### Framework reference
> **R** – 7T5, 7C3

AT 1.4 | **1 Regarde le vidéo-blog. Choisis 1 ou 2 pour Yasmina.**

* Students watch Yasmina's video diary and choose 1 or 2 in answer to each question. Pause the video after each section to allow students time to answer.

Answers: a 1; b 1; c 2; d 1; e 1: f 2; g 2; h 1

 Video clip 11　　　　　page 94, activité 1

Moteur! Action! Bonjour! Bienvenue sur mon vidéo-blog! Aujourd'hui, c'est un grand jour pour ma famille. C'est le mariage de ma sœur Amina!

a En général, dans la maison, on est six: mon père, ma mère, mon frère et mes deux sœurs. Tu as des frères et sœurs, toi?

b Oh là là! Aujourd'hui, dans la maison, on est 13 personnes! Il y a mon oncle, ma tante, ma cousine. Il y a aussi mes trois cousins et ma grand-mère. En général, ma grand-mère n'habite pas avec nous, elle habite en Algérie. Tu habites avec qui, toi?

c Avec 13 personnes dans la maison, il faut s'organiser le matin! Mes parents, se lèvent à six heures. À six heures trente, mes sœurs et ma cousine se douchent. À sept heures, mon frère et mes cousins se douchent. Moi, je me réveille à sept heures trente. Et toi, en général, tu te lèves à quelle heure?

d Moi, je suis prête en dix minutes! Je m'habille, je me brosse les dents et voilà! Je prends ma douche le soir, je préfère. Et toi, tu fais quoi le matin?

e – Yasmina? Yasmina? Tu t'habilles? Aujourd'hui, pour le mariage de ta sœur, tu mets ta robe!
Ça, c'est maman...
– Oui maman, je m'habille.
Ah, une robe, je n'aime pas ça. Moi, je suis grande, mince, sportive! Je suis belle avec un jean et un tee-shirt! Pas une robe! Et toi, tu es comment physiquement? Grand, mince, sportif...?

f Oh mes cheveux... Je déteste mes cheveux raides! Oh c'est horrible! Je veux des cheveux frisés. Ma sœur a les cheveux courts et frisés.

Elle porte des lunettes aussi. Et toi, tes cheveux sont comment? Tu aimes tes cheveux? Tu portes des lunettes?
Bon... je m'habille... excusez-moi, hein! Une minute!...

g Hum hum... re-bonjour! Alors, je suis belle! Regarde, j'ai de beaux yeux marron! Et toi, de quelle couleur sont tes yeux?

h Bon, mais je suis très bavarde, hein, trop bavarde! C'est mon gros défaut! J'ai un défaut, mais j'ai beaucoup de qualités... je suis drôle, gentille, généreuse, travailleuse et surtout, je suis très très modeste! Et toi, tu as quelles qualités? Et quels défauts!
– Yasmina! Yasmina! Tu es prête?! On t'attend, dépêche-toi!
– OK, j'arrive!
Allez, j'y vais! Salut!

AT 4.3 | **2 À toi de répondre!**

* Students write their own answers to questions a–h.

Follow-up:

These activities may be suitable for more able students only:

* Students interview each other using questions a–h.
* Students use their answers from ex. 2 to help them write their own blog. If the appropriate technology is available, allow students to record their own video blogs and play them to the class.

C50
 W72 | A checklist summarising the language of the unit is provided on Copymaster 50 and on page 72 of the *En solo* Workbook. It could be used in tandem with the *Blog-notes* page or at an appropriate point towards the end of the unit. It provides an opportunity for students to review what they have learned and reflect on areas for improvement.

Tu sais tout?

Planner

> **Objectives**
> • To enable students to recap on the language and structures of the unit
> • To provide an opportunity for quick testing of all four skills

The page is divided into four sections: listening, speaking, reading and writing. Each section can be marked out of 5 to give a total score out of 20.

> **Resources**
> Students' Book, page 95
> CD 3, track 12

AT 1.3 | **1 Listen and match each conversation to a symbol.**

Answers: 1 f; 2 a; 3 c; 4 d; 5 b; 6 e

 CD 3, track 12 page 95, activité 1

1 – Tu es comment? Grande? Petite?
– Je suis petite.
2 – Tu habites avec qui?
– J'habite avec mon père et ma mère.
3 – De quelle couleur sont tes yeux?
– J'ai les yeux marron.
4 – Ta sœur est brune, non?
– Non, ma sœur est blonde. Elle a les cheveux longs et frisés.
5 – Tu portes des lunettes?
– Oui, je porte des lunettes.
6 – Ta cousine a les cheveux longs?
– Non, elle a les cheveux courts et raides.
– Elle est brune?
– Oui, elle est brune.

AT 2.3 | **2 Say five things to describe your appearance and personality.**

• Encourage students to use connectives and *assez*, *très* and *un peu*.

AT 3.3 | **3 Read what Claire says about her father's work. Note in English what he does at the times below (a–f).**

Answers: a he arrives at the bakery; b he brushes his teeth, has a shower and gets dressed (in the bathroom); c he wakes up; d he leaves the house; e he gets up; f he has his breakfast (in his pyjamas in the kitchen)

AT 4.3 | **4 Invent a family for Lucas and write a speech bubble for him. Mention at least five different family members.**

This activity could replace task A or B in a Grade 2 Asset Languages teacher assessment.

• Students imagine and describe Lucas's family. If appropriate, suggest that they try to link in a few daily routine phrases too, e.g. *Ma mère* (+ description of appearance). *Elle est très travailleuse et elle se lève à six heures trente.*

En plus

Planner

> **Objectives**
> - To provide extension material for more able students who are confident with the core language of the unit, and to introduce new language where appropriate
> - To provide alternative class and homework material for students who finish other activities quickly

> **Resources**
> Students' Book, page 96

> **Key language**
> *s'entendre avec*

On s'entend bien!

 1 Read and decide what the chat is about.

Answer: c

 2 Find in the text the French for…

Answers: a Tu t'entends bien avec elles? b On s'entend bien. c Je ne m'entends pas bien avec elle.

 3 Answer in English.

- Encourage students to give as much detail as they can, e.g. explain why Manon does or doesn't get on with the different people mentioned.

Answers: a because her grandmother is very patient; b she usually gets on with her mother, but not with her father (her parents are divorced, she sees her father at weekends but she thinks he isn't interested in her); c she gets on with Max (he's the same age as her and they have fun together) but not with Annabelle (she's only three years old and too young)

 4 Say who you get on with in your family.

 - Students could do this orally in pairs (e.g. *Tu t'entends bien avec…?*), then follow it up in writing.

Follow-up: The grammar notes on reflexive verbs focus on *s'entendre avec*. Ask students to find two more reflexive verbs in Manon's text (*il ne s'intéresse pas à moi, on s'amuse bien*). If appropriate, ask students to work out other persons of these verbs, e.g. *je ne m'intéresse pas, tu ne t'intéresses pas*, etc.

Clic.fr

Planner

> ### Objectives
> - To raise awareness of France and French culture
> - To promote intercultural understanding by providing opportunities to compare French culture with students' own culture

> ### Resources
> Students' Book, page 97
> Copymaster 60

> ### Framework reference
> **R** – 7C2

Les noms de famille

 This page looks at some common French surnames and their origins.

1 How many different surnames are there in France?

Answer: 400,000

2 Name five French surnames which can also be first names.

Answers: Martin, Bernard, Thomas, Robert, Richard

3 Which of the surnames above do you think was originally given to a person who...?

Answers: a Petit; b Boulanger; c Lebrun; d Laforêt

 Follow-up:

- Students work out the meanings/origins of the other French surnames listed, using a dictionary: <u>Legrand</u>: someone who is tall; <u>Dubois</u>: someone who lives in the woods; <u>Berger</u>: a shepherd; <u>Mercier</u>: a haberdasher (literally means "haberdasher", but the closest equivalent British surname would probably be Tailor). Point out that they need to remove the initial Le- and Du- from Legrand and Dubois before they look them up in a dictionary.
- Students compare the French surnames on this page with any British equivalents, e.g. Baker and Shepherd are quite common British surnames.
- Students research some of the most common British surnames and their origins.
- If you have a partner school in a French-speaking country, carry out a survey about their surnames.
- Either using the Internet or by looking on a street map of a French town, students search for French streets that are named after famous people and find out more about these people.
- Students list any streets in your town that are named after famous people.

 Further activities focusing on French surnames are provided on Copymaster 60.

Vocabulaire

Planner

> **Objectives**
> - *Vocabulaire*: to provide a theme-based summary of the key language of the unit, which students can use as a reference or as an aid to learning
> - To develop language learning strategies
> - *On chante!*: to reinforce the language of the unit in a fun way

> **Resources**
> Students' Book, pages 98–99
> CD 3, track 13
> *En solo* Workbook, pages 74–75;
> *En solo* CD, track 43
> Copymaster 49

> **Framework reference**
> **R** – 7S3, 7C4

  A list of key language from the unit, with associated activities, is also provided on Copymaster 49 and on pages 74–75 of the *En solo* Workbook.

Say it your way!

- *Aim*: To encourage students to re-use and adapt language they've met.
- Students search pages 98–99 for sentences that they can adapt by substituting different words and phrases.

Answers: a Tu as des oncles et des tantes? b J'habite avec mon frère. c Je me douche tous les jours. d Il est un peu têtu.

On chante!

AT 1.2 **1 Écoute et lis.**

AT 3.2 - Students read and listen to the song. They select an adjective to describe Toto.

Answer: b paresseux

🔘 **CD 3, track 13**   page 99, activité 1

Toto, où es-tu?

Toto, où es-tu? Toto, tu es là?
Moi, je me lève
Mais tu ne te lèves pas
Toi, tu restes au lit
Au lit, au lit, au lit
Toi, tu restes au lit.

Toto, où es-tu? Toto, tu es là?
Moi, je me douche
Mais tu ne te douches pas
Toi, tu restes au lit
Au lit, au lit, au lit
Toi, tu restes au lit.

Toto, où es-tu? Toto, tu es là?
Moi, je m'habille
Mais tu ne t'habilles pas
Toi, tu restes au lit
Au lit, au lit, au lit
Toi, tu restes au lit.

Toto, où es-tu? Toto, tu es là?
Moi, je m'amuse
Mais tu ne t'amuses pas
Toi, tu restes au lit
Au lit, au lit, au lit
Toi, tu restes au lit.

AT 3.2 **2 Trouve...**

- Students search the song lyrics for the French translations of the English phrases.

Answers: a Où es tu? b Tu restes au lit. c Tu ne t'amuses pas.

AT 2.2 **3 Chante avec le CD!**

- Students sing along with the recording.

Lecture

Planner

> **Objectives**
> * To encourage independent reading and develop reading strategies
> * To provide alternative class and homework material for students who finish other activities quickly
>
> The texts and activities on *Lecture A* should be suitable for all; *Lecture B* is more challenging and may be suitable for more able students only.

> **Resources**
> * Students' Book, pages 126–127

> **Framework reference**
> **R – 7T3**

Lecture A

Tu es du matin ou du soir?

 1 Read and find out how to say in French...
* Encourage students to do this activity without a dictionary, using different techniques to work out meanings, e.g. context, cognates, French words that look similar to other French words they already know.

Answers: a le réveil sonne; b je n'ai pas le temps; c à l'heure; d en retard

 2 Are you a morning or an evening person? Do the quiz, choosing a or b.
* Students do the quiz either individually or in pairs, comparing their answers with those of a partner.

Lecture B

Plus belle la vie

This page is based on a real French TV series, *Plus belle la vie*, about the Marci family.

 1 How many different members of the Marci family are mentioned in the article?

Answers: six (le grand-père, la mère, le père, deux enfants, l'oncle)

 2 Who is this?

Answer: Thomas

 Défi!
* Students summarise in English the personality and appearance of the other Marci family members.

Answers: Roland (the grandfather) has grey hair, brown eyes, is stubborn but generous; Blanche (the mother) has long dark curly hair, is sporty, intelligent and generous, interested in politics; Lucas (the son) is artistic, a bit shy, very intelligent, is quite tall, has long dark hair; Johanna (the daughter) has long dark straight hair, is romantic and quite talkative

Follow-up:
* Individually or in pairs, students write comprehension questions on the text to exchange with their partner or another pair.
* If appropriate, return to the opening spread of Unit 5 (Students' Book pages 82–83). Students should now be able to describe in much more detail the TV families pictured there, or any other TV families they are interested in.

Copymasters

Feuille 49 Vocabulaire

A list of key language from the unit is provided here as well as on pages 98–99 of the Students' Book and pages 74–75 of the *En solo* Workbook.

Feuille 50 Je sais…

Use this checklist with *Blog-notes* (Students' Book page 94) or towards the end of the unit. It provides an opportunity for students to review what they have learned and reflect on areas for improvement. This checklist is also provided on page 72 of the *En solo* Workbook.

Feuille 51 À vos marques!

These starter activities are intended for use with the following Students' Book pages:
- Use ex. 1 and 2 with pages 84–85.
- Use ex. 3 with pages 90–91.

1 Relie les parties du mot. Trouve six membres de la famille.

- Students match the word halves to find six family members.

Answers: une sœur, les parents, une cousine, un père, les enfants, un oncle

2 Complète les phrases avec des mots de l'encadré.

- Students complete sentences on the theme of family, using the words provided.

Answers: a qui; b parents; c unique; d sœur; e frère

3 Remplis chaque case avec un mot de l'unité 5.

- Students fill in the grid using words from Unit 5. For each letter B, C, G, P and T, they need to find a family member, an adjective to describe appearance, and an adjective to describe personality.

Possible answers:

	famille	apparence	personnalité
B	beau-père, belle-mère (beau-frère, belle-sœur)	blond, beau (belle), bleus, brun(e)	bavard(e)
C	cousin(e)	cheveux, courts, couleur	calme
G	grand-mère, grand-père, grands-parents	grand(e), gros(se), gris	gentil(le), généreux(euse)
P	père (papa), parents	petit(e)	paresseux(euse)
T	tante		timide, têtu(e), travailleur(euse)

Feuille 52 Bilan de leçon

These plenary activities are intended for use with the following Students' Book pages:
- Use ex. 1 and 2 with Students' Book pages 90–91.
- Use ex. 3 with Students' Book pages 86–87.

1 Crée et décris un extraterrestre. Utilise l'exemple pour t'aider.

- Students make up a description of an alien, using the model text to help them.

2 Présente ton extraterrestre à la classe: fais une petite présentation ou un poster.

- Students give a presentation about the alien they created in ex. 1.

3 Choisis deux images pour chaque phrase.

- Students choose a picture and a clock time to represent each sentence about morning routine.

Answers: 1 b, h; 2 d, m; 3 a, j; 4 f, i; 5 g, n; 6 c, k; 7 e, l

Feuille 53 Écouter

- Use ex. 1 with Students' Book pages 88–89.
- Use ex. 2 with Students' Book pages 84–85.
- Use ex. 3 with Students' Book pages 86–87.

AT 1.2 **1 C'est qui? Écoute et écris la bonne lettre.**

- Students choose a picture to represent each description of appearance.

Answers: 1 b; 2 c; 3 a

 CD 3, track 14 Feuille 53, activité 1

1 Mon frère est blond. Il a les cheveux courts et raides. Il a un petit nez et il porte des lunettes.
2 Mon cousin est brun. Il a les cheveux longs et raides. Il porte des lunettes et il a un grand nez.
3 Mon copain est roux et il a un petit nez. Il a les cheveux courts et frisés.

AT 1.2 **2 Écoute. Trouve la famille correcte et encercle a ou b.**

- Students listen and choose an image to represent each of the families described.

Answers: 1 a; 2 b; 3 b; 4 a; 5 a

 CD 3, track 15 Feuille 53, activité 2

1 – Quentin, tu as des frères et sœurs?
  – Oui. J'ai deux sœurs. J'habite avec elles et avec ma mère.

2 – Et toi, Thiane?
– J'ai deux frères. Nous habitons avec notre père.
3 – Tu habites avec qui, Sarah?
– J'habite avec mes parents et mon grand frère.
4 – Tu as des frères et sœurs, Damla?
– Je suis fille unique, et j'habite avec mes parents.
5 – Dario, tu habites avec ton grand-père, n'est-ce pas?
– Oui, et aussi avec mon père et ma sœur.

 3 Regarde les images. Écoute Loïc. Vrai ou faux?

- Students listen to Loïc describing his morning routine. They look at the pictures and work out whether his statements are true or false.

Answers: 1 vrai; 2 faux; 3 faux; 4 faux; 5 vrai

🎧 **CD 3, track 16**   Feuille 53, activité 3

1 Je me réveille à six heures trente.
2 Je me lève à six heures quarante-cinq.
3 À sept heures quinze, je prends mon petit déjeuner.
4 Je quitte la maison avec ma mère à sept heures trente.
5 J'arrive au collège à sept heures cinquante-cinq.

Feuille 54   Parler

- Use ex. 1 with Students' Book pages 88–89.
- Use ex. 2 with Students' Book pages 90–91.

 1 À deux.

- Working in pairs, each student draws three different people, showing what type of hair they have, their eye colour, size of nose and body shape. They keep the drawings hidden from their partner.
- Students then take turns to describe their drawings to their partner, who draws them.

 2 Un peu de théâtre! Choisis un adjectif. Lis une phrase de la liste. Ton/Ta partenaire doit deviner l'adjectif!

- Students choose an adjective from the list, keeping it secret from their partner.
- They then read out one of the sentences in the style of the adjective, e.g. if they select *timide*, they read out the sentence as if they are a very shy person.
- Their partner tries to identify the adjective.

Feuille 55   Lire et écrire 1

- Use with Students' Book pages 84–85.

AT 3.2 **1a Regarde l'arbre généalogique. Lis les phrases: vrai ou faux?**

- Students look at the family tree and work out whether the statements about it are true or false.

Answers: 1 vrai; 2 faux; 3 faux; 4 faux; 5 vrai; 6 vrai; 7 faux; 8 vrai

AT 3.3 **1b Lis les phrases, regarde l'arbre généalogique et écris les prénoms.**

- Students fill in the names of family members, referring to the family tree for the information required.

Answers: a Romain; b Mathilde; c Ludovic; d Céline; e Françoise; f Robert; g Mathilde; h Clément; i Marie, Céline; j Franck, Vincent; k Marie, Franck, Céline; l Léa, Laura; m Romain

Feuille 56   Lire et écrire 2

- Use ex. 1 with Students' Book pages 90–91.
- Use ex. 2 with Students' Book pages 86–87.

AT 3.2 **1 Complète chaque phrase avec le mot correct.**

- Students use the words provided to complete gap-fill sentences describing an inhabitant of the planet Pluto.

Answers: 1 appelle; 2 famille; 3 cheveux; 4 égoïste; 5 ma; 6 quinze; 7 est; 8 je; 9 les

AT 3.2 **2 La routine de Vanda le vampire! Regarde l'agenda. Mets les phrases dans le bon ordre.**

- Students use the information given on the diary page to help them sort the daily routine sentences into the correct order.

Answers: Je me réveille à neuf heures. Je me lève à neuf heures quinze. Je me douche à neuf heures trente. Je prends le petit déjeuner à neuf heures quarante-cinq. Je quitte la maison à dix heures trente. J'arrive au collège à dix heures quarante-cinq. Je rentre à la maison à cinq heures vingt-cinq.

Feuille 57   Labo-langue

- Use with Students' Book page 92.

1 Remplis les blancs.

- Students fill in the missing words to complete the present tense conjugation of *remplir* and *vendre*.

Answers: <u>remplir</u>: je remplis, tu remplis, il/elle/on remplit, nous remplissons, vous remplissez, ils/elles remplissent
<u>vendre</u>: je vends, tu vends, il/elle/on vend, nous vendons, vous vendez, ils/elles vendent

2 Écris les verbes en français dans la grille.

- Students work out the present tense reflexive verbs and complete the crossword puzzle.

Answers: 1 je me douche; 2 nous nous habillons; 3 elle se brosse; 4 vous vous levez; 5 ils se douchent; 6 tu te lèves; 7 elles s'habillent; 8 nous nous levons; 9 je me réveille

Feuille 58   Bien apprendre!

- Use with *Bien apprendre!* on Students' Book page 93.

1a So far, you have met three connectives. Can you remember what they are? Fill in the French words in the spaces below.

Answers: and – *et*; but – *mais*; or – *ou*

1b Put the most appropriate connective from the box into each gap.

Answers: 1 et; 2 ou; 3 mais

2 Here is a text composed of lots of short sentences. Add some connectives to make it more interesting to read.

Possible answer: Je m'appelle Katia, j'ai douze ans et j'habite à Lyon en France. J'habite avec mes parents et mon frère. Je suis timide mais mon frère est bavard.
Je suis petite et assez mince. Je suis rousse et j'ai les cheveux longs et raides. Je porte des lunettes, mais je n'aime pas porter des lunettes.
Je me lève à six heures trente et je me douche. Je quitte la maison à sept heures cinquante et j'arrive au collège à huit heures cinq.

Feuille 59   Bien parler!

- Use with *Bien parler!* on Students' Book page 93.

1a Lis les mots à haute voix et souligne le mot sans le son è.

- Students read the words aloud and identify the word in each set that doesn't contain the è sound.

Answers: 1 sœur; 2 livre; 3 cousin; 4 histoire; 5 petit; 6 chambre

1b Écoute et vérifie.

- Students listen to check their answers to ex. 1a.

 CD 3, track 17   Feuille 59, activité 1b

1 mère – sœur – père
2 matière – fenêtre – livre
3 cousin – règle – treize
4 collège – anglais – histoire
5 chaise – petit – crayon
6 aime – fête – chambre

2a Combien de mots avec le son è trouves-tu?

- Students identify the words in the box that contain the è sound.

Answers: anniversaire, derrière, deuxième, français, mais, pièce

 2b Vérifie ta réponse avec ton/ta partenaire.

- Students check their answers to ex. 2a with their partner.

3 Tongue-twisters: listen and practise!

 CD 3, track 18   Feuille 59, activité 3

– Mon père est maire, mon frère est serveur.
– Le ver vert va vers le verre vert.
– Seize chaises sèchent.

Feuille 60   Culture

- Use with Students' Book page 97.

1 Can you match up these surnames with descriptions 1–8?

Answers: 1 Brun; 2 Roux; 3 Rousseau; 4 Depaul; 5 Laurent; 6 Boucher; 7 Chevalier; 8 Lisle

2 Use a dictionary to help you to match up the English and French surnames.

Answers:

1	Baker	Boulanger
2	Cowan	Vachon
3	Fields	Deschamps
4	Greenwood	Boisvert
5	Hill	Lamontagne
6	King	Leroy
7	Newton	Villeneuve
8	Smith	Laforge
9	White	Leblanc
10	Young	Lejeune

En solo Workbook

Pages 62–63   5.1 Voici ma famille

• Use with Students' Book pages 84–85.

AT 1.2 | **1 Listen and tick a or b to show how many brothers and sisters each person has.**

Answers: 1 a; 2 a; 3 b; 4 b

 En solo CD, track 38   page 62, activité 1

1 – J'ai un frère… mais je n'ai pas de sœurs.
2 – Maxime, tu as des frères et sœurs?
  – Non, je n'ai pas de frères et sœurs. Je suis fils unique.
3 – Ophélie, tu as des frères et sœurs?
  – Oui, oui… moi, j'ai trois frères, mais je n'ai pas de sœurs.
  – Tu n'as pas de sœurs?
  – Non.
4 – Quentin, tu as des frères et sœurs?
  – Euh, oui!
  – Ah bon! Par exemple…? Tu as des frères?
  – Oui… j'ai deux frères.
  – OK. Et… tu as des sœurs?
  – Oui.
  – Tu as combien de sœurs?
  – J'ai une sœur.
  – Alors, deux frères et une sœur… c'est ça?
  – Oui, c'est exact.
  – Bon, OK, merci, Quentin!

AT 3.2 | **2 Tick the right caption for each picture.**

Answers: 1 a; 2 a; 3 b; 4 a

AT 4.2 | **3 Write captions for these pictures.**

Answers: a J'ai un frère. Je n'ai pas de sœurs. b J'ai une sœur. Je n'ai pas de frères. c J'ai deux sœurs et un frère.

AT 3.2 | **4 Read about Didier Drogba. Underline all the words for family members.**

Answers: son oncle, son père, sa mère, six frères et sœurs, il est père, trois enfants, deux fils, une fille

AT 3.3 | **5 Answer in English: you'll find the answers in the text above.**

Answers: a Didier Drogba; b his uncle; c six; d three (two sons and a daughter); e because he always phones them before he plays in a match

Pages 64–65   5.2 Le matin, chez moi

• Use with Students' Book pages 86–87.

AT 3.2 | **1 Find and copy out the right caption for each picture.**

Answers: a Eddy se réveille. b Il se lève. c Il se douche. d Il s'habille. e Il prend son petit déjeuner. f Il se brosse les dents. g Il quitte la maison.

AT 1.2 | **2 Listen and number the pictures of Eddy in the order you hear them mentioned.**

Answers: a 1; b 5; c 3; d 6; e 2; f 7; g 4

 En solo CD, track 39   page 64, activité 2

Numéro un: Eddy se réveille… brr… il n'aime pas ça!
Numéro deux: Il prend son petit déjeuner.
Numéro trois: il se douche.
Numéro quatre: il quitte la maison.
Numéro cinq: il se lève.
Numéro six: il s'habille.
Numéro sept: il se brosse les dents.

AT 3.2
AT 4.2 | **3 Find a route through each set of clouds to make a sentence. Write it down.**

Answers: a Je me réveille à sept heures. b Je me brosse les dents. c Mon frère se lève à sept heures trente. d Je ne me douche pas.

AT 3.2 | **4 What do sentences a–d mean in English?**

Answers: a I wake up at seven o'clock. b I brush my teeth. c My brother gets up at seven thirty. d I don't have a shower.

AT 4.2 | **Défi!**

• Students write five sentences to describe their own morning routine.

Pages 66–67   5.3 Il est comment?

• Use with Students' Book pages 88–89.

AT 3.1 | **1 Find the French equivalents in the cloud and write them in.**

Answers: short: *petit(e)*; tall: *grand(e)*; slim: *mince*; well-built: *gros(se)*; dark-haired: *brun(e)*; fair-haired: *blond(e)*; short hair: *les cheveux courts*; curly hair: *les cheveux frisés*; brown eyes: *les yeux marron*; blue eyes: *les yeux bleus*

AT 3.2 | **2 Read the descriptions. Who is the girl in the picture? Write her name.**

Answer: Océane

3 Describe what one of your friends looks like.

- Students use the prompts to help them write a description of one of their friends.

AT 3.2 / AT 4.2 **4 Play the game to invent a new computer game character.**

- This game is based on inventing a character for an imaginary new computer game. It could be done individually, but is best played in pairs. Each pair will need a die and coloured pencils.
- Each student decides in advance whether their character will be male or female.
- They work their way through the numbered categories from 1–8. For each category, they throw the die: the number they throw corresponds to a description. Depending on whether their character is male or female, they choose either the masculine or the feminine version of the description, read it aloud and write it down.
- When students have completed all eight categories, they will have eight statements.
- They draw their character so that he/she matches the description built up in statements 1–8. The drawing could be done for homework.
- If no dice are available, students could prepare a card spinner with numbers on or a set of numbered tokens to pick at random out of a bag or envelope.

AT 4.3 **Follow-up:** Students draw a second character and write a description of him/her.

Pages 68–69 5.4 Qui es-tu?

- Use with Students' Book pages 90–91.

AT 3.1 **1 Circle the 12 adjectives that describe personality.**

Answers: généreux(euse), intelligent(e), bavard(e), drôle, égoïste, sportif(ive), têtu(e), timide, travailleur(euse), gentil(le), optimiste, paresseux(euse)

Défi!

- Students sort the remaining words into groups, using different colours to identify the different groupings.
- Accept any appropriate groupings, e.g. colour adjectives, family members, nouns connected with school, etc.

AT 1.2 / AT 3.2 **2 Read and listen to what Francine Stein says about herself and her family. Answer the questions in English.**

Answers: a tall; b no; c very intelligent; d nice/kind and generous; e shy; f very talkative; g funny

 En solo CD, track 40   page 69, activité 2

Je m'appelle Francine Stein. Je suis grande et je suis belle, et je ne suis pas violente.
Ma mère est très intelligente. Mon père est sympa et généreux.
Mon frère est timide. Ma sœur est très bavarde.
Mon grand-père est drôle.

AT 1.2 / AT 3.2 **3 Listen to Francine talking about her dog. Write the missing words into the text below.**

Answers: see underlining in transcript

 En solo CD, track 41   page 69, activité 3

Mon chien est super! Il est <u>petit</u>… et il est très <u>drôle</u>. Il est toujours <u>sympa</u>. Il est très gentil. Et il est très <u>intelligent</u>. Il n'est pas du tout <u>violent</u>.

Pages 70–71 Labo-langue

- Use with Students' Book pages 92–93.

1 Do the quiz on irregular and reflexive verbs. Explain your choices.

Answers: 1 c (it isn't a reflexive verb); 2 a (it doesn't follow the pattern of a regular -er verb); 3 c (it doesn't follow the pattern of a regular -ir verb); 4 c (it's the third person plural of *faire*); 5 c (it's the third person plural of *vouloir*); 6 a (*fais* is the first and second person singular of *faire*); 7 c (the correct pronouns are *je me…, tu te…* and *il/elle/on se…*); 8 a (*me* becomes *m'* before a vowel)

2 Tick the sentences that contain reflexive verbs.

Answers: a, c, e

3 Choose and underline the correct verb.

Answers: a vas; b vais; c fait; d prend; e venez; f voit; g veux; h va; i faisons; j finissent

4 Write in the correct form of the reflexive verb given at the end.

Answers: a me douche; b me brosse; c t'habilles; d se lève; e s'amuse; f s'entend; g me prépare

Page 72 Checklist

- Use with *Blog-notes* (Students' Book page 94) or towards the end of the unit.

The checklist, recording and follow-up activities provide opportunities for students to review what they have learned, test themselves orally on key language and reflect on areas for improvement.

En solo CD, track 42 page 72, activité 2

1 grandmother, grandfather *[beep]* grand-mère, grand-père
2 I haven't got any sisters. *[beep]* Je n'ai pas de sœurs.
3 I live with my mum and my stepdad. *[beep]* J'habite avec ma mère et mon beau-père.
4 Have you got any brothers? *[beep]* Tu as des frères?
5 I arrive at school at nine o'clock. *[beep]* J'arrive au collège à neuf heures.
6 What time do you wake up? *[beep]* À quelle heure tu te réveilles?
7 I'm short. *[beep]* Je suis petit *(if you're a boy, or)* je suis petite *(if you're a girl)*.
8 I'm well-built. *[beep]* Je suis gros *(for a boy, or)* je suis grosse *(for a girl)*.
9 I've got grey eyes. *[beep]* J'ai les yeux gris.
10 I've got long hair. *[beep]* J'ai les cheveux longs.
11 What colour are your eyes? *[beep]* De quelle couleur sont tes yeux?
12 I wear glasses. *[beep]* Je porte des lunettes.
13 My mother is hard-working. *[beep]* Ma mère est travailleuse.
14 My father is very tall. *[beep]* Mon père est très grand.
15 I wake up, you wake up *[beep]* je me réveille, tu te réveilles

Follow-up: Encourage students to draw up their own individual action plan of steps they could take to help them improve. Provide a checklist of suggestions for them to choose from, e.g. try harder to learn vocabulary, read the grammar notes again and make sure they understand them/ask for help if they don't understand, check written work carefully for mistakes, etc.

Page 73 Top tips and strategies

Speaking

This section provides students with tips on how to cope when they want to say something but don't know the language for it, e.g. by trying to plan ahead, by rephrasing or by using mime/gestures. It could be used at any appropriate point during Unit 5.

1 Imagine that you want to tell a French visitor what you do at the weekend. Think ahead. Make a list of words or phrases you think would be useful.

• Students are encouraged to plan ahead for a situation in which they might find themselves and to list any language they might need.

Follow-up: Ask them to repeat ex. 1 for other situations, e.g. telling a French penfriend about school in this country or about where they live.

2 Say these sentences in French, rephrasing the message if necessary to use words you know.

• This activity shows students how they can often avoid language they don't know by rephrasing it.

Possible answers: a Je range ma chambre souvent. b Je me réveille à sept heures. c Le film n'est pas très intéressant/Je n'aime pas le film/Le film est nul/Le film est ennuyeux. (NB Although *ennuyeux* hasn't been introduced as key language, students may have come across it in Unit 3 when researching adjectives to describe school subjects.) d Mon père n'est pas généreux.

 Follow-up: Students play Charades to practise communicating through mime/gesture. They choose a theme (e.g. daily routine, opinions of school subjects) and take turns to mime words and phrases within this theme. Tell them they must choose language they already know, so that they person working out the mime can give the corresponding French word or phrase.

Reading

This section suggests tips to help with reading, e.g. looking for any clues provided by the text type, title or pictures, reading through for gist, using context to work out meanings. It could be used at any appropriate point during Unit 5.

3 What do you think the nonsense word *scoubidou* might mean in each of these sentences?

• Students use context to try to work out possible meanings of the unknown word in each sentence.

Answers: a must be a type of pet; b likely to be "hate"; c any adjective that might be used to describe a house

Pages 74–75 Vocabulaire

• Use with Students' Book pages 98–99.

A list of key language from the unit is provided here as well as in the Students' Book and on Copymaster 49.

1 Listen and tick the phrases you hear.

 En solo CD, track 43 page 75, activité 1

Je suis fils unique.
les enfants
une cousine
Mes parents sont divorcés.
Je me lève.
Tous les jours.
Elle est brune.
J'ai les yeux marron.
généreux, généreuse
Il est un peu timide.

2 Underline in coloured pencil...

- Students search the list for key language items.

3 What's your favourite word or phrase in this unit?

- Challenge students to make up some sentences using their favourite words/phrases.

Unité 6: On mange!   Overview grid

Page reference	Contexts and objectives	Grammar	Language strategies and pronunciation	Key language	Framework	AT Level
102–103 **6.1 On va au café?**	• Eating out	• *au, à la* • Present tense of *aller*		le café, le restaurant, le fast-food, la pizzeria, la crêperie, la cafétéria Je mange au/à la… Je vais au/à la… On va au restaurant? Oui, d'accord. Non…. Je voudrais…. un sandwich, un hamburger, un croque-monsieur, un steak-frites, une crêpe, une pizza	**R** – 7W5, 7L3	1.2–4, 2.2–3, 3.2, 4.2–3
104–105 **6.2 S'il vous plaît!**	• Ordering food	• *au, à l', à la, aux*		Numbers 70–100 *Vous désirez? Je voudrais…, s'il vous plaît. C'est tout? C'est combien? C'est… euros. Voilà.* *Merci, au revoir.* *le chocolat, le fromage, l'orange, la vanille, la tomate, les olives, les fruits de mer, une crêpe au chocolat, une glace à l'orange, une pizza à la tomate, un sandwich aux fruits de mer*	**R** – 7W3, 7T2, 7C5	1.1–3, 2.1–3, 3.2, 4.2–3
106–107 **6.3 Ma recette préférée**	• Recipes: ingredients and quantities	• *du, de l', de la, des* • *… pas de/d'* (revision)		Numbers above 100 *C'est très bon! C'est très facile à faire! Il faut + infinitive.* *il y a/il n'y a pas de…* *de la farine, du sucre en poudre, du lait, du pain, du fromage râpé, du jambon, du beurre, du sel, du poivre, de l'huile d'olive, des œufs, des cerises* *cent grammes (de), un kilo/litre (de), un demi-kilo/demi-litre* *beurrer, mélanger, ajouter* *un plat, un four chaud* *d'abord, ensuite, puis, pour finir*	**R** – 7S5, 7S7, 7T1	1.1–3, 2.2–4, 3.3, 4.2–4
108–109 **6.4 Mange bien!**	• Healthy eating	• *aller* + infinitive		*pour être en forme, je bois, je vais manger* *plus de, moins de* *le poisson, les légumes, les chips, les pâtes, les barres de céréales, le café, le jus de fruit, le chocolat chaud, le soda, l'eau* *en général, de temps en temps* *le matin, le midi, l'après-midi, le soir* *Tu prends un goûter?* *Est-ce que tu manges…? Qu'est-ce que tu manges? Tu manges quoi?*	**R** – 7W5, 7S7	1.2–4, 2.3, 3.3, 4.2–4
110–111 **Labo-langue**	• Grammar • Skills • Pronunciation	• *au, à l', à la, aux* • *du, de l', de la, des*	• Asking questions • Intonation **Workbook:** • How to prepare for listening tasks • Checking written work		**R** – 7W2, 7S4, 7T4, 7T5, 7T7, 7L2, 7L6	
112–115 **Blog-notes / Tu sais tout? / En plus / Clic.fr**	• End-of-unit summary and assessment • Extension • **Cultural focus:** French food			**En plus:** *un paquet de, une tranche de, un morceau de, une boîte de, une bouteille de*	**R** – 7S4, 7T6, 7C2, 7C3, 7C4	1.1, 1.3–4, 2.2–3, 3.1–3, 4.3–4

CLIC! 1 STAR UNIT 6 MEDIUM TERM PLAN

About Unit 6, *On mange!* This unit focuses on different aspects of food, including eating out, meals and mealtimes, recipes, healthy eating, and typical French foods. Students learn how to order/pay for food in a café/restaurant using polite language, describe ingredients and give recipe instructions, and talk about eating habits and healthy resolutions. They are introduced to the conditional (*je voudrais*) and the near future (*aller* + infinitive), focus on different ways of asking questions, get to grips with *au/à l'/à la/aux* and *du/de l'/de la/des*, and practise intonation in questions and statements. Additional teaching and learning includes quantities and numbers 70–100 and above.

Framework objectives (reinforce)	Teaching and learning	Week-by-week overview (assuming 6 weeks' work or approximately 10–12.5 hours)
7W2: High-frequency words	Use of *du/de l'/de la/des, au/à l'/à la/aux* (p. 110).	**Week 1 – Opening spread/6.1 On va au café?** Opening spread: introduction to unit themes and objectives, focusing on typical French foods and eating habits
7W5: Verbs present (+ past)	Present tense of *aller* (p. 103 ex. 7); the conditional: *je voudrais* (pp. 103–105); the near future: *aller* + infinitive (p. 109).	Spread 6.1: eating out; different types of eating place
7S4: Basic questions	Question words (*quand, qui, quoi, où, comment, combien, est-ce que, qu'est-ce que*) and different ways to ask questions, e.g. inversion, intonation (p. 111, p. 117).	**Week 2 – 6.2 S'il vous plaît!** Ordering/Paying for food in a café or restaurant, using polite forms; numbers 70–100
7S5: Basic negatives	Use of *ne… pas* with the near future: *Je ne vais pas manger* (p. 109); revision and recycling of *il n'y a pas de/d'…* in recipe ingredients, e.g. *il n'y a pas de sel* (p. 106).	**Week 3 – 6.3 Ma recette préférée** Recipes, quantities and ingredients; *il faut* + noun; *il faut* + infinitive; sequencers (*d'abord, ensuite,* etc.); numbers above 100
7S7: Time and tenses	Use sequencers, e.g. *d'abord, ensuite, pour finir* (p. 107); talk about resolutions for the future using *aller* + infinitive (p. 109).	
7T1: Reading using cues	Use context and cognates/near-cognates to understand recipes (p. 107 ex. 7).	
7T2: Reading aloud	Read aloud a dialogue ordering food and drink, varying the moods of the speakers, e.g. angry, sad, happy (p. 105 ex. 9).	**Week 4 – 6.4 Mange bien!** Healthy eating, eating habits and mealtimes; healthy resolutions for the future (*aller* + infinitive)
7T4: Using resources	Use a dictionary or the glossary to check food vocabulary; use a range of resources to check for mistakes in written work (Workbook p. 87).	
7T5: Assembling text	Use question words provided to construct as many questions as possible about a photo (p. 111).	**Week 5 – Labo-langue** *au, à l', à la, aux; du, de l', de la, des*; asking questions; intonation
7T6: Texts as prompts for writing	Adapt the answers to questions about Thomas's video blog (p. 112) to compile own personal answers to the same questions. If appropriate, encourage students to build a continuous text from their answers and create their own video blog.	
7T7: Improving written work	Check written work for spellings, genders, agreement, etc. (Workbook p. 87).	**Week 6 – Blog-notes, Tu sais tout?, En plus, Clic.fr, On chante!, Lecture** Reinforcement and extension of the language of the unit; review of progress via the Checklist in the Workbook/on Copymaster; revision and assessment
7L2: Following speech	How to prepare for listening activities (Workbook p. 87).	
7L3: Gist and detail	Watch video clip in which people discuss eating out: identify the places mentioned, then watch the clip again and note down additional details (p. 102).	
7L6: Improving speech	Use of correct intonation in questions and statements (p. 111).	
7C2: Everyday culture	French food and comparing with food in the UK.	
7C3: Contact with native speakers	Video clip in which native speakers talk about eating out (p. 102); video blog (p. 112).	
7C4: Stories and songs	Song on the theme of shopping for food (p. 117).	
7C5: Social conventions	Use of *madame/monsieur* and *vous* for politeness.	

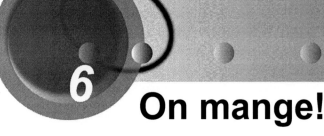

6 On mange!

Unit objectives

Contexts: Food and meals
Grammar: *du, de l', de la, des*; *au, à l', à la, aux*
Language learning: Asking questions
Pronunciation: Intonation
Cultural focus: French food

Assessment opportunities

Listening: Students' Book, page 105, activities 8a and 8b
Speaking: Students' Book, page 108, activity 4

See also **Clic! 1** OxBox Assessment CD-ROM

AT 3.1

C

1 Regarde les photos. C'est quoi?

- *Aim*: To introduce the themes of the unit and develop cultural awareness, reinforcing Framework Objective 7C2.
- Students match the captions to the photos of food. Ask them to take note of whether the items are *un/une* or *des*, e.g. *une paëlla, des escargots.*
- Many of the words are cognates or near-cognates, so students should be able to work out their meanings without using a dictionary.

Answers: 1 b; 2 a; 3 g; 4 c; 5 e; 6 h; 7 d; 8 f; 9 i

Follow-up: Use the photos as an opportunity to focus on the influence of other countries on French food. Ask students which of the foods shown here are from other countries: *une pizza (un plat italien/la cuisine italienne), une paëlla (un plat espagnol), des nems (un plat vietnamien), un couscous (un plat nord-africain), un hamburger (un plat américain).*

Can students identify similar influences in Britain? Which dishes are popular in Britain and which countries do they come from?

AT 4.2

2 Complète!

- Students use the sentences provided as a writing frame for expressing their opinions of the food in the photos.
- Encourage them to use the exclamations *beurk, bof* and *miam miam* in addition to more articulate ways of expressing opinions!

Follow-up:

- Students exchange their opinions of *la cuisine anglaise, la cuisine écossaise, la cuisine indienne,* etc.
- Use this spread as an opportunity to tackle clichés about French food (snails, etc.). Discuss specialities from other countries and cultures. What do people in some countries eat that we in Britain don't? What do we eat that other cultures wouldn't find very appetising? For example, the French aren't particularly keen on Marmite and baked beans!

6.1 On va au café?

pages 102–103

Planner

> **Objectives**
  - Eating out

> **Resources**
  Students' Book, pages 102–103
  CD 3, tracks 20–21
  Video clip 12
  En solo Workbook, pages 76–77;
  En solo CD, track 44
  Copymaster 64

> **Key language**
  Tu manges où en ville?
  le café, le restaurant, le fast-food
  la pizzeria, la crêperie, la cafétéria
  Je mange au/à la… Je vais au/à la…
  On va au restaurant?
  Oui, d'accord. Non,…

  Je voudrais…
  un sandwich, un hamburger, un croque-monsieur,
  un steak-frites
  une crêpe, une pizza

> **Grammar**
  au, à la
  Present tense of *aller*

> **Framework reference**
  R – 7W5, 7L3

> **Starters**
  - Students draw out two columns, with *au* at the head of one column and *à la* at the head of the other. Display the words for the six places to eat (without genders) and set a time limit for students to list them in the correct columns. They swap with a partner and check each other's lists.
  - In small groups (e.g. three to five), students play a chain game to build up sentences using *Je voudrais* + food and *On va* + place to eat. Provide support by writing different categories of words on the board for them to choose from, e.g.

  - subject pronouns (*je, tu, on*)
  - verbs (*voudrais, va*)
  - food items (*une crêpe, un hamburger,* etc.)
  - places to eat (*au restaurant, à la crêperie,* etc.)

  To play the game, each student chooses one word only, e.g.
  A: *Je…*; B: *voudrais…*; C *une…*; D *crêpe*.
  E: *On…*; A: *va…*; B: *à…*; C: *la…*; D: *crêperie?*
  E: *Je…*; A: *voudrais…*, etc.
  They need to concentrate on choosing a food word and eating place that are the correct gender to match what the preceding person has said (*un* or *une, au* or *à la*). They also need to make sure they don't end up with any unlikely combinations, e.g. *steak-frites* and *crêperie*! To make this competitive, anyone who makes a grammatical error or an unlikely combination is out of the game. Eventually only one person (the winner) will remain.

> **Plenaries**
  - Write out the lines from a dialogue (similar to the one in ex. 4) in jumbled order on the board or an OHT, e.g.
    - *On mange où?*
    - *On va à la crêperie? Je voudrais une crêpe.*
    - *Bof! Je n'aime pas les crêpes. Je préfère les hamburgers. On va au fast-food?*
    - *Non, merci. Je déteste les hamburgers. On va à la pizzeria?*
    - *Oui, d'accord. Je voudrais une pizza. On va à la pizzeria!*

    Give students a time limit to sort the dialogue into the correct order. Pairs read it aloud.
  - Focus on how important it is to learn the gender of nouns in French. In pairs, student reflect on issues that are affected by gender, e.g. definite and indefinite articles, adjective agreement, and on this spread they have learned *au/à la* to talk about going to places. Allow time for whole-class feedback.
  - Copymaster 64 *Bilan de leçon* ex. 2.

---

1 Regarde. Note dans l'ordre.

  - The video clip shows people being interviewed about where they like to eat out. Students note down the places from the photos in the order they are mentioned.

  Answers: 2 (le restaurant), 3 (le fast-food), 5 (la crêperie), 6 (la cafétéria), 4 (la pizzeria), 1 (le café)

▶ **Video clip 12**   page 102, activité 1

  Aujourd'hui, on va parler de là où tu manges quand tu vas en ville…

  - Tu manges où quand tu vas en ville?
  - En ville? Je mange au restaurant avec ma famille. Mes parents aiment bien manger au restaurant.

  - Tu manges où quand tu vas en ville?
  - En général, avec des copains, on va au fast-food, au Flunch, au MacDo, au Quick. C'est sympa.

  - Bonjour! Alors tu aimes manger à la crêperie quand tu vas en ville?

6 On mange!

> - Oui, j'adore manger à la crêperie quand je vais en ville avec des copines. On adore les crêpes!
>
> - Tu manges où quand tu vas en ville?
> - Quand je vais au supermarché avec mes parents, je mange à la cafétéria. C'est pratique.
>
> - Salut! Tu manges où quand tu vas en ville?
> - Je vais à la pizzeria. La pizza, c'est mon plat préféré.
>
> - Salut! Tu manges où quand tu vas en ville?
> - Des fois, on mange au café. C'est rapide. On prend un sandwich et après on va au cinéma!

AT 1.3–4

Follow-up: Play the video clip again. Students note down the reasons given for eating at the different places. Ask them to listen out for any additional information, e.g. number 4 says he eats at the cafeteria in the supermarket with his parents, and number 6 says she has a sandwich and then goes on to the cinema.

AT 2.2 **2 À deux, avec un dé. (B → A)**
- Students take turns to throw a die and practise saying the key vocabulary.
- The numbers on the die correspond to the numbered places in the key language list, e.g. 1 = *le café*, 2 = *le restaurant*. For example:
  Student A (throws a 5): *Je mange à la crêperie!*
  Student B (throws a 3): *Je vais au fast-food!*
- The first student to throw all six numbers and correctly say six sentences is the winner.
- Emphasise that students should try to say a complete sentence including the verb (*Je mange* or *Je vais*) and concentrate on using *au* and *à la* correctly. Point out the information panel on *au/à la*.

AT 4.2 **3 Écris.**
- Students use the jigsaw words to build sentences practising *au* and *à la*. Accept any appropriate answers.
- This activity provides support in forming longer sentences that include a time phrase, e.g. *le lundi, je mange à la cantine*.

Preparation: Before doing ex. 4, revise the question words used: *Qui? Quand? Où? Quoi?* Revise times, if necessary, and make sure that students recognise the parts of *aller* used in the text.

AT 1.2 **4 Écoute, lis et réponds.**
AT 3.2
- Students read the script while listening to the recording: the three teenagers are discussing where in town to eat.

- Students focus on finding specific details: Who is it? When is this taking place? Where are they going to eat? What are they going to eat?

Answers: a C'est Claire, Sara et Marie. b C'est samedi, à 13 heures. c Ils vont à la pizzeria. d Ils mangent une pizza.

 CD 3, track 20 page 103, activité 4
> - Samedi, 13 heures. Claire, Sara et Marie vont en ville…
> - On mange où?
> - Je voudrais un hamburger. On va au fast-food?
> - Bof! Moi, je n'aime pas les hamburgers. Je préfère les pizzas. On va à la pizzeria?
> - Miam! Miam! J'aime les pizzas!
> - Oui, d'accord.

AT 1.2 **5a Écoute (1–3).**
- Students listen to three short conversations focusing on food and places to eat. They note down the food (from the photos provided) mentioned in each conversation.

Answers: 1 d, a; 2 b, e; 3 c, f, d

 CD 3, track 21 page 103, activité 5
> **1** - Il est 18 heures. On mange où?
> - Je voudrais un steak-frites. On va au restaurant?
> - Non, je suis végétarien. Je préfère les crêpes.
> - Bon, ben, on va à la crêperie!
> **2** - Papa, il est midi trente. On mange où?
> - Je voudrais juste un sandwich. Et toi?
> - Moi, je voudrais un croque-monsieur.
> - OK, d'accord! On va au café. Un croque-monsieur pour la demoiselle, un!
> **3** - Oh là là, déjà 14 heures. Maman, on mange?
> - Oui, d'accord. On va au fast-food? Je voudrais un hamburger.
> - Oh non, merci! Je déteste les hamburgers!
> - Alors, une pizza, à la pizzeria? C'est cool.
> - Ah non, moi, je préfère un bon steak-frites et une salade au restaurant!

AT 1.3 **5b Réécoute et réponds.**
- Play the recording again. Students answer questions a–d from ex. 4 for each conversation.

Answers:
1 a C'est un homme et une femme. b Il est 18 heures. c Ils vont à la crêperie. d Ils mangent des crêpes.

2 a C'est un père et sa fille. b Il est midi trente. c Ils vont au café. d Ils mangent un croque-monsieur.

3 a C'est une mère et son fils. b Il est 14 heures. c Ils vont au restaurant. d Ils mangent un steak-frites.

168

AT 2.3

AT 4.3

6 À deux: adaptez la conversation.
(B ➤ A)
- Students adapt the conversation in ex. 4, changing the highlighted words and phrases.

Follow-up:

- Students repeat the game from ex. 2 to practise *Je voudrais* + the food items shown in photos a–f. Tell them to imagine that the photos are numbered 1–6 (to correspond with the numbers on the die) instead of a–f:
  Student A (throws a 3): *Je voudrais un hamburger!*
  Student B (throws a 6): *Je voudrais une pizza!*
- More ambitious students could add an appropriate place, e.g.
  Student A (throws a 3): *Je voudrais un hamburger! On va au fast-food?*
  Student B (throws a 6): *Je voudrais une pizza! On va à la pizzeria?*

**7 Grammaire: trouve les formes du verbe *aller*
(pages 102–103).**
- Students search pages 102–103 for different forms of the verb *aller*.
- The answers are partially provided, with missing letters for students to fill in.

Answers: je vais, tu vas, on va, ils vont

Défi!
- *Aim*: To encourage students to think about language patterns.
- Students use their knowledge of present tense verb endings to help them complete the *il*, *elle*, *nous* and *vous* forms of *aller*.

Answers: il va, elle va, nous allons, vous allez

**W
76–77** Pages 76–77 of the *En solo* Workbook provide further activities to practise the present tense of *aller*, *au/à la* and places to eat out.

6.2 S'il vous plaît!

pages 104–105

Planner

> ### Objectives
> • Ordering food

> ### Resources
> Students' Book, pages 104–105
> CD 3, tracks 22–25
> *En solo* Workbook, pages 78–79;
> *En solo* CD, tracks 45–47
> Copymasters 63, 64, 65, 66, 68; CD 3, tracks 41–43

> ### Key language
> Numbers 70–100
>
> *Vous désirez?*
> *Je voudrais…, s'il vous plaît.*
> *C'est tout?*
> *C'est combien?*
> *C'est… euros.*
> *Voilà. Merci, au revoir.*
>
> *le chocolat, l'orange, l'ananas, la vanille, le fromage, la tomate, les fruits de mer, les olives une crêpe au chocolat, une glace à l'orange, une pizza à la tomate, un sandwich aux fruits de mer*

> ### Grammar
> *au, à l', à la, aux*

> ### Framework reference
> R – 7W3, 7T2, 7C5

> ### Starters
> • Play Hand-on-the-Buzzer. Call out numbers between 70 and 100 very slowly, e.g. *soix…*

ante… et… onze, quatre-… vingt-… dix-… sept. The first student to call out the correct number in English wins. The dilemma is that students have to wait long enough to hear the end of the word, but they can't wait too long or an opponent might call out the number first!

• Write the following jumble of words on the board or OHP. Give students 30 seconds to match them up into appropriate combinations. They must use all the words once only, and each item must be grammatically correct as well as something you'd want to eat!
un sandwich / un sandwich / une glace / une glace / une crêpe / une pizza
au / au / à la / à la / à l' / aux
fromage / tomate / vanille / chocolat / orange / olives

• Copymaster 63 *À tes marques!* ex. 3.

> ### Plenaries
> • Display a café dialogue on the board, OHP or interactive whiteboard, incorporating key language from the spread. Read it with the whole class, then erase one or two words/phrases. Challenge pairs to read the dialogue aloud, filling in the missing words. Erase even more words/phrases, then challenge pairs to read it again. Continue until only a few words/phrases remain. Can any pairs reconstruct the whole dialogue from memory?
> • Pairs brainstorm other situations in which they might be able to use some of the transactional language of this spread (e.g. *Je voudrais*, asking/saying prices, *voilà/merci*, etc.). Collect ideas on the board.
> • Copymaster 64 *Bilan de leçon* ex. 1.

---

1 Écoute. C'est quoi?

• Students listen to ten people ordering different flavours of ice cream, sandwiches, pizzas and pancakes. They note down the letters and numbers of the corresponding pictures.

Answers: 1 a2; 2 b3; 3 d8; 4 c4; 5 d1; 6 b5; 7 a6; 8 c5; 9 a6/7; 10 b2/6

 CD 3 , track 22   page 104, activité 1

1 Une pizza à la tomate, s'il vous plaît.
2 Un sandwich au fromage, s'il vous plaît.
3 Une glace à l'orange, s'il vous plaît.
4 Pour moi, une crêpe au chocolat.
5 Pour moi, une glace à la vanille.
6 Pour moi, un sandwich aux fruits de mer, s'il vous plaît.
7 Je voudrais une pizza aux olives.

---

8 Je voudrais une crêpe aux fruits de mer.
9 Je voudrais une pizza aux olives et à l'ananas.
10 Je voudrais un sandwich à la tomate et aux olives.

---

2 Tu aimes?

• Students play a dice game to practise fillings, flavours and opinions. Two dice are needed.
• First, students choose a food item a–d (a pizza, sandwich, pancake or ice cream). To determine the filling or flavour, they then throw either one die (for items 1–6) or two dice (for numbers 7 and 8):
Student A (chooses D, then throws a 6): *Une glace aux olives! Beurk! Je déteste ça!*
Student B: (chooses B, then throws a 3): *Un sandwich au fromage! Miam miam! J'aime ça!*

---

3 Grammaire: invente des menus!

- Students invent weird menus for each other or for famous people/cartoon characters.
- Encourage them to research additional flavours and fillings using a dictionary.

 4 Compte!

- *Aim*: To revise numbers up to 70 before higher numbers are introduced in ex. 5.
- Students read aloud the sums and work out the missing numbers.

Answers: a dix-sept plus dix-sept égalent <u>trente-quatre</u>; b vingt-quatre plus <u>quarante-cinq</u> égalent soixante-neuf; c <u>quarante et un</u> moins trente et un égalent vingt et un; d seize plus quarante-deux égalent <u>cinquante-huit</u>; e quarante et un moins quinze égalent <u>vingt-six</u>; f *accept any numbers that add up to 56*

 5 Écoute et note.

- Students listen and supply the six numbers that are missing from the sequence 70–100.

Answers: soixante-quatorze, soixante-dix-huit, quatre-vingt-trois, quatre-vingt-six, quatre-vingt-quinze, quatre-vingt-dix-huit

---

CD 3, track 23   page 105, activité 5

70, 71, 72, 73, ..., 75,
76, 77, ..., 79, 80,
81, 82, ..., 84, 85,
..., 87, 88, 89, 90,
91, 92, 93, 94, ...,
96, 97, ..., 99, 100

Follow-up:

- Play the recording again. Keep pausing it and ask students to supply the next number in the sequence.
- To increase the challenge, keep replaying the recording and ask students to supply the next two numbers in the sequence, then the next three numbers, and so on.

   6 À deux. (B ➔ A)

- Students play a guessing game to practise numbers 70–100. Student A thinks of a number and secretly writes it down; B guesses which number it is. When B has guessed correctly, the pair swap roles.

C65   Ex. 1 on Copymaster 65 is a listening activity on numbers.

 7 Écoute et lis. Trouve.

- Students read and listen to a dialogue in which someone orders food in a café. They search the text for key phrases.

Answers: a Vous désirez? b C'est tout? c C'est combien?

CD 3, track 24   page 105, activité 7

– Bonjour. Vous désirez?
– Je voudrais un sandwich au fromage et aux olives, s'il vous plaît.
– C'est tout?
– Oui. C'est combien?
– C'est 4,75 euros.
– Voilà. 4,75 euros, Merci.
– Merci. Au revoir!

 8a Écoute (1–4) et note le plat (voir page 104).

- Students listen to four conversations in which people order food. They note down the corresponding numbers and letters (from the pictures on page 104) of each person's order.
- This recording extends the basic model dialogue (from ex. 7) for students who may have learned this language already at primary school.

Answers: 1 a2/3; 2 d1; 3 c5, d4; 4 c4, d1

CD 3, track 25   page 105, activité 8

1 – Bonjour. Vous désirez?
   – Je voudrais une pizza à la tomate et au fromage, s'il vous plaît.
   – C'est tout?
   – Oui. C'est combien?
   – C'est 6,85 euros.
   – 6,85 euros. Voilà. Merci.
   – Merci. Au revoir!
2 – Bonjour. Vous désirez?
   – Euh... Je voudrais une glace au chocolat, s'il vous plaît.
   – Désolée. Il n'y a pas de glace au chocolat.
   – Il y a une glace à la vanille?
   – Oui!
   – Alors, une glace à la vanille.
   – C'est tout?
   – Oui. C'est combien?
   – C'est 3,90 euros.
   – Voilà. 3,90 euros. Merci.
   – OK. Au revoir.
3 – Bonjour. Vous désirez?
   – Je voudrais une crêpe aux fruits de mer, s'il vous plaît.
   – C'est tout?
   – Non, je voudrais aussi une glace au chocolat.
   – Voilà. C'est tout?
   – Oui. C'est combien?

> – Alors… 3,75 euros et 2,15 euros. C'est 5,90 euros, s'il vous plaît.
> – 5,90 euros. Voilà. Merci.
> – Merci. Au revoir!
> **4** – Bonjour. Vous désirez?
> – Je voudrais une crêpe, s'il vous plaît.
> – Oui, une crêpe, c'est super bon, hein! Vous désirez une crêpe au chocolat? À l'ananas? Au chocolat? Oui! Ou bien une crêpe au fromage? Aux fruits de mer? Au…
> – Une crêpe au chocolat.
> – Oui, très bien. Une crêpe au chocolat avec de la glace?
> – Oui, d'accord.
> – Alors, il y a de la glace au chocolat, de la glace à la vanille, de la glace…
> – Avec de la glace à la vanille, s'il vous plaît.
> – Très bien. C'est tout?
> – Oui. C'est combien?
> – C'est 5,85 euros, s'il vous plaît.
> – Voilà. 5,85 euros. Merci.
> – Merci à vous. Et bon appétit! Au revoir! Au revoir!

AT 1.2 **8b Réécoute et note le prix.**

• Play the recording again. Students note down the prices.

Answers: 1 6,85 euros; 2 3,90 euros; 3 3,75 + 2,15 = 5,90 euros; 4 5,85 euros

AT 2.3 **9 À deux: inventez!**

AT 4.3

• Students adapt and perform the model conversation (ex. 7), changing the highlighted words and phrases.
• Encourage them to assign a mood or personality to the customer and waiter/waitress, e.g. sad, very grumpy, deaf, over-enthusiastic, very polite or impolite, etc. Explain that it is more polite to use complete sentences (e.g. *Je voudrais…, s'il vous plaît*) than to give a short statement of what you want (e.g. *Une crêpe, s'il vous plaît*).

C65

C66

C68

Ex. 2 and 3 on Copymaster 65 are listening activities on places to eat and ordering food. Speaking activities to practise this language are provided on Copymaster 66, ex. 1–3. Copymaster 68 is a reading/writing activity based on a menu.

W 78–79 Pages 78–79 of the *En solo* Workbook provide further activities to practise numbers 70–100, ordering food and asking for different flavours/fillings.

6.3   Ma recette préférée

Planner

> ### Objectives
> - Recipes: ingredients and quantities

> ### Resources
> Students' Book, pages 106–107
> CD 3, tracks 26–29
> *En solo* Workbook, pages 80–81;
> *En solo* CD, tracks 48–49
> Copymasters 63

> ### Key language
> Numbers above 100
>
> *Ma recette préférée*
> *C'est très bon! C'est très2   2 facile à faire!*
> *Il faut* + noun
> *Il faut* + infinitive
>
> *il y a/il n'y a pas de*
> *de la farine*
> *du sucre en poudre, du lait, du pain, du fromage*
> *râpé, du jambon, du beurre, du sel, du poivre*
> *de l'huile d'olive*
> *des œufs, des cerises*
>
> *cent grammes (de), un kilo (de), un litre (de)*
> *un demi-kilo, un demi-litre*
> *beurrer, mélanger, ajouter*
> *un plat*
> *un four chaud*
>
> *d'abord, ensuite, puis, pour finir*

> ### Grammar
> *du, de l', de la, des*
> *… pas de/d'*

> ### Framework reference
> R – 7S5, 7S7, 7T1

> ### Starters
> - Play Number Noughts and Crosses as a class to revise numbers up to 100 and/or to practise numbers above 100. Draw a Noughts and Crosses grid on the board and divide the class into two teams. Players from each team take turns to say the numbers aloud to win squares.

The first team to win three squares in a row is the winner.
This could be done in groups of three: two students play the game and the third checks against a list of numbers to make sure they are saying them correctly. Make sure they swap roles.
- Play "Food Shoot-out". Two students stand up. Call out a food item from page 106, in English. The pair compete to say the word in French with the correct form of *du/de l'/de la/des*. The first person to answer correctly remains standing; the loser sits down and is replaced with another challenger.
- In pairs, students play Contradictions. If one student says a positive sentence, their partner has to deny it, and vice versa, e.g.
Student A: *Il y a du pain.*
Student B: *Il n'y a pas de pain!*
Student A: *Il n'y a pas de cerises.*
Student B: *Il y a des cerises!*
- Copymaster 63 *À tes marques!* ex. 2.

> ### Plenaries
> - Give students a few new food/drink words in English (e.g. rice, lemon, jam, spinach, fish, chicken, soup, potatoes, salad, water). Challenge them to find the French words in a dictionary and to write them down with *du/de l'/de la/des*. Set a time limit. Students compare their answers with a partner and discuss how to pronounce the words. Allow time for feedback, to check answers and pronunciation.
> - In pairs, students share their understanding of *du/de l'/de la/des*. How do they know when to use each one? When should they use *de/d'* instead? They write down some example sentences in French to show correct usage.
> - Pairs reflect on what they have learned from working on the recipes (apart from how to make the two dishes!), e.g. reading strategies, ways to give instructions in French, new vocabulary, how to use sequencers. Ask them to brainstorm other contexts in which they could use the sequencers, e.g. describing weekend activities, school timetable and daily routine. Allow time for whole-class feedback and discussion.

1 Écoute et note.

This activity would be suitable as part of preparation for external assessment at Breakthrough stage.
- Students listen and note down the numbers of the ingredients. They tick or cross each item to show which ingredients the speakers do and don't have.
- Point out the notes on the partitive and the use of *de/d'* after a negative.

Answers: 1 ✓; 2 ✓; 3 ✗; 4 ✗; 5 ✗; 6 ✓; 7 ✓; 8 ✓; 9 ✓;
10 ✗; 11 ✓; 12 ✗

  CD 3, track 26   page 106, activité 1

> **1** – Il y a de la farine?
>   – Oui, il y a de la farine.
> **2** – Est-ce qu'il y a des œufs?
>   – Oui, il y a des œufs.

3 – Il y a des cerises?
  – Non, il n'y a pas de cerises.
4 – Est-ce qu'il y a du sucre en poudre?
  – Non, il n'y a pas de sucre en poudre.
5 – Il y a du lait?
  – Non, il n'y a pas de lait.
6 – Est-ce qu'il y a du sel?
  – Oui, il y a du sel.
7 – Il y a du poivre?
  – Oui, il y a du poivre.
8 – Est-ce qu'il y a du beurre?
  – Oui, il y a du beurre.
9 – Il y a du pain?
  – Oui, il y a du pain.
10 – Est-ce qu'il y a du fromage râpé?
  – Non, il n'y a pas de fromage râpé.
11 – Il y a du jambon?
  – Oui, il y a du jambon.
12 – Est-ce qu'il y a de l'huile d'olive?
  – Non, il n'y a pas d'huile d'olive.

 2 Grammaire: à deux. (B ➤ A)

- Students play a guessing game to practise the partitive. Each student chooses six food items and writes them down, keeping them hidden from their partner.
- They then ask questions to work out what they each have on their lists, e.g.
  Student A: *Il y a du pain?*
  Student B: *Non, il n'y a pas de pain.*
  Student A: *Il y a du beurre?*
  Student B: *Oui, il y a du beurre!*
  The winner is the first student to guess all the items on their partner's list.

 3 Lis. Complète.

- Students look at the ingredients needed to make the recipes on page 107. They compare these with the ingredients they already have (i.e. the items they ticked in ex. 1) and write a shopping list of what they need to buy (i.e. the items they put a cross beside in ex. 1).
- Draw attention to *Il faut* + noun.

Answers: Il faut du sucre en poudre, du lait, des cerises, du fromage et de l'huile d'olive.

 4 Écoute (1–4) et note.

- Students listen to four sequences of numbers and fill in the missing number in each one.

Answers: 1 sept cents; 2 cent quatre; 3 cent douze; 4 cent soixante

 CD 3, track 27   page 106, activité 4

1 100, 200, 300, 400, 500, 600, ..., 800, 900
2 101, 102, 103, ..., 105, 106, 107, 108, 109, 110
3 111, ..., 113, 114, 115, 116, 117, 118, 119
4 120, 130, 140, 150, ..., 170, 180, 190, 200

 Follow-up: Students make up their own missing number sequences for a partner, similar to those in ex. 4.

 5 À deux. (B ➤ A)

- Students take turns to read out the sums for each other to work out, e.g.
  Student A: *Soixante-quinze plus trente-cinq!*
  Student B: *Cent dix!*

 Follow-up: Students make up similar sums for each other.

 6 Écoute et note.

- First, students list the ingredients for the two recipes given in the Students' Book.
- Play the recording: Manon and Thomas give the quantities of ingredients required. Students listen and fill in the missing quantities.

Answers: see underlining in transcript

 CD 3, track 28   page 107, activité 6

– Ma recette préférée, c'est le clafoutis aux cerises. C'est très bon! Miam miam! Comme ingrédients, il faut: <u>150</u> grammes de farine, <u>quatre</u> œufs, <u>120</u> grammes de sucre en poudre, <u>un demi</u>-litre de lait, <u>un demi</u>-kilo de cerises, du sel et du beurre.
– Moi, ma recette préférée, c'est les croque-monsieur. C'est très facile à faire! Comme ingrédients, il faut <u>huit</u> tranches de pain, <u>quatre</u> tranches de jambon, <u>300</u> grammes de fromage râpé, du beurre, du poivre et de l'huile d'olive.

 7 Lis les recettes. Trouve...

- Students read the recipes and find the French equivalents of the English words.
- Encourage them to try doing this without a dictionary, using cognates (what English word does *plat* look like, even though it sounds completely different?) and context.

Answers: a ajouter; b beurrer; c mélanger; d mettre; e un plat; f la pâte; g un four; h une tranche

  8 Écoute et note.

This activity could replace task C in a Grade 2 Asset Languages teacher assessment.

- Play the recording: Manon and Thomas describe how to make their favourite recipes. Students listen while reading the jumbled sequence of instructions (a–d) for each recipe. They note down each sequence of instructions in the correct order.
- Alternatively, students try to work out the correct sequence of instructions before listening. Once they've done this, play the recording so that they can check their answers.

Answers: <u>le clafoutis aux cerises</u>: c, b, d, a; <u>le croque-monsieur</u>: c, a, b, d

CD 3, track 29   page 107, activité 8

– Alors, pour faire un clafoutis…
D'abord, il faut mélanger la farine, le sucre, les
œufs, le sel et ajouter le lait. Ensuite, il faut
beurrer un plat. Puis, il faut mettre les cerises
et la pâte dans le plat. Pour finir, il faut mettre
45 minutes dans un four chaud (200° C,
thermostat 7). Et voilà!

– Voici la recette des croque-monsieur…
D'abord, il faut beurrer le pain. Ensuite, il faut
mettre une tranche de jambon et du fromage
râpé entre deux tranches de pain et ajouter un
peu de poivre. Puis, il faut mettre un peu de
fromage râpé sur les croque-monsieur et
ajouter un peu d'huile d'olive. Pour finir, il faut
le mettre dix minutes dans un four à 220° C
(thermostat 7–8). Voilà, c'est prêt!

AT 2.3

9 À deux: comparez. (B ➤ A)

- Students talk about the recipe instructions, using
  the sequencers *d'abord, ensuite, puis* and *pour
  finir*, e.g.
  Student A: *D'abord, il faut mélanger la farine, le
  sucre…*
  Student B: *Oui. Ensuite, il faut beurrer un plat.*
- Point out that the recipe instructions in the
  Students' Book use the infinitive, whereas they
  will need to use *Il faut* + infinitive.

AT 2.3–4
AT 4.3–4

Défi!

- Students pretend to be TV chefs and present one of
  the recipes as if it's a cookery programme on
  television. If possible, record the presentations on
  video, with students holding up autocue cards for
  each other.
- More able students could present a recipe of their
  own choice instead of using the ones in the
  Students' Book. If appropriate, allow them to
  choose their own way of presenting their recipes,
  e.g. in the form of a poster, written instructions and
  photos, a video or a PowerPoint presentation.
- Encourage students to use sequencers (as in ex. 9)
  as a framework for their demonstration.

W 80–81 Pages 80–81 of the *En solo* Workbook provide
further activities to practise the language of this
spread.

6.4 Mange bien!

Planner

> ### Objectives
> • Healthy eating

> ### Resources
> Students' Book, pages 108–109
> CD 3, tracks 30–33
> *En solo* Workbook, pages 82–83;
> *En solo* CD, tracks 50–51
> Copymasters 63, 67

> ### Key language
> *Bien manger*
> *pour être en forme*
> *je bois*
> *je vais manger*
> *plus de, moins de*
>
> *le poisson, les légumes, les chips, les pâtes, les barres de céréales*
> *le café, le jus de fruit, le chocolat chaud, le soda, l'eau*
>
> *en général, de temps en temps*
>
> *le matin, le midi, l'après-midi, le soir*
> *Tu prends un goûter?*
>
> *Questions*
> *Est-ce que tu manges…? Qu'est-ce que tu manges?*
> *Tu manges quoi?*

> ### Grammar
> *aller* + infinitive

> ### Framework reference
> R – 7W5, 7S7

> ### Starters
> • Hold a short discussion about healthy eating. Ask students whether their own idea of healthy eating differs from that of their parents. Who is the healthiest person in their family?

• Word Tennis. Call out a mealtime (*le matin, le soir*, etc.); a student responds with an appropriate food or drink item in French, including the correct determiner. Alternatively, ask them to respond with a full sentence, e.g. *Je mange des fruits*. Repeat around the class.
• Display some anagrams of food and drink items. Students solve the anagrams, work out whether each word is *du, de l', de la* or *des*, then write the words out in two columns: *C'est bien pour la santé* and *Ce n'est pas bien pour la santé*.
• Copymaster 63 *À tes marques!* ex. 1.

> ### Plenaries
> • Display the following incomplete sentences together with jumbled missing words:
> *Je vais manger moins de…*
> *Je vais faire plus de…*
> *Je vais boire moins de…*
> *Je vais manger plus…*
> *Je ne vais pas manger…*
> *Je vais manger plus de…*
> *Je vais boire plus d'…*
> *Je vais mettre moins de… sur les légumes.*
> Missing words: *chocolat / sport / soda / le matin / au fast-food / fruits / eau / sel*
> Set a time limit for students, working in pairs, to complete the sentences to make a set of healthy resolutions. Allow time to check answers.
> • Display a few single words/phrases from the lesson; in pairs, students write both a question and an answer containing each word/phrase. They compare their ideas with those of another pair. Collect in suggestions and write them up on the board.
> • Students tell each other what they feel are the most important and/or interesting things they have learned in Unit 6, in terms of either language or cultural information. Can they think of any language or grammar from Unit 6 that could be transferred to other contexts? Allow time for whole-class feedback and discussion.

---

1 Écoute et note. C'est bien ou ce n'est pas bien?
• Students listen and note down the letter of each food item mentioned, using tick and cross symbols to show whether the items are described as healthy or unhealthy.

Answers: ✓ b, c, e, f, h, j; ✗ a, d, g, i

CD 3, track 30   page 108, activité 1

Qu'est-ce qui est bien pour la santé?
Le poisson, c'est bien; les légumes, c'est bien; les pâtes, c'est bien; le jus de fruit, c'est bien; le chocolat chaud, c'est bien; et l'eau, c'est bien.
Qu'est-ce qui n'est pas bien pour la santé?
Les barres de céréales, ce n'est pas bien; les chips, ce n'est pas bien; le café, ce n'est pas bien; et le soda, ce n'est pas bien.

2 Écoute et lis.

- Students read and listen to an interview with Thomas about his eating habits.
- They work out the meanings of the underlined words and phrases. They should be able to do this without a dictionary, using context and cognates to work out meanings.

Answers: *je bois*: I drink; *en général*: in general/ usually; *de temps en temps*: from time to time/ sometimes; *ça dépend*: it depends

---

 CD 3, track 31   page 108, activité 2

  – Est-ce que tu manges le matin?
  – Oui! Le matin, je mange du pain avec du Nutella. Je bois du chocolat chaud.
  – Qu'est-ce que tu manges le midi?
  – En général, je mange des frites et je bois de l'eau!
  – Tu prends un goûter l'après-midi?
  – Oui, de temps en temps: je mange des barres de céréales et je bois du soda.
  – Tu manges quoi le soir?
  – Ça dépend. J'aime bien manger des pâtes.

 3a Lis. À deux: imaginez l'interview de Yasmina. (B ➤ A)

- Students read Yasmina's text to find out how she would answer the interview questions. They copy out the questions together with Yasmina's answers.

Answers: see transcript in ex. 3b

 3b Écoute et vérifie.

- Students compare their own version of Yasmina's interview with the recorded version.

CD 3, track 32   page 108, activité 3b

  – Est-ce que tu manges le matin?
  – Le matin, je ne mange pas mais en général, je bois du café.
  – Qu'est-ce que tu manges le midi?
  – Le midi, en général, je mange un sandwich et des chips.
  – Tu prends un goûter l'après-midi?
  – L'après-midi, après le collège, je ne mange pas mais je bois du jus de fruit.
  – Tu manges quoi le soir?
  – Le soir, ça dépend, j'aime bien manger du poisson et des légumes.

---

 4 À deux. (B ➤ A)

- Students interview each other about their own eating habits, using Thomas's and Yasmina's interviews as a model.

C67 Additional reading/writing activities on diet and eating habits are provided on Copymaster 67.

---

 5 Lis et choisis.

- Students read the magazine-style feature about healthy eating and select the appropriate word or phrase (*plus* or *moins*, *Je vais* or *Je ne vais pas*) to complete each statement 1–8.
- They then choose resolutions for themselves.

Answers: 1 plus; 2 moins; 3 plus; 4 plus; 5 moins; 6 moins; 7 Je vais; 8 Je ne vais pas

---

 6 À deux. (B ➤ A)

- Students question each other about their healthy resolutions, based on sentences 1–8. They note down their partner's responses.

AT 1.3–4 **7 Écoute et note.**

- Students listen to the radio phone-in: a dietician gives advice on healthy eating to a series of teenagers. Her eight points correspond with sentences 1–8 from ex. 5.
- Students look at their eight sentences in ex. 5 and note briefly beside each one what the dietician says, e.g. by ticking or crossing to show whether she agrees or disagrees. Students compare the dietician's advice with their own and their partner's responses.

CD 3, track 33   page 109, activité 7

  – Bienvenue sur Radio Clic! Le sondage aujourd'hui: Qu'est-ce que tu vas faire pour être en forme? Alors, on écoute les messages et les conseils de notre diététicienne.
  1 – Je vais manger plus le matin.
  – Oui, très bien, il faut bien manger le matin.
  2 – Je vais manger moins vite le midi.
  – Excellent! Il ne faut pas manger vite.
  3 – Je vais manger moins de pain et de pâtes.
  – Ah non, il faut manger plus de pain et de pâtes!
  4 – Je vais boire moins d'eau.
  – Ah non! Au contraire! Il faut boire plus d'eau! C'est très important!
  5 – Je vais boire moins de soda.
  – Excellente résolution. Il faut boire moins de soda. C'est très mauvais!
  6 – Je vais mettre plus de sel sur les légumes.
  – Ah non non non! Il faut mettre moins de sel. Le sel, ce n'est pas bon, ce n'est pas bon du tout!
  7 – Je vais prendre des vitamines.
  – Oui, il faut des vitamines! N'oublie pas, il y a des vitamines dans les fruits et les légumes!
  8 – Je vais faire un régime.
  – Non, il ne faut pas faire de régime. Ce n'est pas une bonne idée quand on a 12 ans!
  – Eh bien, merci pour vos appels et merci pour les conseils! A bientôt!

8 Grammaire: futur ou pas?

- Students work out which of sentences a–d refer to the future.
- Point out the grammar notes on *aller* + infinitive.

Answers: sentences b and d refer to the future

 Défi!

- Students write five more healthy resolutions and compare with a partner.
- Encourage them to adapt sentences 1–8 from ex. 5 by substituting different vocabulary items, e.g. *Je vais manger moins de chocolat. Je vais manger plus de légumes.*

Page 82–83 of the *En solo* Workbook provide further activities to practise asking questions, *aller* + infinitive and *plus de/moins de*.

Labo-langue

Planner

> ### Objectives
> - *au, à l', à la, aux; du, de l', de la, des*
> - Asking questions
> - Intonation

> ### Resources
> Students' Book, pages 110–111
> CD 3, tracks 34–36
> *En solo* Workbook, pages 84–85, 87;
> *En solo* CD, track 53
> Copymasters 66, 69, 70, 71; CD 3, tracks 44–46

> ### Framework reference
> **R** – 7W2, 7S4, 7T4 (via Workbook), 7T5, 7T7 (via Workbook), 7L2 (via Workbook), 7L6

Bien comprendre!

au, à l', à la, aux; du, de l', de la, des

 1 Choose a word to complete each sentence.

- Make sure students realise that in each case they need to choose a word of the correct gender and number to match the preceding *au* or *du*.

Answers: 1 café; 2 fromage; 3 gâteau

2 Make other sentences using the words that are left over.

This activity would be suitable as part of preparation for external assessment at Breakthrough stage.
- Accept any appropriate answers.

 See Copymaster 69 for additional grammar practice of *au/à l'/à la/aux*, *du/de l'/de la/des* and *de/d'* after a negative.

 Page 84–85 of the *En solo* Workbook provide further activities to practise these grammar points.

Bien apprendre!

Asking questions

1 How many questions can you ask about this photo, using the question words above?

This activity would be suitable as part of preparation for external assessment at Breakthrough stage.
- Don't give students any background information about the photo: they will find this out for themselves when they listen to the ex. 2 recording.

2 Listen. Which question words do you hear? List them.

- This recording features a series of questions and answers about the *Fête de l'Omelette géante*. On the first listening, students note the question words they hear (see underlining in the transcript).

They compare these with their own list of questions in ex. 1.
- Play the recording again: students note down the answers to the questions. Do they have any questions that have been left unanswered?
- The *Fête de l'Omelette géante* takes place every year in September at the little town of Saint-Aygulf on the Côte d'Azur, when chefs from the local area prepare a huge omelette in the market place. The omelette, made in a pan measuring about 3 metres in diameter, contains 10,000 eggs, about 30 litres of oil and several kilos of herbs. It takes about three hours to cook and is then shared between hundreds of visitors.

 CD 3, track 34 page 111, Bien apprendre! activité 2

- C'est <u>quoi</u>?
- C'est la Fête de l'Omelette géante!
- C'est <u>où</u>?
- C'est à Saint-Aygulf, une petite ville dans le sud de la France.
- C'est <u>quand</u>?
- C'est en septembre.
- Il faut <u>combien</u> d'œufs pour faire l'omelette?
- Il faut 10 000 œufs pour faire cette omelette!
- <u>Qui</u> fait l'omelette?
- Des chefs de la région font l'omelette.

 Défi!

- *Aim*: To reinforce question forms in a range of contexts and recycle previously learned language.
- Students write eight questions to ask their partner. Point out that the questions can be on any topic.

See Copymaster 70 for further activities to practise question forms.

Ex. 4 on Copymaster 66 provides a speaking activity to practise questions and answers from the whole of **Clic! 1**. It could be used at any point towards the end of Unit 6.

W87 Further language learning strategies are provided on page 87 of the *En solo* Workbook, which could be used at any appropriate point during Unit 6:

- *Listening*: preparing for listening tasks
- *Writing*: tips on checking written work

Bien parler!

Intonation

1 What is the difference in the way these sentences are said?

- Make sure students realise that although the words in a/b and c/d are identical, the intonation of the questions is different from that of the statements.

2 Listen. In which order do you hear items a–d from activity 1?

Answers: 1 a; 2 b; 3 d; 4 c

 CD 3, track 35   page 111, Bien parler! activité 2

1 Tu aimes le chocolat.
2 Tu aimes le chocolat?
3 Il y a de l'eau?
4 Il y a de l'eau.

3 Listen. Raise your hand only when you hear a question.

- As in ex. 1 and 2, the wording in each pair of sentences is identical (or, in the case of items 1 and 2, almost identical). By focusing on the intonation, students will be able to work out which items are questions and which are statements.

Answers: see transcript

 CD 3, track 36   page 111, Bien parler! activité 3

1 Je me lève à huit heures.
2 Tu te lèves à huit heures?
3 Elle n'aime pas le chocolat.
4 Elle n'aime pas le chocolat?
5 On fait du shopping ce week-end?
6 On fait du shopping ce week-end.
7 Vous habitez dans une grande maison.
8 Vous habitez dans une grande maison?

Défi!

- Students write four sentences on any topic. There must be a mixture of questions and statements.
- They read them out to the class, who work out from the intonation which are questions and which are statements.

C71 See Copymaster 71 for further pronunciation practice, focusing on intonation.

Blog-notes

Planner

> **Objectives**
> * To summarise the main points of the unit in context, in a format that is fun and familiar to students, i.e. a video blog
> * To provide a model enabling students to personalise the language of the unit
> * To provide opportunities for students to ask as well as answer questions
> * To provide extended listening practice recycling the language of the whole unit

> **Resources**
> Students' Book, page 112
> Video clip 13
> *En solo* Workbook, page 86;
> *En solo* CD, track 52
> Copymaster 62

> **Framework reference**
> **R** – 7T6, 7C3

---

 1 Regarde le vidéo-blog de Thomas. Choisis 1 ou 2.

* Students watch Thomas's video diary and choose 1 or 2 in answer to each question about his eating habits. Pause the video after each section to allow students time to answer.

Answers: a 1; b 1; c 2; d 2; e 2; f 2; g 1; h 1

Video clip 13 page 112, activité 1

Salut! Yo, c'est moi! Thomas Garnier. Ça va?
a Hmmm… désolé! Je mange mon petit déjeuner! Le matin, au petit déjeuner, je mange une tranche de pain et du Nutella. C'est bon le Nutella! Et toi, qu'est-ce que tu manges le matin?
b Moi, j'aime bien manger en ville, avec mes copains. En général, on va à la pizzeria près du collège. Et toi, tu manges où quand tu vas en ville?
c Je vais souvent au restaurant avec mes parents, le dimanche en général. Il y a de très bons restaurants dans la région. Et toi, tu vas quand au restaurant?
d Moi, j'aime bien manger! Pas toi? Mon plat préféré, c'est le couscous. J'adore ça! C'est de la viande, des légumes et du couscous. Hum! Ton plat préféré, c'est quoi?
e J'aime bien faire des gâteaux. Ma recette de gâteau préféré, c'est le quatre-quarts. Comme ingrédients, il faut quatre œufs, 250 g de farine, 250 g de sucre, 250 g de beurre et un peu de sel.
f – Thomas? Je vais faire les courses. Qu'est-ce que tu voudrais manger ce soir?
Ça, c'est ma mère. Qu'est-ce que je voudrais manger ce soir? Euh… je ne sais pas… euh, ah oui, je sais!
– Maman! Je voudrais une pizza aux fruits de mer avec de la salade.
– Ah oui! D'accord. Bonne idée! À plus!
– Salut, maman!
Et toi, qu'est-ce que tu voudrais manger ce soir?

g Je ne mange pas souvent de pizza. La pizza, ce n'est pas "très" bien. Mais bon, je mange bien en général, alors une pizza de temps en temps, ça va! Et toi, tu manges bien en général?
h Moi, je voudrais être en forme. Alors, j'ai pris deux bonnes résolutions : je vais faire plus de sport et je vais manger moins de Nutella! Et toi, qu'est-ce que tu vas faire pour être plus en forme? Allez, salut!

 2 À toi de répondre!
* Students write their own answers to questions a–h.

Follow-up:
These activities may be suitable for more able students only:

* Students interview each other using questions a–h.
* Students use their answers from ex. 2 to help them write their own blog. If the appropriate technology is available, allow students to record their own video blogs and play them to the class.

 A checklist summarising the language of the unit is provided on Copymaster 62 and on page 86 of the *En solo* Workbook. It could be used in tandem with the *Blog-notes* page or at an appropriate point towards the end of the unit. It provides an opportunity for students to review what they have learned and reflect on areas for improvement.

Tu sais tout?

Planner

> **Objectives**
> • To enable students to recap on the language and
>   structures of the unit
> • To provide an opportunity for quick testing of all
>   four skills

The page is divided into four sections:
listening, speaking, reading and writing. Each
section can be marked out of 5 to give a total
score out of 20.

> **Resources**
> Students' Book, page 113
> CD 3, track 38

AT 1.3 **1 Listen. Who does what to be healthy? Match
up speakers 1–6 with bubbles a–f.**

Answers: 1 a; 2 d; 3 f; 4 e; 5 b; 6 c

 CD 3, track 38   page 113, activité 1

  – Qu'est-ce que tu fais pour être en forme?
1 Pour être en forme, je mange beaucoup le
    matin au petit déjeuner.
2 En général, l'après-midi, je mange un fruit ou
    une barre de céréales.
3 Quand je mange en ville, je ne vais pas au
    fast-food.
4 Le soir, je mange des pâtes ou du riz.
5 Je mange des fruits et des légumes tous les
    jours.
6 Je bois du jus de fruit mais je ne bois pas de
    soda.

AT 3.3 **2 Read the recipe and list the pictures in the
correct order.**

Answers: f, a, b, e, c, d

AT 4.3 **3 Answer the questions.**

• Students write their own answers to questions
  about food preferences and eating habits.

AT 2.3 **4 Order the items ticked in the grid.
Remember, be very polite!**

• Point out the features of the example answer that
  help to make it polite, e.g. it's a full sentence, and
  the speaker uses *Bonjour, Je voudrais…* and *s'il
  vous plaît*. Tell students it is even more polite to
  address the person you're speaking to as *monsieur*
  or *madame*.

Answers: Bonjour, monsieur/madame, je voudrais
une crêpe au fromage/un sandwich au fromage/une
pizza aux olives/une glace à la vanille/une glace à
l'ananas/une pizza à l'ananas, s'il vous plaît

En plus

Planner

> ### Objectives
> * To provide extension material for more able students who are confident with the core language of the unit, and to introduce new language where appropriate
> * To provide alternative class and homework material for students who finish other activities quickly

> ### Resources
> Students' Book, page 114
> CD 3, track 39

> ### Key language
> *un paquet de, une tranche de, un morceau de, une boîte de, une bouteille de*

Une tranche de jambon

This page introduces some additional quantities, packaging and containers.

1 Relie. Écoute et vérifie.

* Students match the food pictures to the captions, then listen to the recording to check their answers.

Answers: 1 b – une tranche de jambon; 2 c – un morceau de fromage; 3 g – une bouteille d'eau; 4 e – une boîte de cerises; 5 a – un paquet de sucre; 6 f – un kilo de tomates; 7 d – un litre de lait

CD 3, track 39   page 114, activité 1

1 b – une tranche de jambon
2 c – un morceau de fromage
3 g – une bouteille d'eau
4 e – une boîte de cerises
5 a – un paquet de sucre
6 f – un kilo de tomates
7 d – un litre de lait

2 À deux: jouez.

* Students play Three-in-a-Row to practise asking politely for food items.
* Point out that in order to win a square, they need to focus on three things: ask for the item politely (*Je voudrais…, s'il vous plaît*), name the food item correctly, and state an appropriate quantity or container/packaging.

Clic.fr

Planner

➢ **Objectives**
- To raise awareness of France and French culture
- To promote intercultural understanding by providing opportunities to compare French culture with students' own culture

➢ **Resources**
Students' Book, page 115
Copymaster 72

➢ **Framework reference**
R – 7C2

Not many people know that...

 This page provides various "food facts" in English relating to France and the French: the inventor of the traditional chef's hat, the opening of the first restaurant, the first tinned food, and the popularity of bread in France.

Students begin by searching the French headings/captions for key words.

Answers: a une toque; b les auberges; c des boîtes; d les boulangers

 Students discuss the food facts and reflect on what they've learned about French food in Unit 6.

 Further activities on the theme of French food are provided on Copymaster 72.

Vocabulaire

Planner

> **Objectives**
> * *Vocabulaire*: to provide a theme-based summary of the key language of the unit, which students can use as a reference or as an aid to learning
> * To develop language learning strategies
> * *On chante!*: to reinforce the language of the unit in a fun way

> **Resources**
> Students' Book, pages 116–117
> CD 3, track 40
> *En solo* Workbook, pages 88–89;
> *En solo* CD, track 54
> Copymaster 61

> **Framework reference**
> **R** – 7S4, 7C4

  A list of key language from the unit, with associated activities, is also provided on Copymaster 61 and on pages 88–89 of the *En solo* Workbook.

Question time!

* *Aim*: To encourage students to ask as well as answer questions.
* Students search page 117 for question words that begin with a "k" sound (all apart from *où* and *est-ce que*).
* They then translate some questions into French using only the vocabulary on pages 116–117.

Answers: a C'est facile à faire? Est-ce que c'est facile à faire? b Qui va au restaurant? c On va où? d Il faut quoi? Qu'est-ce qu'il faut?

On chante!

AT 3.2 **1 Lis et trouve…**

* Students search the song lyrics for the French translations of the English phrases.

Answers: a au marché; b je fais les courses; c j'ai fait les courses; d je vais acheter; e j'ai oublié d'acheter

AT 3.2 **2 À deux. Traduisez.**

* Students translate all the food items mentioned in the song into English, using a dictionary for anything they are unable to guess.

Answers: des épinards: spinach; *une ou deux poires*: one or two pears; *du camembert*: Camembert; *de la bière*: beer; *un bout de gruyère*: a piece of Gruyère; *des champignons*: mushrooms; *un gros melon*: a large melon; *du saucisson*: cold cooked/dried sausage or salami; *des citrons*: lemons; *six tranches de jambon*: six slices of ham; *un ananas*: a pineapple; *de la glace*: ice cream; *des avocats*: avocados; *de la pizza*: pizza; *des crêpes au chocolat*: chocolate pancakes

AT 1.2 AT 2.2 **3 Écoute et chante!**

* Students listen and join in with song.

 CD 3, track 40 page 117, activité 3

Au marché

Aujourd'hui, je fais les courses
Et au marché, je vais acheter…

… des épinards, une ou deux poires
du camembert et de la bière
et un bout de gruyère
… des champignons, un gros melon
du saucisson et des citrons
et six tranches de jambon
… un ananas et de la glace
des avocats, de la pizza
des crêpes au chocolat.

Aujourd'hui, j'ai fait les courses
mais j'ai oublié d'acheter…

… des épinards, une ou deux poires
du camembert et de la bière
et un bout de gruyère
… des champignons, un gros melon
du saucisson et des citrons
et six tranches de jambon
… un ananas et de la glace
des avocats, de la pizza
des crêpes au chocolat.

Aïe aïe aïe aïe aïe!

Lecture

Planner

> **Objectives**
> • To encourage independent reading and develop reading strategies
> • To provide alternative class and homework material for students who finish other activities quickly

The texts and activities on *Lecture A* should be suitable for all; *Lecture B* is more challenging and may be suitable for more able students only.

> **Resources**
> Students' Book, pages 128–129

> **Framework reference**
> **R** – 7C2

Lecture A

Quiz-santé!

1 Read the quiz and find...

• Students search the quiz for the French translations of the English words and phrases.

Answers: meat: *de la viande*; potatoes: *des pommes de terre*; a drink: *une boisson*; a plate/a plate full of food: *une assiette*; to eat a lot of fat: *manger beaucoup de gras*; never: *jamais*; from time to time: *de temps en temps*; once a day: *une fois par jour*; several times a day: *plusieurs fois par jour*; every day: *tous les jours*

2 In pairs, do the quiz. (B ➝ A)

• Students do the quiz and work out their score.

Lecture B

Les repas au Burkina Faso

This page provides cultural information about typical food and eating habits in Burkina Faso. It focuses on Nora from a little village in Burkina Faso, who was introduced in Unit 4.

1 Reading race! Find...

Answers: <u>family members</u>: ma mère, mes frères, mon père, mes sœurs; <u>names of food</u>: du tô, la farine de mil, du couscous, des fruits, des sauces, du poulet, du poisson, des œufs, des omelettes, du riz, les légumes; <u>drinks</u>: du lait, de l'eau; <u>times of the day</u>: le matin, le midi, le soir; <u>regular -er verbs</u>: manger, préparer, apporter; <u>irregular verbs</u>: boire, aller, avoir, être, faire; <u>how many du?</u>: six; <u>how many de la?</u>: two

2 Match a paragraph to each photo.

Answers: a 2/4; b 3; c 5

3 Discuss in English.

• Students discuss what have learned about African food from Nora's text. Is there anything here that they find surprising?

Copymasters

Feuille 61 Vocabulaire

A list of key language from the unit is provided here as well as on pages 116–117 of the Students' Book and pages 88–89 of the *En solo* Workbook.

Feuille 62 Je sais…

Use this checklist with *Blog-notes* (Students' Book page 112) or towards the end of the unit. It provides an opportunity for students to review what they have learned and reflect on areas for improvement. This checklist is also provided on page 86 of the *En solo* Workbook.

Feuille 63 À vos marques!

These starter activities are intended for use with the following Students' Book pages:
- Use ex. 1 with pages 108–109.
- Use ex. 2 with pages 106–107.
- Use ex. 3 with pages 104–105.

1 Trouve l'intrus et donne une raison.
- Students choose the odd-one-out in each set of words, giving a reason for each choice.

Possible answers: a *la vanille*, because it's a flavour and not a place to eat, or *le fast-food* because it's masculine; b *une glace*, because it's a dessert and not a main course; c *les fruits de mer*, because it's the only savoury dish or because it isn't a flavour of ice cream; d *du lait*, because it's a drink, or *une crêpe* because it's feminine; e *la cantine*, because it's a place to eat and not a mealtime; f *un gâteau*, because it's a food item and not a quantity

2 Écris le nom de chaque ingrédient.
- Students label the food pictures using the words provided.

Answers: a des œufs; b du fromage; c du pain; d de l'huile d'olive; e du jambon; f du beurre; g du sucre; h du lait

3 Écris les nombres en chiffres.
- Students write the numbers in figures.

Answers: a 72; b 100; c 80; d 83; e 68; f 95; g 99; h 76

Feuille 64 Bilan de leçon

These plenary activities are intended for use with the following Students' Book pages:
- Use ex. 1 with Students' Book pages 104–105.
- Use ex. 2 with Students' Book pages 102–103.

1a Complète les phrases.
- Students fill in the gaps in the sentences, replacing the food pictures with words.

Answers: a une pizza; b une glace; c un coca; d un hamburger, un jus de fruit; e fast-food

1b Écris cinq phrases, en remplaçant les mots soulignés et les images.
- Students rewrite the five sentences from ex. 1a, replacing the underlined items with new words of their own choice.

2 Mets le dialogue dans le ordre.
- Students sort the lines of the French conversation into the correct order so that it matches the English version.

Answers: 1 d; 2 f; 3 a; 4 g; 5 c; 6 e; 7 b

Feuille 65 Écouter
- Use with Students' Book pages 104–105.

1 Écoute et encercle le nombre que tu entends.
- Students listen and circle the numbers that are called out.

Answer: a 72; b 80; c 91; d 100; e 60; f 83; g 73; h 77

 CD 3, track 41   Feuille 65, activité 1
- a soixante-douze
- b quatre-vingts
- c quatre-vingt-onze
- d cent
- e soixante
- f quatre-vingt-trois
- g soixante-treize
- h soixante-dix-sept

2 Écoute et mets les images dans le bon ordre.
- Students listen and note the food and drink items in the order they are mentioned.

Answers: b, c, a, f, e, d

 CD 3, track 42   Feuille 65, activité 2

Un coca… un hamburger avec des frites… un sandwich au jambon… une crêpe… une eau minérale… un croque-monsieur.

6 On mange!

 3a Écoute les quatre conversations. Ils mangent où?

* Students listen to four conversations and identify the place where the people are eating.

Answers: 1 b; 2 d; 3 a; 4 c

 CD 3, track 43   Feuille 65, activité 3

1 – Bonjour! Vous désirez?
  – Je prends un hamburger et un coca, s'il vous plaît.
2 – Bonjour, monsieur. Vous désirez?
  – Je voudrais une soupe, s'il vous plaît.
  – Et comme plat principal?
  – Je vais prendre un steak-frites.
  – Et comme dessert?
  – Une glace à la vanille, s'il vous plaît.
3 – Bonjour. Vous désirez?
  – Pour moi, un croque-monsieur et un café.
  – Et pour moi, un sandwich au jambon et un jus de fruit.
4 – Bonjour, vous désirez?
  – Je vais prendre une pizza végétarienne.
  – Et avec ça?
  – Une salade, s'il vous plaît… et de l'eau minérale.

 3b Réécoute. Les clients commandent quoi?

* Students listen again and tick the food/drink pictures to show what the customers order.

Answers: 1 a; 2 a; 3 b; 4 b

Feuille 66   Parler

* Use ex. 1, 2 and 3 with Students' Book pages 104–105.
* Ex. 4 practises language from the whole of **Clic! 1** so can be used at any point towards the end of the unit, e.g. as a follow-up to the *Bien apprendre!* section on asking questions on Students' Book page 111.

 1 Complète le dialogue.

 * Students complete the café dialogue using their own choice of items from the menu.

 2 Lis le dialogue avec ton/ta partenaire. Puis, changez de rôles.

 * Students practise reading the dialogue from ex. 1 with their partner.

 3 À deux. Faites un autre dialogue au café. Jouez-le pour la classe.

 * In pairs, students make up another café dialogue
 and perform it for the class.

---

 4 Révisez tout! À deux, répondez aux questions.

 * In pairs, students take turns to interview each other on a range of topics from the whole of **Clic! 1**.

Feuille 67   Lire et écrire 1

* Use with Students' Book pages 108–109.

AT 3.2 **1 Lis et réponds aux questions.**

* Students read the text about Jean-Christophe's diet and answer questions in English.

Answers: a cereal; b ham sandwich and fruit; c yes, cake/biscuit and a Coke; d an omelette and a salad; e he doesn't have a pudding; f quite healthy, but the cake/biscuit and Coke that he has for his afternoon snack aren't healthy

AT 3.3 **2 Corrige les erreurs.**

AT 4.2 * Students correct the errors in statements about Jean-Christophe's diet.

Answers: a Jean-Christophe mange des céréales le matin. b À midi, il mange un sandwich. c À midi, il mange aussi un fruit. d L'après-midi, il boit un coca. e Le soir, il mange une omelette. f Le soir, il ne mange pas de dessert.

AT 4.2–3 **3 Utilise le texte de Jean-Christophe et écris un texte pour toi.**

* Students write a text about their own diet, using Jean-Christophe's text as a model.

Feuille 68   Lire et écrire 2

* Use with Students' Book pages 104–105.

AT 3.2 **1 Regarde le menu. Trouve le français.**

* Students read the menu and find the French for the English words and phrases.

Answers: a pâtisseries; b selection, assortiment; c poisson; d soupe à l'oignon; e tarte aux abricots; f riz; g poulet; h glace à la menthe; i legumes

AT 3.3 **2 Lis les phrases a–h. Vrai, faux ou pas mentionné?**

* Students read statements a–h and work out whether they are true, false or not mentioned in the menu.

Answers: a faux; b pas mentionné; c vrai; d faux; e faux; f pas mentionné

AT 4.2–3 **3 Qu'est-ce que tu choisis pour le petit déjeuner, le déjeuner et le dîner?**

* Students write down what they themselves would choose from the menu for breakfast, lunch and dinner.

Feuille 69   Labo-langue

- Use with Students' Book page 110.

1 Complète les phrases avec *au, à la, à l'* ou *aux*.

- Students complete the sentences using *au, à la, à l'* or *aux*.

Answers: a à l'; b aux; c au; d à la; e au

2 Classe les articles.

- Students write the food items in the correct place: *du, de la, de l'* or *des*.

Answers: du: chocolat, jambon, fromage, lait; de la: soupe, salade; de l': eau, huile d'olive; des: œufs, cerises

3 Il n'y a pas de…

- Students write sentences using *il n'y a pas de/d'*, in response to the picture prompts.

Answers: a Il n'y a pas de pain. b Il n'y a pas de frites. c Il n'y a pas d'œufs. d Il n'y a pas d'eau minérale.

Feuille 70   Bien apprendre!

- Use with *Bien apprendre!* on Students' Book page 111.

1a Turn these statements into questions using *Est-ce que…?*

Answers: see transcript

1b Listen to check.

CD 3, track 44   Feuille 70, activité 1b

a Est-ce que tu aimes les pizzas?
b Est-ce qu'il est végétarien?
c Est-ce qu'elle prend une crêpe?
d Est-ce qu'on mange des céréales pour le petit déjeuner?
e Est-ce qu'il y a un café en ville?
f Est-ce qu'on va au restaurant?

2a Underline the question word in each sentence.

Answers: 1 quelle; 2 quoi; 3 qui; 4 où; 5 comment; 6 combien

2b Now match each question from 2a to the correct answer.

Answers: a 3; b 2; c 6; d 4; e 1; f 5

Feuille 71   Bien parler!

- Use with *Bien parler!* on Students' Book page 111.

1a Listen and decide whether you hear a statement or a question. Add a full stop or a question mark at the end of each one.

Answers: see transcript

CD 3, track 45   Feuille 71, activité 1a

Tu habites à la campagne?
Il boit un coca.
Je suis en forme.
Il y a du lait?
C'est bon?
Il faut manger des fruits.
Tu viens au restaurant?
Elle voudrait un sandwich?

1b In pairs, practise reading items 1–8 aloud using the correct intonation.

2a Practise reading these questions aloud with your partner.

2b Listen to a conversation that includes five of the questions in 2a. Tick the ones you hear.

Answers: a, d, f, g, i

CD 3, track 46   Feuille 71, activité 2b

– Tu veux aller en ville?
– Oui, je veux bien. On mange en ville?
– D'accord. Tu veux aller à la crêperie?
– Non, je n'aime pas les crêpes. On va au café?
– Bonne idée! Je vais prendre un sandwich au jambon. Et toi?
– Moi, je préfère les sandwiches au fromage.

3 In pairs, make up three questions and statements for each other. Take turns to read them out. Your partner has to decide if you are reading a statement or question. How many does he/she get right?

Feuille 72   Culture

- Use with Students' Book page 115.

1 Read the food and drink names (1–8). Do some research and find out what these dishes are. Match them up to definitions a–h. You may know some of them already.

Answers: 1 b; 2 g; 3 f; 4 e; 5 c; 6 d; 7 h; 8 a

**2 Find out about three more French dishes,
desserts or drinks. How many can your class
find altogether?**

**3 What dishes/drinks are typical of your region
or nationality?**

En solo Workbook

Pages 76–77 6.1 On va au café?

- Use with Students' Book pages 102–103.

AT 4.2 **1a Complete the captions: fill the gaps with the correct form of the verb *aller* and the place name. Use the words in clouds to help you.**

Answers: 1 Je vais à la crêperie. 2 Tu vas à la cafétéria. 3 Il va au café. 4 Nous allons au restaurant. 5 Vous allez au fast-food. 6 Ils vont à la pizzeria.

AT 3.2 **1b Then say what each sentence means in English.**

Answers: 1 I'm going to the pancake restaurant. 2 You're going to the cafeteria. 3 He's going to the café. 4 We're going to the restaurant. 5 You're going to the fast-food restaurant. 6 They're going to the pizzeria.

AT 1.2 **2 Listen to three conversations and fill in the**
AT 3.2 **gaps.**

Answers: see underlining in transcript

🔘 **En solo CD, track 44**   page 77, activité 2

1 – Je voudrais <u>un hamburger</u>. On va <u>au fast-food</u>?
  – Oui, d'accord. J'adore les <u>hamburgers</u>!
  – D'accord, alors, on va <u>au fast-food</u>!
2 – Je voudrais <u>une pizza</u>. On va <u>à la pizzeria</u>?
  – Bof! Je n'aime pas <u>les pizzas</u>. On va <u>à la cafétéria</u>?
  – D'accord, alors, on va <u>à la cafétéria</u>!
3 – Je voudrais <u>une crêpe</u>. On va <u>à la crêperie</u>?
  – Non, merci. Je préfère <u>les croque-monsieur</u>.
  – D'accord, alors, on va <u>au café</u>!

Pages 78–79 6.2 S'il vous plaît!

- Use with Students' Book pages 104–105.

AT 1.2 **1 Listen to six people ordering food. Draw lines to join up the words and pictures to show what they ask for. Use different colours.**

Answers: see transcript

🔘 **En solo CD, track 45**   page 78, activité 1

1 S'il vous plaît! Une pizza aux fruits de mer!
2 Je voudrais un sandwich au fromage.
3 Pour moi, une crêpe au chocolat.
4 Je voudrais une glace à la vanille.
5 Pour moi, une glace à l'orange.
6 S'il vous plaît! Une crêpe aux fruits de mer!

AT 4.2 **2 Write a sentence for each person.**

Answers: 1 Je voudrais une crêpe à la tomate. 2 Je voudrais un sandwich aux fruits de mer. 3 Je voudrais une glace à l'orange. 4 Je voudrais une pizza au fromage.

AT 3.1 **3a Read these numbers and write them in figures in the boxes.**

Answers: soixante-dix 70; soixante et onze 71; soixante-douze 72; soixante-dix-neuf 79; quatre-vingt-un 81; quatre-vingt-quatre 84; quatre-vingt-dix 90; quatre-vingt-onze 91; quatre-vingt-treize 93

AT 1.1 **3b Listen and cross out the ones you hear.**

Answers: see transcript

🔘 **En solo CD, track 46**   page 79, activité 3b

93, 72, 79, 81, 71, 90

AT 4.1 **3c Write out the numbers that are left over in the boxes.**

Answers: soixante-dix, quatre-vingt-quatre, quatre-vingt-onze

AT 1.2 **4 Listen and number the eating places (1–3) in the order Toto phones them. Where will he be eating tonight?**

Answers: 1 crêperie; 2 pizzeria; 3 restaurant; Toto va au restaurant

---

🔘 **En solo CD, track 47**   page 79, activité 4

– Bon alors, numéro 1: 02 87 62 24 69; alors, 02 87 62 24 69…
  Oh non! Bon. Numéro 2: 02 87 72 80 79.
  Voilà: 02 87 72 80 79…
  Aahahahah! Numéro 3: 02 97 72 81 69.
  Donc 02 97 72 81 69…
– Allô oui! J'écoute?
– Ahhh super! Allô, oui… bonjour, monsieur …

Pages 80–81 6.3 Ma recette préférée

- Use with Students' Book pages 106–107.

AT 4.1 **1 Write out the shopping list, using *du, de la, de l', des*.**

Answers: du lait, de la farine, du sucre, des œufs, de la vanille, du sel, du chocolat, de la glace

AT 4.1 **2a Now look at the shopping basket. What's missing?**

Answers: il n'y a pas de lait, de farine, d'œufs

AT 1.2 **2b Listen and check your answers to activities 1 and 2a.**

 En solo CD, track 48   page 80, activité 2b

Alors, pour la recette, il faut… du lait, de la farine, du sucre, des œufs, de la vanille, du sel, du chocolat et de la glace.
Alors… voilà. Il y a du sucre, de la vanille, du sel, du chocolat, de la glace. Mais… Mais… Mais… il n'y a pas de lait, il n'y a pas de farine et il n'y a pas d'œufs! Oh non!

AT 3.2 **3a Before listening to the recipe, try to predict the missing words in the ingredients and the instructions. Write them in pencil.**

Answers: see transcript for ex. 3b

AT 4.1 **3b Listen and check your guesses. Did you predict correctly?**

 En solo CD, track 49   page 81, activité 3b

Voici la recette des gaufres…
Comme ingrédients, il faut:
300 g de <u>farine</u>, deux <u>œufs</u>, 40 centilitres de <u>lait</u>, un peu de <u>levure</u>, un peu de <u>sucre</u>, de la <u>vanille</u>, du <u>sel</u>.
Alors, la recette:
a   <u>Mélanger</u> les œufs.
b   <u>Ajouter</u> tous les ingrédients et bien <u>mélanger</u>.
c   <u>Mettre</u> la pâte dans le gaufrier.
d   Manger avec du <u>chocolat</u> ou de la <u>glace</u>. Bon appétit!

Pages 82–83   6.4 Mange bien!

• Use with Students' Book pages 108–109.

AT 3.3 **1 This is an interview with a young tennis player. Read questions 1–4 and find the matching answers (A–D).**

Answers: 1 C; 2 D; 3 A; 4 B

AT 1.3 **2 Listen to the interview and check whether you were right!**

 En solo CD, track 50   page 82, activité 2

– Qu'est-ce que tu manges au petit déjeuner?
– En général, le matin, je mange des céréales, du pain et des fruits!

– Qu'est-ce que tu bois pour avoir de l'énergie?
– Je bois surtout du jus de fruit frais et du lait.
– Qu'est-ce que tu manges avant un match?
– Je mange des pâtes et des bananes. C'est bon pour l'énergie!
– Est-ce que tu bois beaucoup pendant un match?
– Oui, je bois de l'eau, c'est très important quand je joue.

AT 4.3 **3 Complete the resolutions with correct forms of the verb *aller* and an infinitive.**

Answers: see transcript for ex. 4

AT 1.2 **4 Listen and check your answers.**

 En solo CD, track 51   page 83, activité 4

1   Je vais manger plus de fruits!
2   Tu vas boire moins de soda!
3   Il va manger moins de bonbons!
4   Nous allons manger moins de frites!
5   Vous allez faire plus de sport!
6   Elles vont boire plus de lait!

AT 4.3 **Follow-up**: Ask students to draw two more cartoons and write captions for them. Encourage them to include a comment/opinion in each caption, e.g. *C'est très important!*

Pages 84–85   Labo-langue

• Use with Students' Book pages 110–111.

1 Do the quiz on *à* and *de*. Explain your choices.

Answers: 1 a (must be a feminine noun after *à la*); 2 c (must be *du* before a masculine noun); 3 c (must be *de la* before a feminine noun); 4 c (*de* is used after a negative); 5 c (a and b would need to be followed by <u>*du beurre*</u>); 6 c (*aux* must be followed by a plural noun); 7 b, c (*au* is followed by a masculine noun); 8 b (*de/d'* is used after a negative)

2 Fill the gaps with the words in the box. You'll need some more than once.

Answers: 1 au; 2 aux; 3 à l'; 4 à la; 5 à; 6 à la, au; 7 du; 8 de la; 9 de; 10 des; 11 de; 12 de l'

3 Translate the sentences in activity 2 into English. What do you notice about the translation of *à* and *de*?

Answers: Students should realise that these words are used differently in English (e.g. *au/à l'/à la/aux* can mean "to the" or "in the"), and sometimes they are not translated at all (e.g. *une glace à l'orange* – orange ice cream, *du sucre* – sugar).

1 Are you going to the seaside? 2 My dream is to go to the United States. 3 I like orange ice cream. 4 It's a restaurant in the countryside. 5 She lives in Paris. 6 When I go to the pancake restaurant, I often eat a pancake with sugar. 7 To make a cake, you need sugar. 8 Do you want some more pizza? 9 You need a kilo of apples. 10 Are there any eggs? 11 I never eat mushrooms. 12 Are you drinking water?

4 Make up your own answers to these questions. Make sure what you write matches the forms of *à* and *de*!

- Students complete the sentences. Accept any answers that are grammatically correct.

 Follow-up: Challenge students to make up four sentences showing correct use of *au/à l'/à la/aux*, *du/de l'/de la/des* and *de/d'*. They swap with a partner and award each other points for each example of correct usage. Suggest that they award bonus points for any sentences that include more than one example.

Page 86 Checklist

- Use with *Blog-notes* (Students' Book page 112) or towards the end of the unit.

The checklist, recording and follow-up activities provide opportunities for students to review what they have learned, test themselves orally on key language and reflect on areas for improvement.

 En solo CD, track 52   page 86, activité 2

1 Where do you eat in town? [*beep*] Tu manges où en ville?
2 I eat in a pancake restaurant. [*beep*] Je mange à la crêperie.
3 a ham and cheese toasted sandwich [*beep*] un croque-monsieur
4 I'd like a sandwich. [*beep*] Je voudrais un sandwich.
5 Shall we go to a restaurant? [*beep*] On va au restaurant?
6 Yes, OK. [*beep*] Oui, d'accord.
7 a vanilla ice cream [*beep*] une glace à la vanille
8 I'd like a cheese sandwich, please. [*beep*] Je voudrais un sandwich au fromage, s'il vous plaît.
9 How much is it? [*beep*] C'est combien?
10 three hundred and sixty [*beep*] trois cent soixante
11 some milk, some flour and some eggs [*beep*] du lait, de la farine et des œufs
12 You must mix the sugar and the eggs. [*beep*] Il faut mélanger le sucre et les œufs.
13 What do you eat in the morning? [*beep*] Qu'est-ce que tu manges le matin?
14 I'm going to drink fewer fizzy drinks. [*beep*] Je vais boire moins de soda.
15 When do you eat? [*beep*] Tu manges quand?

Follow-up: Encourage students to draw up their own individual action plan of steps they could take to help them improve. Provide a checklist of suggestions for them to choose from, e.g. try harder to learn vocabulary, read the grammar notes again and make sure they understand them/ask for help if they don't understand, check written work carefully for mistakes, etc.

Page 87 Top tips and strategies

Listening

This section provides tips on how to prepare for listening tasks, e.g. reading the questions carefully before listening, looking for clues in the title or introduction, using prior knowledge to try to predict language that might come up. It could be used at any appropriate point during Unit 6.

1a Try out tips 1–3 while you do this listening task.

Answers: a yes; b She usually eats salad or fish. She drinks water.

 En solo CD, track 53   page 87, activité 1a

À midi, je mange au collège. Je vais à la cantine. On mange bien à la cantine, très bien. C'est toujours très bon. Normalement, je prends une salade, ou du poisson. Je bois de l'eau.

 1b Discuss your results with a partner. Did you find any clues before listening? Did you predict any words, and did that help?

- Students should spot several clues in the questions, e.g. they know they will hear some food and drink vocabulary and that it will be the sort of food/drink you might have for lunch in a school canteen, and they know that Julie will express an opinion because one of the questions asks whether she enjoys school lunches.

Writing

This section provides tips on how to achieve greater accuracy in written work, e.g. by checking spellings, accents, genders, and agreement of adjectives and verbs. It could be used at any appropriate point during Unit 6.

3 Check this piece of writing. Circle eight words that have mistakes.

- This could be done together as a class, or completed individually before checking as a whole class.

193

Answers: mistakes are underlined, with corrections in brackets:

J'ai un problème avec mes <u>parent</u> (parents). Il y a <u>une</u> (un) ordinateur et une <u>telêvision</u> (télévision) dans le salon. Je <u>veut</u> (veux) un ordinateur et une télé dans <u>mon</u> (ma) chambre, parce que ma chambre est <u>grand</u> (grande). Le soir, <u>j'aim</u> (j'aime) visiter des sites Internet, regarder la télé et jouer sur <u>mon</u> (ma) console.

Pages 88–89   Vocabulaire

• Use with Students' Book pages 116–117.

A list of key language from the unit is provided here as well as in the Students' Book and on Copymaster 61.

1 Listen and tick the phrases you hear.

 En solo CD, track 54   page 89, activité 1

Je mange au fast-food
Je voudrais… un steak-frites, s'il vous plaît.
C'est combien?
C'est vingt euros.
une pizza à la tomate
Ma recette préférée,… c'est très facile à faire.
C'est très bon!
Il faut… mélanger… de la farine,… du beurre,… des œufs.
Pour être en forme,… je vais manger… plus… au petit déjeuner.

2 Underline in coloured pencil…

• Students search the list for key language items.

3 Note: a) your favourite word/phrase in this unit; b) 3 key words/phrases to remember.

• Challenge students to make up some sentences using these words.